THE FANNI

THE LIFE AND LETTERS OF KATHARINE FANNIN
1902 - 1970

Mrs Katharine Fannin

JUDY ALDRICK

Old Africa Books
Kenya

The Fannin Papers

Old Africa Books
A Division of Kifaru Educational and Editorial Consultants
PO Box 65
Kijabe - 00220 - Kenya

First Old Africa Books edition 2010

ISBN 978-9966-7204-2-9

Printed by Regal Press
Nairobi, Kenya

CONTENTS

ACKNOWLEDGEMENTS

There are many debts to acknowledge. First there is the late Edward Rodwell, without whom this biography could not have been written. It was he who put the Fannin papers at my disposal, encouraged me to write the story and acted as mentor and adviser throughout. Almost every week I would visit him to glean more information, borrow books and papers from his archives and sit with him and his wife Olivia on the verandah over tea and biscuits, reminiscing and reviving memories of a former age. I thank his heirs for their kind permission to reproduce photographs, letters and maps from the Rodwell Archive.

I would like to thank my late husband, Richard, for purchasing a computer, supplying me with reams of paper and encouraging me to write, my parents who read the manuscript in an early stage and my children, Philip and Katy, who bore with me. Special mention should be given to Desmond and Phyllida Forbes-Cockell, who provided me with important additional information for the first and final chapters and to Richard Pankhurst, who kindly corrected and checked my chapters on Ethiopia. I owe a debt of gratitude to the staff of the SOAS Library, The India Office Records and the Public Record Office, Kew, who at short notice provided me with reader's tickets and patiently pointed me in the right direction for the research material required.

Then there are the people in England and Mombasa, who have shared with me their personal memories of Katharine Fannin and described particular incidents and meetings that I have mentioned in this account. I list them in no particular order and thank them for time and effort unstintingly given. Olivia Rodwell, Dorothy Kirkman, Jean Wallwork, June Knowles, Arthur Ratcliff, Dixie Dean, Millicent Reeve,

Nicole Benazeth, Roland MacVicar, Lorna Hayes, Juanita Carberry, Ann de Souza, Tom and Doreen Miller, Eddie Gregory, Daphne Bagshaw, Sheila Unwin, Judy Forbes, Barry and Maeve Mitchell, Susan Adcock, and the Nyali Fish Shop.

Last but not least I would like to thank my dear friend Cynthia Salvadori, who through her generosity made this book possible, when I had lost all hope of publication. She recommended me to Shel Arensen, who agreed to take me on and make this the first title of his new publishing company Old Africa Books, specialising in lives lived in Africa.

Judy Aldrick
Kent, 2010

FOREWORD

Edward Rodwell first introduced me to Katharine Fannin, or at least her papers. After Katharine's death, her papers were given to Rodwell for his archives in Mombasa. He roughly sorted them, placed them into 25 large brown envelopes, labelled them and put them in a filing cabinet pending action. There they had waited for more than 20 years until time had softened the edges and had matured the events into history and the story of Katharine Fannin could be told.

Roddy, as he was known to his friends, was a well known Mombasa character. Trained as a journalist, he came to Mombasa in 1933 at the age of 24 as general manager and editor for the *Mombasa Times*. When this newspaper was amalgamated with the *East African Standard* in the 1950s, he continued on the staff and wrote a weekly column for that same newspaper. When I visited him in July 1991 at his home on Mtwapa Creek, he sat surrounded by books and memories of events and people long gone. I wanted to tap this mine of information and he produced what I required in a few short seconds and our conversation turned to other matters. He suddenly pointed to an ancient rusting filing cabinet in a corner of the room and said, "Pull out that drawer." I found 25 large brown envelopes containing the life and letters of a brave and remarkable woman. "See, there are the Fannin Papers," Rodwell said. "Why don't you take them, read them and see if you can write anything from them." Rodwell had always hoped to do the project himself, he knew he never would. I agreed to read the Fannin Papers.

We piled them into the back seat of my car. For the next eight weeks, whenever I had a few minutes spare, I pulled out an envelope and perused more material. It was like a lucky dip - you never knew what would come to light next; old photographs, invitations to official functions, newspaper clippings, a share certificate for a now defunct Kavirondo goldmine and hundreds of letters to family, acquaintances and high authorities. Katharine was an inveterate letter writer who did not believe in pulling punches or keeping it brief when stating her point of view or registering a complaint. In some letters she had written so intensely and pressed down so hard with her pen that the ink had eaten through the yellowed and brittle paper and the letters almost crumbled in my hand. Slowly a picture emerged of Katharine and her life.

Of particular interest were letters sent to her uncle, when she first came to Kenya. I read the articles she wrote for *The Kenya Weekly News*, her column for the *Mombasa Times*, written under the pseudonym 'Shellback' and the six-part broadcast series she made in 1960 for the Kenya Broadcasting Service, entitled 'Memories of the Twenties and Thirties in Kenya.' But the most important find were the papers and the reports relating to her two Ethiopian journeys of 1938 and 1939, when she travelled through Somalia, Ethiopia and Etritrea as a secret agent collecting information for British Intelligence. This interlude, which apparently she rarely referred to in later life, gave insight into the fascinating profession of spying. At this point I knew I had to tell her story. How did a respectable middle-aged housewife become a spy? What led her to take this unusual step?

However, the papers I had left large gaps in Katharine's life. For example, there is very little in the Fannin papers directly relating to Katharine's family background or childhood. The material for the first chapter has been largely put together from snippets of information taken from her Saturday column written for the *Mombasa Times* between 1949-51, from her early letters and the reminiscences of Desmond Forbes-Cockell, a distant relative on her mother's side.

I went back to Edward Rodwell, who searched his memory for relevant details. He and Katharine had both been journalists working in Mombasa. He lent me background reading from his archives and gave me addresses of people who had known her. One contact led to another. I followed many false trails and dead ends, but occasionally one more puzzling piece fell into place. On my home leaves I stole away from my protesting family to visit the Public Record Office (PRO) in London, as well as the Library of the School of Oriental and African Studies

(SOAS) and The India Office Records (IOR). By 1991 fifty years had passed since the beginning of World War II and the classified papers of that period had just been released, so I was delighted to find Katharine's intelligence reports for the Foreign Office open for public viewing, under the files for Ethiopia. Back in Mombasa, I ransacked the libraries of the Mombasa Club and Fort Jesus Museum for historical information and source material and pestered elderly residents for reminiscences of Katharine and old Mombasa.

Despite her volubility and energy, I discovered Katharine had been a very private person. She had many acquaintances but none who knew her really well. She had no close family and when she came to Kenya she had cut herself off completely from her former life. I had a hard time tracking down information about her background. Her family had not approved of her marriage to Charles Fannin and she never developed friendly relations with the family of Charles' first wife. Charles' own immediate family had consisted of several unmarried elder sisters, none of which provided much meat for a hopeful biographer.

As I wrote myself through her life, I found I needed more historical background as Katharine developed from a frivolous girl only interested in society and having a good time, into a serious minded and mature woman deeply immersed in the politics of the period. What started as a few light-hearted descriptions of conditions in colonial Kenya taken from her delightfully breezy letters to her uncle inadvertently grew into a more serious project describing the social and political changes experienced in East Africa based on Katharine's writings and strongly held views.

Unlike many Kenyan characters of the colonial period, whose adventures have proved so fashionable in the West, Katharine was not a glamorous figure: She was not a famous sportswoman, nor a stunning beauty. Her antecedents were distinctly middle class, and despite her undoubted intelligence and varied talents, she had to work hard for her living, and could not rely on powerful friends to see her through the bleak times. The story of Katharine Fannin is not one to excite the imaginations of those who revel in escapist fantasy. It is the story of an ordinary woman pitting her wits against a cruel world full of prejudice and injustice, who cared about Africa and its people. There is no happy ending, only sad decline and death. But the living along the way is worth the telling, portraying the idealism, visionary hopes and final disillusionment of many of those who made their life in Africa and lived through decolonisation and the 'End of Empire.'

Almost every East African memoir I had read had been based up-country. Many had been the reminiscences of retired colonial officials wishing to vindicate their actions and the policies they had carried out, or sentimental tales of white farmers, forced to leave their land after back-breaking effort and sacrifice. In Katharine's story I found something different – a new perspective on a well-trodden period of history. Katharine spent most of her life on the Coast of Kenya, an area not many had written about. Her spying interlude in Ethiopia sheds light on the Abyssinian Campaign, an almost entirely forgotten episode of World War II. I hope Katharine's story will fill in a few small gaps and give the reader a new view of East Africa's history as seen through the eyes of a determined and resourceful woman.

INTRODUCTION

Katharine Fannin is chiefly remembered for the two journeys she made in 1938 and 1939 across Italian East Africa. Armed only with an invitation from the Viceroy, her silver lamé evening dress and an antiquarian guidebook, she gathered vital information for British Intelligence. Her maps, details of military installations and reports of conditions, proved invaluable in the Abyssinian campaign of 1941, when British troops defeated the Italians in Eritrea, Somalia and Ethiopia.

As a talented journalist, Katharine's writings on Africa remain fresh and direct. She gave pleasure to many readers and her sometimes controversial views left her out of favour with the authorities of the period. Her writings can now be read with new appreciation for their prescience and honesty.

Born 1902 in the foothills of the Himalayas on a tea estate in India, Katharine Mary was the eldest daughter of William Trood and his wife Maude. Educated in England, Katharine came out to Kenya in 1926 at the age of 23. Intelligent and ambitious, she wanted to make something of her life and thought the colonies would offer her the opportunity she sought. "Where else," she asks, "but in the British Colonial Service can you find such opportunities, congenial surroundings and companions, combined with productive and rewarding employment?" From an early age she had a fervent belief in the British Empire, and was a great patriot. She felt it her Christian duty to assist and direct those less fortunate than herself. She believed the strong should protect the weak and the rich should support the poor. She thought the benevolent paternalism practised by the British Empire would bring the most benefit to the people of Africa.

Though Katharine Fannin belonged to a past age, the story of her life has a relevancy that bridges the passage of time. It reveals the struggle of an intelligent woman determined to escape the drudgery and boredom of genteel poverty in England in the aftermath of World War I. Capable and ambitious, Katharine Fannin, if she'd lived in more enlightened times, would have succeeded in any career she chose. She might have become an internationally known journalist, without resorting to the subterfuge of marriage in order to see the world and secure a better chance for herself. Africa gave Katharine the opportunity she would never have had in England. She first tried her hand at social work and received a medal. The special circumstances of war gave her the break she needed to prove her true abilities, first as a secret agent and then as a journalist and broadcaster.

Her story provides intimate glimpses into society and conditions of colonial life in Kenya and the politics behind it, giving a fresh insight into an important period of African history. It is often forgotten what East Africa was like in the early 1900s. The input of the colonising powers and pioneering settlers from all over Europe transformed the face of this part of Africa beyond all recognition. Whether or not the transformation has been to the African's ultimate benefit is a debatable point, but there is no doubt that at the time those concerned believed they were working for everyone's best interests. Colonialists built the roads, the railways, the schools, the hospitals, the industries and big farming concerns where previously there had been scattered villages on the vast plains and forested hillsides, alongside teeming herds of animal life. Many spent and lost fortunes on the visionary scheme of 'opening up Kenya' as a profitable branch of the British Empire.

All her life Katharine remained dedicated to the colonial ideal, where the prime considerations of the administration were justice for all, peace, prosperity and the well-being of its subjects. At first she thought introducing western civilisation to Africa was a good thing, but in later life she had serious doubts about the benefits of westernization in Africa and questioned the wisdom of tampering with the traditional structures of society and age old systems of organisation. She preferred the methods of old-fashioned colonialism and the concept of indirect rule to the modern form of neo-colonialism, where the forced imposition of western style government was wrapped up in the guise of self-determinism and independence. Nowadays it is fashionable to express horror at the sheer arrogance of the colonialist way of thought and shudder at the moral certainty of the Victorian ethos that claimed a superior right to rule the world. The fact is many people in England were brought up to think this way and in order to understand the history of the West's involvement in Africa, these views cannot be ignored.

In 1926, full of hope, Katharine Fannin went forth with determination and complete faith in the rightness of her mission in Africa. The plump and sturdy solidity of her 5 foot 3 inch figure and her forthright utterances quelled all but the most foolhardy of disbelievers. She thought she could help create a better society in an untouched land by her willingness to work hard and be involved. With great courage and initiative she travelled across Italian East Africa and wrote detailed reports for the Foreign Office. She did this out of love of adventure and a sense of patriotism to the Empire. She had such confidence in the 'God-given' superiority of the British and their proven administrative qualities, that she hoped to see the whole map of Africa painted in pink, the colour used on maps of that period to represent the British Empire. She completely approved of The Duke of Aosta, the Italian ruler of Ethiopia, and a profound Anglophile. She genuinely believed his rule benefited the majority of Ethiopians.

She had a great affection and sympathy for the people of Africa. Both she and her husband spent most of their lives working for the betterment of living and social conditions of Africans. Charles Fannin, surveyor and town planner, spent 16 years laying out Mombasa town as we see it today, with all its roads and infrastructure, none of which existed when he started in 1920. Katharine, distressed by instances of extreme poverty and neglect, raised the money and organised alms houses for the destitute and homeless in Mombasa.

They were never well off, despite Charles' 35 years with the Surveying Department of the Colonial Office, and after his death, his widow struggled unsuccessfully to make ends meet. This is in contrast to some Kenya pioneers, who returned after their African experiences to comfortable homes in Europe to write up a fashionably romantic view of White Man's Africa. Katharine Fannin had no home to go back to. She had committed herself to Africa.

Katharine Fannin saw herself as a lady of principle. Her Victorian sense of duty, her strong belief in the paramount values of truth and justice, instilled into her during early childhood, remained with her throughout her life. She tried to live according to what she thought was right. Unencumbered by self-doubt, she had complete faith in the correctness of her beliefs and voiced her views openly.

In later life Katharine became very critical of the decolonisation process in East Africa. She didn't like the way the British Government disposed of their colonies and their responsibilities and felt the transition caused unnecessary hardship not only for the white settler communities but also for the indigenous peoples. She could not agree with the post-war policies on Africa and felt the new recipes for self-rule and economic development based exclusively on western experience were doomed to failure. The imposition of Western systems of government and administration as a prerequisite for independence, without taking into account local traditions and custom, affronted common sense and the African peoples. She deplored the way the wishes and welfare of people became secondary to abstract policies formulated by cynical politicians seated in the capitals of the West. Katharine felt the politicians supported the calls for self-determination not through a genuine concern for the good of Africa but for selfish reasons of political expediency and who then hastily put together ramshackle independent governments and passed the plate, with a sigh of relief. With retrospect it is possible to see the policies of the post-war period have in fact been worse than the colonialist policies of the pre-war period. The continued interference of outsiders in African affairs has in many cases led to deeper dependency and poverty. Today many African states find their western style administrative systems have not been able to cope with conditions in Africa and a number of sub-Saharan countries have no functioning government at all. A radical rethinking of the West's involvement in Africa is needed. The voices of those with long experience in Africa are needed for the process to start. Katharine Fannin's voice is one that needs to be heard again.

CHAPTER ONE

Childhood days in India and Devon 1902-1926

"I was destined to arrive late on Christmas Eve in a remote part of India far beyond a railhead and where our customary method of reaching the nearest station was to mount an ancient and docile lady elephant. I can only just remember it, for like all English children then born in India, I was wrapped away when very small and sent to uncles and aunts at home to be brought up. We lived not far from the Tibetan border. My father loved gardening and was a keen naturalist and a good shot. He was so much under the spell of the country where he spent nearly forty years, that in all that long time he passed less than three years in his native country, preferring after my mother's untimely death, to wander about Bhutan and the fringes of Tibet perfecting an encyclopaedic knowledge of the local dialects and gathering together a fascinating collection of objects of all kinds."[1]

Katharine Fannin wrote this recollection of her early childhood in India. She was baptised Katharine Mary Trood into the Scottish Kirk by a minister called Cameron,[2] who arrived on the back of the lady elephant and saw in the New Year in with "our frivolous household." "My people were English and Church of England," she explained, "but we had no chaplain to serve the scattered district so this good Scot, who was ever ready to snatch small brands, such as myself, from the burning came hurrying at my parents' invitation."[3] Robert Carmichael, later to become Lord Carmichael and Governor of Bengal, stood in as Katharine's godfather.

Her father, William Trood, wrote her a letter dated May 1, 1922. It is headed Nedeem Tea Co., Dalsingpara Division, Alipur Dooars, and enclosed inside is a present of a ticket for the Royal Calcutta Turf Club

Sweep. "My darling Kitty," her father wrote, "I hope the glasses are doing your headaches good and that you are taking your medicine, like a dear girl. Very busy this morning, please excuse short note only, fondest love Dad." This was the last letter he wrote to her for he died in August that year and was buried in India.[4] Katharine loved her father and shared his facility for languages, his interest in books and his collector's instinct and curiosity. One can feel the distant charm of this obviously kindly but selfish man, whose only known legacy to his daughter was a raffle ticket and who preferred to spend his leaves travelling on the fringes of Tibet, rather than coming home to see his motherless children who were parcelled out to long suffering relatives and boarding schools.

William Trood went out to India to work on a tea estate. His name appears in Thackers Indian Directory for 1892, when he is listed as an Assistant Manager for the Cachar Tea Company. By 1898 he had moved to the Nedeem Tea Company, where he first managed their tea garden at Toorsa and from 1913 became manager at Dalsingpara. The Nedeem Tea Company started in Dooars in 1882, but the big expansion of tea production in the region did not begin until the 1890s. The tea garden of Toorsa was founded in 1895. Dooars in Jalpaiguri district had been annexed by the British in 1869, a frontier tract bordering on Nepal, Bhutan and Sikkim. Remote and far from civilisation, nevertheless it was good tea growing country and produced tea almost as good as that from Darjeeling. When the tea was first planted, the gardens had to be hacked out of dense jungle and only the boldest and most adventurous of pioneers came to Dooars in those early days. Innumerable rivers and streams traversed the district from north to south, becoming raging torrents in the rainy season. Dooars was an unhealthy and dangerous district where malaria (and malaria's final stage 'blackwater fever') was rife.[5] William Trood survived to be one of the oldest planters in the region and his death is recorded in the minutes of the Dooars Planters Association Annual Report for 1922. However, he was not apparently an active member of the Dooars Planters Association, preferring to spend his time far from the trammels of civilisation.

Katharine left no portrait of her mother and only once mentioned the fact of her "untimely death,"[6] but this phrase may betray Katharine's feeling of abandonment. Maude Elizabeth Trood died in India in 1915[7], but the last time Katharine saw her mother was in 1911 as a little girl of

8, when the Troods were on leave in England. Katharine described her childhood as 'grim' on at least one occasion.[8] Her parents sent her back to England from India, probably at the age of four or five, to be brought up by aunts, who showed her very little love or affection. Virtually nothing is known about Katharine's mother, but an old photograph album turned up, battered and coverless, amongst the Fannin papers, which contains pictures of both her father and mother in India.

It is easy to imagine the motherless child, treasuring these pictures of a half-remembered life. First of all is the bungalow, firmly labelled "Katharine's parents' home in India." Pictures of two white horses come next. The label reads: "Kanchee and Honesty, Dalsingpara." One is harnessed to a light carriage, possibly Katharine's mother's. The other is a sturdy hack with docked tail, surely her father's usual mount. Another photo shows Katharine aged about two in her father's lap seated on the ground beside a tent, while an elegant Edwardian lady sits posed on a stool beside them. In another picture a large elephant stands beside a ramshackle reed shelter while Katharine's parents sit amongst scattered camping equipment. Further on comes a photograph of a party of Europeans carried in dhoolies[9]. In the foreground a small child sits in front of a lady in a large hat. These are the only pictures of what, one presumes, is Katharine's mother. At all times her face is shaded by her hat. Her father, on the other hand, stands out clearly, a solid, short figure with his pipe firmly clamped between his teeth.

A loose photograph stuck between the pages of the album shows Katharine aged about twelve with long fair hair seated in a pony trap in front of an English country cottage. On the back is written: "At Rose Cottage."

Katharine had one brother, Geoffrey, also known as 'the Boy,' who was a couple of years younger than her.[10] He was educated at Clifton School, Bristol, one of a crop of boarding schools that sprang up in the wake of the celebrated Dr Arnold of Rugby, which aimed to train boys for overseas service within the British Empire. The schools emphasised moral rectitude and 'playing the game' and, as one recent writer has described, instilled the pupils with 'that discreet arrogance and lack of self-doubt that was required to fight the Great War or administer thousands of square miles of frontier territory with the aid of nothing but a clipped voice and a light rattan cane.'[11] However Clifton's creed of

Muscular Christianity and emphasis on patriotic service in distant parts failed to inspire Geoffrey Trood, who preferred the easy life of a man about town. He lacked the drive and intelligence of his energetic elder sister. In early manhood Geoffrey Trood lived in London and made a show of studying for accountancy exams, which he never passed and later dabbled in various business ventures, none of which succeeded. Though very close as children, Katharine's affection for Geoffrey diminished as the years went on, and it became clear he would never amount to anything. He appears to have lived a precarious existence scrounging off relatives, which infuriated his sister and eventually turned her sisterly feeling into active dislike. Geoffrey joined the Royal Air Force (RAF) and was killed in World War II.

A resumé amongst her wartime papers gives the bare facts of Katharine's education:

> Educated in France
> Southlands School, Exmouth, Devon 1914-18
> Lausanne University 2 years
> Gloucester School of Domestic Science

A passing mention in one of her *Mombasa Times* Saturday articles suggests Katharine was brought up with cousins to begin with. They spent much of their time in France and had a French governess who had great difficulty keeping them under control and was the butt of their practical jokes. Katharine described the childish games they used to enjoy and the pranks they played. She often spoke of the happy time she and her brother spent in France. This changed, presumably with the onset of World War I, when Katharine was sent to boarding school in Devon and put in the care of her father's sisters, who lived in a small Devonshire village called Exton, not far from Exeter. There were eight of these aunts, whom she described as Victorian ladies of rigidly unimaginative upbringing and outlook.[12] They made Katharine's life miserable with their strict, and to her, unreasonable discipline. As an avid reader, she particularly disliked their inflexible rule that allowed no reading until 2.30 pm, - "no books until after luncheon." The account she gave of a Victorian household was almost certainly based on personal experience of living with her aunts. She described how the last meal of the day was served at 5.00 pm, whatever the time of year, and how after dinner the women sat and embroidered or sewed while listening to readings from the daily newspaper and Bible. To a lively teenager, it must have seemed a dreadfully dull and restricted existence.

Her closest ally during this gloomy period of her life was Uncle John, her 'dearest Runcle.' How he was related is unclear, but John Jones Esq, who lived at Eastcliff, Exton, was the nearest thing she had to a father.[13] Reminiscing many years later about her childhood, she wrote in the *Mombasa Times* of "an old uncle whose study was lined with enchanting old books, tall, green and stately, or short, fat and bound in pebbly patterned boards with leather backs and corners,"[14] and recalled how he gave her a copy of Milton's poetic works, published in 1720, for a present on her fifteenth birthday. She treasured this book all her life and kept it with her on her travels. He allowed her to read whatever caught her fancy from his extensive shelves of classics, travel books and early Victorian novels. One typical tale of virtue triumphant that stuck in her memory was entitled **Mildred of the Starry Eyes and Nut Brown Hair**, whose preoccupation with a fate "worse than death" completely mystified her.[15] Katharine at this age was a lonely and studious girl, full of romantic imagining, who escaped from the dreariness of the war years and the company of her unsympathetic aunts into a fairy tale world of heroic literature.

One of Katharine's favourite books was Rudyard Kipling's famous novel **Kim**, which told the tale of an orphan boy, who worked as a spy for the British Empire - working for the "Great Game" as it was called. Kim found his spiritual mentor and replacement father figure, was sent to boarding school and given the chance to succeed in life. The "Great Game" was the term given to the battle of wits, which was played between Russia and Britain for control over the uncharted territory of High Asia, consisting of Afghanistan, Nepal, Bhutan and Tibet. It epitomised the high imperialistic mood of the late Victorian age and as a romantic image it captured the imagination of many young minds brought up on a diet of adventurous tales of derring-do, featuring the utopian world of Shangri La and the mysterious Dalai Lama, where fair play and superior British intelligence always wins the day against the forces of evil. Katharine, who had spent her early childhood on the North West Frontier, supreme "Great Game" country, found such tales particularly fascinating. Another author she read was Sir Francis Younghusband, whose books described his daring exploits amongst the mountains of the Himalayas and his expedition through Sikkim into Tibet. His love of the mountain scenery and mystical affinity for the region must have reminded her of her father and his travels and great affection for that part of India. These books gave Katharine a sense of belonging and helped justify in her own mind her parents' absence and supplied her with role models she could identify with.[16]

Her kindly uncle encouraged her reading and they had long discussions together. An old fashioned and very learned gentleman, he liked to pepper his speech with Latin tags and apposite quotations and aphorisms. The philosophies of her 'best Runcle' and the talks they had in his study lined with books, provided the basis of her beliefs in life. It seems he is the one who instilled in her a complete faith in the British Empire and fuelled her ambitions for an adventurous life in the colonies.

After the war, Katharine spent two years at a finishing school at Lausanne, in Switzerland, where she learned to play the piano and sing to a professional standard. Later she rounded off her education as a young lady with a cooking course at Gloucester. Her future seemed bright. She had acquired polish and was witty and accomplished enough to enter society and win the heart of that scarce commodity – a young man, who had survived the war.

In the early 1920s Katharine visited the Great Exhibition at Wembley[17] "a lot and free too, being the fortunate owner of the right sort of cousin who was in charge of the valuable exhibits of the Public Record Office (PRO)."[18] The PRO showed off a double sheet of early New South Wales stamps, which her cousin had come across while going through a folio of dispatches from overseas Governors. Katharine went round looking at the wonderful exhibits, enjoying in particular the jewellery display from Ceylon, seeing Huntley and Palmer bake their famous biscuits and watching a Ford car come off the assembly line every 25 minutes. As a treat she stopped at the Lucullus restaurant where she entered under a Roman arch and received a menu printed in gold. For a few minutes she imagined herself savouring elegant living and dining with the gods.

However, reality was different. The Troods were not a wealthy family and after her father's death in 1922, it became apparent Katharine would have to earn a living or find herself a husband quickly. An old visiting card speaks of one attempt to earn an income:

Miss K.M. Trood
Pianist and Accompanist
13 Nottingham Place
London W.I.

It was hard work keeping up appearances and earning enough to keep going. She had all the outward trappings of elegance – so essential in those days – a full length musquash fur coat with a big collar, her mother's sapphire and diamond ring, the statutory pearls and dressing case with the initials M.E.T. stamped in gold on the front and fitted with silver backed brushes and scent bottles to match. She had been brought up with the expectation of money only to find at the age of 21 she had none.

Katharine felt terribly let down by all her family. Many years later she wrote bitterly: "It is odd how some people can make their families' lives a burden to them. Nothing on this earth can give any child a greater backing than an affectionate and peaceful atmosphere in the home."[19] This cry from her heart touched on something Katharine felt had been lacking in her upbringing. Not long before his own death, Katharine's father had married in India for a second time. His second wife, Ethel Maud, took little interest in the welfare of her husband's children, but inherited everything on his death, while Katharine and her brother, Geoffrey, received only a small legacy from their mother's estate. Katharine never forgave her stepmother and was bitterly disappointed by the injustice of the financial settlement.[20]

But the family did not entirely abandon her. Her mother's side, more affluent and worldly than the Devonshire Troods, came to her rescue. One of Katharine's mother's sisters, Lena, had married a stockbroker, Cedric Forbes-Cockell, who worked at the Royal Exchange, Calcutta, and was relatively well to do. By 1925 they had returned to England and Katharine stayed with them. At this time she was introduced to a young doctor, John Buchanan, who asked her to marry him and to go out to Tanganyika Territory, where he had been posted with the Medical Department of the Colonial Office.[21] Her engagement very properly appeared in The Times:

"April 2nd 1925: The engagement is announced between John Cecil Rankin Buchanan MB ChB son of the late John Buchanan CMG of Blantyre British Central Africa and Katharine Mary Trood only daughter of the late Mr. and Mrs. William Trood of Dalsingpara, Bhutan Dooars, India and Exton, near Exeter, Devon."

'Buckie,' as he was known, was a tall good-looking sportsman and evidently Aunt Lena congratulated herself on finding her sister's daughter a suitable match. It was standard practice in those days for a young man making his career in the colonies to find a bride during his long leave, get engaged, go ahead to make the living arrangements and then send for his fianceé. Often more than a year would go by before they saw each other again. Whilst waiting, Katharine busied herself by gathering together wedding presents from relatives and friends and well-wishers and packing up an enormous trousseau of trunks containing all the equipment thought necessary for setting up home in the tropics. A year passed before Katharine, aged 23, eventually set sail on the passenger liner *SS Morvada* to join her husband-to-be in East Africa.

But somewhere on the high seas, before crossing the line on August 6, 1926, she realised she had made a terrible mistake and could not go through with her intended marriage. The prospect of meeting a man she hardly knew and hadn't seen for over a year on the quayside at Dar es Salaam and then going directly to the church for the wedding, with just a brief stopover on the way to change into her wedding dress, terrified her with its awful finality.[22] The thought of being married to a man she did not truly love in some out-post of Tanganyika must have filled her with despondency. As the ship sailed steadily closer, the idea of working as a doctor's wife and assistant amongst the African sick and needy, which had seemed so glamorous and exciting in England, grew steadily less alluring.

On the voyage out she had met a sympathetic and kindly older man, Charles Fannin, travelling back to Kenya. He told her about the opportunities in Kenya and she confided her doubts about her impending marriage and asked his advice and help. Whether it was from old-fashioned chivalry or pity for a frightened girl or a case of hot-blooded passion, no one will ever know, but Charles threw caution to the winds and offered to marry her instead. In gratitude she turned to him as the solution to her situation. She decided not to marry her Tanganyikan doctor after all, but to stay in Kenya. Charles Fannin had been separated from his wife for some years and he promised to marry Katharine as soon as his divorce came through. He was lonely and no doubt found the high spirited and intelligent Katharine a charming and flattering companion.

Katharine made up her mind to keep all the wedding presents and the vast amounts of equipment she had brought. She was still getting married, even if not to the same man or right away. She would remain in Kenya under Charles' protection. In a long and painful letter written to her uncle just after arriving in Mombasa in August 1926,[23] she tried to justify her astonishing change of plan and naively explained how she had discovered that she "had mistaken her heart and that 'Buckie' would understand and be thankful in the long run." She didn't feel ready for marriage and the time it would take for Charles' divorce to come through, she thought, would make all the difference. She told her uncle she would work hard and get a job and no one must worry about her. Everyone had been very kind and she loved Mombasa. She had adored the ship's voyage and nearly died of sunstroke in Aden. She ended the letter by asking her uncle to please explain everything to the relatives. It was to be five long years before Katharine saw Devon and her uncle again.

CHAPTER TWO

The pioneer: Arrival in Mombasa 1926

In her radio series "Memories of the Twenties and Thirties in Kenya," Katharine Fannin described her embarkation and arrival in East Africa.[24] Always extremely coy about what actually happened between Charles Fannin and her on the voyage, the details of her whirlwind shipboard romance have to be left to the imagination.

> "In England in the 1920s Kenya was hardly more than a name on a map to most people. Like many Devonshire families, mine had relations scattered about in India and South America, but I was the first of us to try out Africa. So when my people saw me off from Exeter in 1926, I was definitely invested with a 'Dr. Livingstone, I presume?' aura and loaded down with a perfect stack of clothes and gear, most of it thoroughly unsuitable, or unnecessary. From this, older listeners will at once deduce, that I, a gullible young fly, had walked only too trustingly into the parlours of those astute London spiders, sundry tropical outfitters, who used to weave their enticing webs round about Piccadilly. In those days there was no air travel to East Africa, one came by sea; a voyage this particular rosy-cheeked innocent of 23 found wholly enchanting; perhaps it's a pity one lives and learns!"
>
> "Anyway one heavenly sunny morning, with the sea all blue and glittering over the reef, Mombasa golf links green and fresh with only a couple of houses poking

their noses over the bushy ridge above, the old B I[25] ship *Morvada* steamed in and dropped anchor. We were quickly beset by hordes of cheerful smiling Swahili in canoes and rowing boats. Fortunately a kindly fellow-passenger offered to see me and my baggage ashore so I hurried to my cabin to clamp on my topi; this was a vast three-decker ocean-going hideously unbecoming khaki affair, which I was assured I must wear to stave off instant sunstroke. We took the sun very seriously in the 1920s. Awful things were prophesied if you were mad enough to venture out in it for even five minutes, unprotected by a topi, or a hot felt double terai, guaranteed to give you a headache and absolute death on your hair. Perhaps as this is a factual account I should tell you briefly what we women customarily wore in those days. Well, when I landed I had on a dreary vest, stays to keep up my stockings, white broderie-anglaise bust bodice and knee-length frilly white cotton drawers all prettied up with satin ribbon; a hand-tucked cotton petticoat came next and the lot was topped by a truly deplorable frock, a sort of tubular loose cover, its waist about half-way between my shins and where it ought to have been - in other words the latest fashion.

"But to return to the port at Kilindini: we passengers were rowed ashore and landed at a small wooden jetty whence we walked over a rough patch of ground to a solitary, fairly large wood-and-corrugated-iron combined Customs and Baggage Shed. Now in 1926, if you can visualise it, that shed and jetty together with a couple of wooden lighterage wharfs, an odd bit of railway track and some rather forlorn sheds dumped down here and there comprised the whole of the leisurely, unruffled port of Kilindini.[26]

"I'll never forget that first arrival; the dazed incredulous look on the face of the young customs officer, who checked my crates and packing cases. You see those outfitters, how I'd trusted them, had assured me that married life in East Africa was unthinkable without, for example 30 pounds of finest white icing sugar. How could one exist away from England without afternoon tea and properly iced birthday and Christmas cakes? Then appeared my banjo and ukelele. In those days banjos played the most important part in any dance band – and I was a passionate Olly Oakley fan. Then came specially made folding tables and chairs, none weighing more than 60 pounds. I had read all about porter's loads on safari, 60 pounds each; you couldn't catch me out there. Next appeared two elegant pairs of knee high grey suede safari boots with clumping great soles, which afterwards wore my poor feet into ribbons and were agony. I soon discarded them. A heavy stoneware filter and candles were all mixed up with pots and pans, mosquito nets, camp beds with long wooden poles and an enormous green lined umbrella. There were cases of sunlight soap and masses of tinned things, which later that same day I was staggered and cross to find could all have been bought locally.

"Finally, to uphold culture in the blue: one mustn't go to the dogs my dear! a vast case full of books and other things I couldn't bear to leave behind. Beatrix Potter, Alice, Lorna Doone, unreadable school prizes in lovely leather bindings that were promptly eaten by white ants – Milton, Kipling, Galsworthy, Jock of the Bushveld and all Rider Haggard. My butterfly catching outfit, my favourite pictures and Granny's lovely old Rockingham tea set and dessert plates – a wedding present. After all, Africa was to be my life and I saw no reason whatsoever to lower my standards. I may say these aids to gracious living and a dash of high thinking were secured by elaborate letter coded padlocks to foil the light fingered. They foiled me too, and had to be hacked off. In the flurry of arrival I lost the list of their open sesame words. However it didn't matter in the least because for the next ten years, I never locked a thing nor had anything stolen.

"Don't imagine the gear I've just told you about was out of the ordinary. Not a bit of it. Another girl, also coming out to get married, had most of my little lot plus saddlery, sporting guns and a patent cooking stove in a crate. We'd become friends, so after the Customs officers had finished with us both, we set out together in the taxi, a 1912 Ford, along the sandy rutted Kilindini earth road under the lovely mango and palm trees until we reached that outpost of civilisation Mr Schwentofsky's Palace Hotel, then standing in two-storeyed solitary state. Almost opposite was the picturesque old French Mission, home of the bearded, brown cassocked, besandalled White Fathers."[27]

Soon after Katharine's arrival she wrote a long letter to her uncle, dated September 10-22, 1926. The full realisation of her behaviour and its consequences did not hit her until she reached dry land. Divorce and breach of promise were viewed very strictly in the 1920s. She had just arrived in a colony, where the Governor, Sir Edward Grigg, later Lord Altrincham, had instructions from King George Vth never to receive a divorcée or invite one to official functions. According to Elspeth Huxley, the Griggs (1925-31) raised the tone of Kenyan colonial society, which previously had been rather lax, both socially and morally.[28] A year or two earlier an illicit shipboard affair between two government servants would have been viewed philosophically, but in 1926, when Kenya was trying to uplift standards, it was considered a serious misdemeanour.

Fortunately, Charles Fannin was a gentleman in the fullest sense of the word. He stood by his Kitty. He had been working in Mombasa since 1920, so had several good friends, who now looked after Miss Trood, while he went on to Dar es Salaam to explain the changed situation to her jilted fiancé. What he said and what actually occurred between the two men on the quayside at Dar es Salaam remains a matter for conjecture. Katharine's understated report to her uncle merely said: "'Buckie' was pretty sore but took it like a gentleman."[29] When Aunt Lena heard all about it, she was furious and washed her hands of her ungrateful niece entirely. The story of the jilted doctor seeing Mrs Fannin many years later, when she had grown considerably in girth, and saying, "There by the Grace of God goes the woman who might have been my wife!"[30] was well remembered within the family circle. The main bone of contention was the trousseau and wedding presents. Katharine had left behind several unpaid debts and had bought various items on Buckie's account, which he refused to pay for. Lawyer's letters were exchanged and nearly two years after the event Katharine's Uncle John was still settling her affairs. Buchanan could legally have sued Charles Fannin for enticement. This would have caused Charles particular embarrassment as in those days notices of all court cases appeared on the Court Circular page of the newspapers and scurrilous gossip about the affair would have spread like wild fire throughout British East Africa.[31] That is probably why Charles Fannin went to see Buchanan personally and presumably an out of court settlement was agreed, in lieu of the damages to which Buchanan was entitled.[32]

East Africa was a small place in those days and despite Charles Fannin's efforts to pre-empt the rumour mongers there is no doubt there was a scandal. It is quite possible Charles Fannin's career suffered because of it – he was not transferred from Mombasa until 1936. He remained 16 years in Mombasa, an unusually long posting, and was only promoted from Assistant to District Surveyor after his remarriage. It is recorded that Clarence Buxton, a District Officer, who ran off with the wife of a Government Analyst a few years later, was posted to Palestine in disgrace.[33] Government officials were supposed to set a good example and the well-known quip "are you married or do you live in Kenya?" might have been acceptable among certain sections of the settler community but was definitely frowned upon in the Colonial Office.

Katharine stayed only a few weeks in Mombasa, where she managed to get sunstroke again although wearing her felt terai. During that time she also went swimming off the sandy beach at English Point and leaves a description of changing behind the bushes into a long thick dark stockinette bathing dress and sponge bag mob cap. Swimwear for men at that time apparently consisted of dark combinations from shoulder to knee.[34]

In 1926 virtually no European women lived in Mombasa[35] and western style accommodation in the town was very limited. Féliciée Benazeth, the wife of the General Manager of the French trading company

Louis Besson & Co., who came in December 1926, found herself one of only twelve women when she attended the New Year's Eve ball at the Mombasa Club. She wrote back home in a letter, that she was so busy dancing at least she didn't have to make English conversation.[36] When Féliciée first arrived with her small son she had to live above the company premises in Treasury Square, with her husband and the three other employees in the 'bachelors mess' until separate married quarters could be found. A 'bachelors mess,' where most unmarried men in Mombasa lived in the 1920s, was a communal dormitory arrangement, where the men slept and ate. They usually shared rooms and conditions were basic. Mombasa had few hotels of any reputation at this period. Smaller hotels, hardly more than boarding houses or rented rooms, were available but these, like the Africa Hotel in the Old Town, were liable to smell of "rancid ghee, curry and other offensive odours of insanitary drains, earth closets, decaying fish and unwashed humanity"[37]and were not considered suitable lodgings for single young ladies.

So until more satisfactory arrangements could be made and to avoid further gossip and speculation, Charles sent Katharine to Kwale, a hill top station in the Shimba Hills some 30 miles South West of Mombasa. Here she stayed with Bar and Billy Marchant, the District Commissioner (DC) and his wife, good friends of Charles'. She slept in a guest hut made from red mud with a grass thatched roof at the Boma[38] (the headquarters of the District Comission), which covered an area of about five acres cut out of the forest. The DC was a young veteran of World War I, badly handicapped by war wounds, who lived with his wife, a former nurse. As DC he ensured order and peace, with the help of a young assistant and 25 native policemen, in an area roughly the size of Wales. As Katharine described it, Marchant had to act as policeman, judge and doctor over twelve potentially warring tribes and spent fifteen days out of every thirty on safari walking through the 89 square miles of untouched bush that comprised his district. Mrs Marchant, who was a "bit knocked up by fever," was glad of company.[39]

Straight out of England, Katharine revelled in the life and found the sights and wildlife fascinating. She described hearing a leopard coughing and barking outside the Boma, while a lion was shot at Tiwi,[40] and seeing waterbuck, buffalo and baboons. "Of course," she said, "whenever I go out I always take my automatic loaded and ready and a good big stick. Billy insists on it. In the Boma we sleep with doors locked, thick wire netting across the windows and our pistols under our pillows. I was awfully thrilled at first, but do it as a matter of course now."[41]

She described the thick forest all around, the sunsets and moonlight and the native villages, clusters of red mud huts – "square built as circular huts aren't the fashion in the Digo District" - with no windows but just a hole in the thatch to let out the smoke. She mentioned the children playing and the small scraggy hens with long legs running all about, while the smells were "magnificent." Katharine was wholly enchanted by it all. She was thrilled by the glorious strong colours of the shrubs and trees and kept her eye open for interesting butterflies and moths. She was not at all put out by the oversize insect life and described the familiar red and black millipede "15 inches long and 2 inches wide" (surely an exaggeration) as "jolly pretty." Soon she could identify six types of ants, several species of beetle and spiders with furry legs of the tarantula breed.[42]

She reported to her uncle that nearly all the Europeans in Mombasa were British, apart from the banks and a few trading and shipping concerns. "The government people have of course picked the best part of the island round the whole front. The houses there are colonial style with thick stone walls and lattice-work enclosed verandahs, good solid government workmanship that will last for ages. Jolly comfortable and all of them are set in gardens." [43] The Government people she referred to were the administrative officers, the top échelon of the Colonial Service. They lived in a front row of large spacious houses overlooking the sea next to the golf course. Charles Fannin, who was an assistant surveyor attached to the Public Works Department (PWD), belonged to one of the least prestigious branches of the Colonial Service and probably lived in a bachelors mess, if not a tent. Elspeth Huxley gives a very clear explanation of the strict grading system that existed within the Colonial Service in her book **Out in the Midday Sun**: "First of all came the men of the administration – provincial and district commissioners, district officers and officials of the secretariat. Next came men of the various technical services – medical, agricultural, veterinary, educational, police and so on; finally at the bottom of the heap, employees of the Public Works Department and the Railway."[44] Wives also had to follow the pecking order and woe betide any unwary lady who infringed these unwritten rules. Charles as a surveyor despite his attachment to the PWD could classify himself as technical.

Katharine's return to Mombasa was delayed when rain made the road completely impassable. This gave her extra time to reflect on her situation. She could not live with Charles in Mombasa and she could not marry him as he still had a wife and child in London. A divorce would take at least eighteen months. Although Charles was comfortably off, earning £800 a year with accommodation, he had the extra expense of a family in England and it was clearly impossible for Katharine to stay alone in Mombasa. She would have to find a way to earn her own living and support herself until he was free to marry her. Hearing of job possibilities in Nairobi for single women, Katharine thought she should go there.

Maybe she regretted her impetuous change of plan, now realising difficulties she had not foreseen in the initial romantic glow, but the die was cast and there was no turning back.

Perhaps it was a case of true love after all, though neither of them were romantic figures. Katharine was plump, high spirited and short sighted, while Charles was lean, reserved and already middle-aged. They were both intellectuals and the attraction seems to have held a strong element of mental compatibility. Charles, born in 1890, the son of an Anglican canon in Natal, South Africa, had been a Rhodes scholar and a fine mathematician, who later trained as a civil engineer in London. He had fought with distinction during World War I and had been awarded the Military Cross for bravery in action. In 1919, his marriage already on the rocks, and with no job prospects or future in England, he had come out to Kenya on the Soldier Settler Scheme to start a new life. The 1919 land settlement scheme, which involved over 2 million acres of land, increased the area of white settlement in Kenya by a third at one stroke. It was run as a lottery, whereby the applicants drew lots for the farms and some individuals were lucky and some were not.

Farms came in two categories: large "A" farms, where the settler was not required to live on the farm and the smaller and more popular "B" farms where 1,000 acres was the basic working unit. Applicants for the "B" farms had to be prepared to put down a minimum of £1000 capital and prove an annual income of £200 and they had to agree to work the land. The Soldier Settlement Scheme of 1919 was not deemed a great success either in land settlement or immigration. Most of the participants were junior officers, who had no farming experience. They sold rather than settled on their farms as in many cases they found that a job with the railways or with the government was worth more than a thousand acres of African bush.[45]

Charles Fannin applied for a "B" category farm and was allocated 1,000 acres of land. Discovering he was no farmer, he sold out in 1920 and found a job with the Kenya Survey Department as a surveyor and was posted to Mombasa.[46] An excellent cricketer, hardworking and good at his job, he was well liked in Mombasa. Friends gave advice on how to stop the scandal-mongers and salvage respectability. Katharine should live in Nairobi until his divorce was final. Bishop and Mrs Heywood of Nairobi came to their rescue. They had daughters of the same age and they offered to house Katharine in Nairobi until she found her feet. Living with the Bishop and his family would restore Katharine's reputation and give her that essential stamp of acceptability in Nairobi society.

CHAPTER THREE
Nairobi 1926-1929

Katharine described her journey up to Nairobi in 1926 on the Uganda Mail in the third talk of her 1960 broadcast series.[47] In those days the twice-weekly train left about tea-time from old Kilindini Station, for ships passengers and luggage, and arrived in Nairobi the following evening.

> "Seasoned passengers knowing what they were in for dressed in their oldest, shabbiest clothes – with the inevitable topis, double terais and spine pads. But newcomers – myself among them – unwarily set off in the usual profusion of hot unsuitable garments and kept our headgear on until dark. There were no corridor coaches or restaurant cars then. At Samburu Station out we tumbled, and were herded by Goan stewards into an old smoky, lamplit railway dining room where, at long trestle tables, we fortified ourselves with what I recognised nostalgically as the typical British Railway Dinner. Watery soup with sinister bits floating in it, sad fish, blue about the fins, inedible meat and string beans, fruit salad with bright yellow custard-powder custard, followed by surprisingly good coffee supplied by the French Mission. After dinner I returned to my carriage to find my personal boy had undone my mattress roll and made my bed. The line was unmetalled then and a stifling cloud of red dust raised by the train was all pervasive. Next morning when we all got down at chilly

> dawn at Kiu Station, we'd managed to wash our hands and faces but otherwise we were sights, smothered from head to foot in a red film. We newcomers, sadly eyeing each other's filthy hair and ruined clothes, then understood why most of our fellow travellers had got themselves up like scarecrows and tied up their heads with scarves. However, after breakfast the small old wood burning engine puffed us bravely along, stopping now and then to take on logs from huge stacks dumped at intervals beside the train. Dirty discomfort was soon forgotten in watching from the windows of the train an endless display of wildlife.
>
> "Arriving in Nairobi, I secured a one-horse shay and in it lurched and bumped over the deep earth ruts and potholes of Government Road to the celebrated Norfolk Hotel. At the Norfolk my upstairs room opened, like all the rest, on to an unpartitioned balcony along which fellow guests seemed to make one cheerful uninhibited family party, with everyone knowing precisely what was going on and being much amused by it."

The strictly brought up Katharine was profoundly shocked by all this and lay in bed with her sheet firmly pulled up to her chin. However, she soon moved to stay with Bishop and Mrs Heywood and their daughters at old Bishopsbourne, a charming rambling bungalow on the Hill.[48] She described the bishop as "a commanding figure in his robes, tall and scholarly and incredibly energetic at getting about his large diocese. He was a petrifying car-driver careering along, often on the wrong side of the road, quite oblivious of on-coming traffic, his mind on higher things." Mrs Heywood was a kindly, motherly soul and no doubt Katharine made herself useful singing in the choir and helping out with her piano playing skills. She stayed at Bishopsbourne until May 1927.

Nairobi, unlike Mombasa, was an entirely new town. Before the advent of the railway and the British, Nairobi had been an uninhabited area of swampland. But its half way position on the railway line between the Coast and Uganda and its proximity to the best farming land in the colony made it the most practical place to build a capital city along purely

British lines. In 1907 the Governor moved his administration from Mombasa to Nairobi and by 1926 Nairobi had become the focal centre for Britain's most fashionable and go-ahead African colony. The Governor and all his chief officials resided there. Commercial enterprises had their headquarters in Nairobi and foreign diplomats and visiting dignitaries lurked close to the corridors of power. Governor Sir Edward Grigg had big ideas, hoping to become the Governor General of a federation of the British possessions in East Africa, (Kenya, Uganda and Tanganyika), which he would rule from Nairobi. During his tenure he set about turning the rather down-at-heel, tin-roofed settler town into a more fitting setting for the main seat of British power in East Africa. He invited architects to build impressive new administrative quarters and to plan parks and gardens. The Governor's wife, Joan Grigg, directed much of her energy into setting up maternity hospitals and medical clinics for African women and their babies. Elspeth Huxley remembered that the Griggs made a notable impact on the raw Colony. Despite their lavish spending, which was frowned upon in certain quarters, their tenure had a certain panache and an unforgettable style, which no other Governor captured.[49] Katharine lived in Nairobi for nearly three years during this Governorship and what she saw and heard during this period very much influenced her subsequent political views. Lord Delamere and Ewart Grogan embodied the imperialist and settler dreams. Ewart Grogan used to hold court with silver-tongued oratory at his Torrs Hotel. His eloquence kept Katharine spellbound as she listened to his plans for a Kenya ruled by white settlers, along the lines of New Zealand or Australia. Nairobi in the 1920s seemed the ideal place for an ambitious young girl wanting to make a new start in life and put the past behind her.

Hamisi, Katharine's personal servant or 'boy,' accompanied her to Nairobi along with her huge mounds of baggage. As she tells us, the first thing practically any European did on arriving in East Africa then was to take on a personal boy. He went with you everywhere, looked after you and your things and when you stayed with people cleaned your room and helped your host's servants. "I too took on a boy and struck it lucky. A friend's headboy had produced a number of raw youths for inspection and I took instinctively to a large shambling Mgiriama with an engaging grin and the innate courtesy of Coast Africans. I signed up his brand new Kipande and hired him for 30/- a month – considered in those days very generous."[50] (All adult male Africans had to carry a kipande, a pass or registration certificate. This served both as an identification card and as a mechanism of labour and movement control. An employer had to sign the kipande, when taking on an employee, and endorse it when terminating employment. Kenyans disliked this system and abolished it at independence). Hamisi stayed with Katharine Fannin for over forty years until he died. He became a greatly valued friend, prop and mainstay of the household. When Katharine first employed him, he had never done a job except help his fisherman father and he didn't speak a word of English.

Katharine first found employment as a bookkeeper with the Anglo-Baltic Shipping Company, but had a stroke of luck by talking to a minor colonial government official at a Christmas party, who offered her a position in the Research Laboratory of the Government Medical Department. She jumped at the opportunity as this guaranteed her £300 a year, plus £60 housing allowance, free dentist, doctor, travelling and a first class passage home with six months leave after two-and-a-half years service. As she herself put it, "socially I have moved from the Polsloe Road of Commerce to the Heavitree of Government Service."[51] As the office was some way out of town she bought herself a second-hand car with the money she had saved from the job at Anglo-Baltic and quickly taught herself to type using the Bishop's typewriter. In February 1927 she sent this excellent news to her uncle by the first airmail from East Africa.

Not much is heard of her for the rest of the year, but we know she disliked the cold months of July and August, after the rains, when the roads became impassable and red mud clogged Nairobi. She had moved into a bungalow, which fortunately did not suffer from the severe earthquake of January 1928.

For Christmas 1927 she took three weeks local leave and drove to the Coast with Charles Fannin and a friend. This was quite a pioneering adventure as L D Galton-Fenzi had only just made his memorable Nairobi-Mombasa safari one year previously in 1926. It was still considered such a hazardous enterprise the local newspaper reported successful drives so everyone would know who had managed to complete the trip. No real road had been built connecting Mombasa and Nairobi and the journey involved nearly 300 miles over parallel ruts roughly following the path of the railway. The Fannin expedition got no further than thirty miles out of Nairobi before the car broke down. They put it on a railway truck and ignominiously finished the journey by train.

On the way back, the car mended, they drove the first seventy miles through the Samburu desert with no mishap, but then the brakes suddenly jammed in a swamp. They managed to unstick the brakes, but for the next sixty miles into Voi they had no brakes at all! Then one tyre burst followed by another just as darkness fell. They lost their way and drove up to the axles into a black cotton soil swamp. "We all swore very loudly and heartily – and then knowing from bitter experience – got out blasphemously and unroped all the kit – petrol, rifles and every blessed thing – to lighten the car. [52] Then we took hatchets and cut down every blinking bush for a hundred yards around – because the swamp was about the worst malaria and blackwater and snake infested place we could have stuck in – and then made a road where there wasn't one. That took us two hours and it took us another half hour of straining and heaving and awful language, to get the car onto firmer ground. I was put on to drive and the men all pushed like mad. Our homemade road held just long enough to get the car over and we carried all the gear back, ankle deep. Anyway, we got to Voi after midnight. I was so done that I fell asleep as I sat in my chair eating some food and don't remember anything until I woke up about three hours later on the bed in the dak bungalow still in my clothes and heavy boots."[53]

After a days rest at Voi to repair the brakes, they continued on to Makindu, admiring the views of Mount Kilimanjaro "soaring into the sky all the way along." They did the remaining 150 miles to Nairobi the next day. The perilous tree trunk bridge over the Kiboko River gave them an anxious time. "We had to build it up by cutting down a couple of small trees, but we got the car across and from there the remaining eighty miles was simple." This memorable drive had also included the rescue of the driver and two passengers of a lorry. They had been attempting the same journey and had been chased and then charged by a couple of rhinos when the lorry stuck in the mud. The terrified travellers had narrowly escaped death by sitting on the roof, while the enraged rhinos made mincemeat of the lower half of the vehicle. Katharine and Charles came upon these unfortunate travellers and gave them lift to the nearest station, but their lorry was a complete wreck.[54]

Katharine arrived back in Nairobi on her 25th birthday. It had taken four days to drive from Mombasa to Nairobi. On Boxing Day she and Charles set out on a camping safari and stalked buck but with no success: "I walked miles and miles with a rifle and made my shoulder sore and never hit a thing. But it's simply topping to knock around in a shirt and a pair of slacks and big boots, (to keep out the damned ticks) and sleep on your camp bed whenever you feel like it."[55]

By March that year she was working hard for a shorthand and typing exam that would earn her a 30/- rise per month. She had also entered 'High Society,' attending a dinner party given by the Chief Justice for members of the Hilton Young Commission, who had come out to Kenya on a fact finding mission and also to examine the possibilities for an East African Federation. The following day she shook hands with Governor and Lady Grigg at a Garden Party, where apparently Sir Hilton Young, the star guest, "wore white spats and stood around looking commanding and picturesque."[56] Only the cream of Nairobi society were invited to the Governor's Garden Parties and being introduced and shaking hands with the Governor was the ultimate seal of social approval, carrying with it almost the same éclat as being presented at Court. Small wonder that Katharine Fannin carefully preserved her invitation amongst her personal papers.[57]

British colonies were microcosms of British society and in the 1920s and 30s class distinctions and social status were taken very seriously. Kenya had a reputation of being particularly snobbish and your chances of promotion and success within the hierarchy of the British community very much depended on whether you were considered socially acceptable or not. Many of the settlers and colonial administrators were ex-officers who had fought in World War I and had come out to Kenya in order to preserve their 'caste' as officers and gentlemen, which with high unemployment and inflation in Britain had become increasingly under strain. Kenya was attractive to younger sons and minor branches of the aristocracy, retired officers and public schoolboys, precisely because it seemed to offer a career with a chance of profit and some certainty of status without too much competition. It was possible in Kenya to live cheaply and yet preserve a semblance of a lifestyle that in Europe they simply could not have afforded. They could have houses full of servants, keep racehorses, play polo and own large tracts of undeveloped bush. Both farming and Government Service were considered socially acceptable occupations for gentlemen while the professions, trade and commerce ranked further down the social scale. Katharine Fannin understood these social distinctions because she fell on the outer edges of the system. She desperately wanted to be part of the social élite, which she considered the key to success. She was extremely ambitious, but with neither birthright, fortune, nor beauty to assist her, she had to rely on wit, hard work and that most elusive and important element of all – luck.

In addition to her interest in entering society and furthering her career, Katharine was also curious about the country and the people. She repeatedly told her Uncle how much she liked the Africans and how interesting she found their customs. In one letter[58] she described how she watched the Maasai procedure for extracting ox-blood for mixing with milk. "An old man with a bow and arrow stands about four feet away from the ox and looses off his arrow just piercing the beast's jugular vein. Certain damsels then dash up with gourds and when the wretched ox shows signs of fainting they cauterize the wound and the animal is turned out to grass for 4-6 months to get over it. The Maasai drink the blood by making a kind of gin-swizzle of it. They mix it straight away, half and half with milk – froth it up with a swizzle stick and drink the lot off with tremendous relish. Tradition says that before our rule here they used prisoners and captives instead of oxen." Later in the same letter, she described the Wakamba as "wonderful workers with their hands making chain mail as fine as any we saw in Spain, all without tools." In another letter she described the Kikuyu, who she spoke of as a small people not usually growing to a height of more that just over five feet. "But the women look very attractive wearing two brown hides made soft with working them under water and bead rings in their ears and coloured chains. On special dance days they also wear bead caps and wide waistcoats."[59] Katharine described her Goan clerk, Nicholas Sebastiano Cavalho Montenez Maximilliano de Souza. (All the government offices employed Goans as clerks as they were considered honest and reliable). "He is my personal clerk and old enough to be my father. A topping old thing as black as your hat and a Portuguese gentleman of the very finest manners." [60] Later on she complained about her roommate at the bungalow, who is "not quite a lady" and won't help her in the garden being entirely occupied in getting on in society.[61]

In another letter[62] she described the visit of the Duke and Duchess of Gloucester to unveil war memorials, when all the tribal chiefs turned out in full splendour. "Chief Kinyanjui of the Kikuyu…was there in full regalia of colobus monkey robe slung round his shoulders, enormous headdress of ostrich feathers dyed green – lots of earrings and nose rings… The Maasai chief Seggi was there 6 feet 5 inches dressed in fur robes and a lion's mane headdress – and paramount chief Malamas, who still holds such a superstitious sway over his subjects that as he walked down the street followed by his witch doctors and headmen, all the Kavirondo in the crowd sank to their knees in respect." Katharine found the display most impressive.

Katharine obviously enjoyed life enormously in Nairobi. She found her job stimulating and whenever she could over a weekend, would take her car and some friends and drive out to the Rift Valley, Embu, Naivasha, Fort Hall or the Ngong Hills to enjoy the magnificent scenery and wildlife. "Heaven preserve me from ever developing into one of those parasitical women of the tropics, who drink tea from 10-12 in the mornings and hog it on their beds from 1-4.30 every afternoon," she wrote.[63] She earned her living and paid her way, but only just. Her credit balance at the end of each month in 1928, was 12/-.

October 1928, when Edward Prince of Wales came on his first celebrated visit to Kenya, marked a high point for Katharine.[64] (Edward, Prince of Wales and the Duke of Gloucester arrived in Mombasa September 28, 1928 on board the *S S Malda* for an informal tour of East Africa, but their visit was cut short by the illness of H M King George Vth). Vivacious and single, Katharine enjoyed a round of endless celebration, fireworks and parties for two weeks. But her constitution, never strong, collapsed at about this time, and for the following year her health was uncertain. The mood of her letters changed. She worried about money matters and wrote bitterly about her rapacious stepmother and the injustice of her father's will. She had attempted to contest the will, but her efforts had failed. In February 1929, she described famine and a swarm of locusts fourteen miles long, which flew over Nairobi. The thick swarm obscured the sun and threw the houses into darkness so they had to turn on the electric lights to see. She spoke of the Governor's unpopularity, especially how the Griggs were spending £120,000 on building two palaces of Government Houses, one in Nairobi and one in Mombasa, instead of improving the roads as originally promised or putting the money to some more public spirited use. Depressed and out of sorts, she had suddenly had enough of Nairobi and thought she would feel better once she settled in Mombasa. She moved out of her bungalow and was back once more at Bishopsbourne, being fed junket by the kindly Bishop's lady.[65]

Katharine gave no exact explanation for her long period of malaise. She mentioned a spell in hospital with malaria, but she also spoke of heart trouble, fatigue and not being allowed to play sport for six months, which perhaps suggests hepatitis or some related illness. Severely depressed, she needed "guts and willpower to fight against ill-health in the tropics."[66]

Charles had gone to England in July 1928 to finalise his divorce, but it seems things did not turn out exactly as expected and it is possible the disappointment may have affected Katharine's well being. The nervous strain of waiting and struggling on her own in Nairobi may also have exacted its toll on her system. Charles paid a visit to Uncle John at Eastcliff and collected various household items for Katharine. Amongst these was her fur coat, an article she had a particular attachment to. Later on she wrote that she never travelled without it and strange as it seems today, took it with her all across Africa. Katharine felt sure her dearest 'Runcle' would like Charles as "he is awfully quiet and keen on walks and cats," but his reaction was not revealed.[67]

Katharine eventually married Charles quietly at the Scottish Church in Nairobi sometime in 1929.[68] It is strange that no marriage certificate or wedding photograph turns up among her papers and there is no reference to this long-awaited event anywhere in her writing. On the other hand she carefully preserved her engagement notice to 'Buckie' in *The Times*. Did she regret her whirlwind shipboard romance with Charles? Had she suffered another change of heart? Or was she simply still feeling unwell? We can't know, but for her there was no turning back. Marriage to Charles Fannin was the only option.[69]

CHAPTER FOUR
Early married life in Mombasa: 1929-1931

Katharine and Charles spent Christmas of 1929 in Malindi. Calling it their honeymoon puts perhaps an over-romantic gloss on events. In her broadcast series of 1960 Katharine described her journey up the North Coast and her stay in Malindi.

> "In 1929 Malindi's District Commissioner, Mr Brailsford, invited us to spend Christmas with him at the Boma. To make sure of getting there in time, we set off a couple of days early. Nyali Bridge was not built. You got to the North Mainland on a contraption of planks laid across a stout wooden boat, which dumped you off on the shore at Kisauni. The main road then was a narrow track, which bumped over coral outcrops, through deep sand, round baobabs, palms and mango trees to the steep approach of Shimo La Tewa Ferry.[70] There the Giriama ferry boys enchanted to welcome the comparatively few cars of those days, staged an impromptu ngoma (dance) on the shore, before getting down to the task of getting you across. Takaungu village, through which the road went next was very picturesque and had been an Arab stronghold.[71] In the 1880s an Indian duka (small shop) had been appointed postal agent and in 1929 they still had in use a post office scales, weights and a little pillar-box all marked V R - Victoria Regina. One crossed Takaungu creek rather perilously on two long iron girders, which joined the ends of the causeway. After that the road went

through sisal plantations until you came to the chain ferry at Kilifi. Between Kilifi and Malindi were long boring stretches of road with grass growing high in a central ridge that scraped the bottom of your car. Then rather unexpectedly there was Malindi. Now in 1929, Malindi itself stopped short at the Boma. It was the last house before the long deserted beach with no other building between it and Mambrui, except one tumble down mud and makuti banda (makuti is the straw thatch that the small huts - bandas - are roofed with), just where the beach curves, which Mr O'Brady had made into a sort of primitive inn. Very different from now!

The Boma, a large two-storey building right on the beach, was much as it is to day.[72] Downstairs was the office and the D C and his guests lived in the cool rooms upstairs, then reached by a broad stepped ladder through a massive trapdoor. A romantic custom of earlier days still prevailed - when we were all upstairs and about to go to bed, an askari (guard) ceremoniously shut that heavy wooden door with a bang and fastened it down with two massive wooden bars. This I may say was to secure us from being rushed in the night by raiding bands or carried off by slavers. I was fearfully impressed; it seemed to bring Rider Haggard's Allan Quartermaine to life.

We spent a wonderful ten days meeting the local Arab and Asian notabilities, who called to wish the District Commissioner a Happy Christmas and New Year."[73]

A letter dated 1931[74] gives further information about Malindi and Mr Brailsford and a second Christmas holiday also spent in Malindi. Katharine described Malindi Town as rather disappointing – consisting of six large Arab houses and about 100 Swahili mud huts. "There is nothing to do except eat fish, bathe in the surf and sleep. All of which Charles and I did for a fortnight and thoroughly enjoyed it. Mr Brailsford, our host, is inclined to be bit trying as his wife is in a loony asylum and he tells you about it all day and every day and bemoans his lot."[75] In the same letter Katharine mentioned a visit by the Liwali of the Coast, Sir Ali bin Salim, who came to tea one day and brought with him a mechanical toy to show the D C. "It was a fat German harridan made of tin, which by a neat arrangement of wheels and emery paper opened her mouth and emitted showers of sparks."[76] Apparently this quite cheered up poor Mr Brailsford. The life of a Government official stuck out in a remote spot, as Malindi was considered in those days, was lonely and uncomfortable with few amusements and no doubt he could be excused somewhat strange and eccentric behaviour.

Later on they visited Mambrui – just a mosque and a collection of mud huts. Here Katharine bought some decorative floor mats for which Mambrui was famous. They had stories, texts from the Koran or lucky signs woven into the rush work patterns and measured about six feet by four feet all most artistically done. She used them to furnish the empty dilapidated government house, where Charles and Katharine lived in Mombasa.

Charles Fannin, who had lived in a tent for the first four years of his stay in Mombasa, was obviously not domesticated and improvements to his bachelor arrangements came high on Katharine's wifely priorities. She started her married life living in the garden, while the Public Works Department foremen thoroughly de-batted and fumigated their house. Sefu, her husband's faithful retainer, who had been with him for ten years, found the new regime too much to cope with and beat a hasty retreat.[77]

At this time Katharine kept a pet mongoose to which she was very attached. The mongoose protected them against snakes and it also ate rats and other small rodents.

To keep herself busy and bring in enough money to live, Katharine worked at the British-American Tobacco Company office in Mombasa as a typist. Although no specific mention is ever made, it is clear Charles had a considerable financial commitment to his earlier marriage. Ill health continued to trouble Katharine. In her letters to her uncle she complained of headaches, attacks of dysentery and malaria as well as unspecified infections, which before the days of antibiotics and modern drugs often took weeks to cure and left her feeling low and depressed. Charles' job as a surveyor took him on frequent foot safaris into the uncharted bush of the coastal area, where he would disappear for weeks on end with his trusted headman, Jascho,[78] and a string of porters.

Katharine describes herself in later years as a Government Servant's chattel, who survived eleven moves in the first fifteen years of marriage.[79] There is no doubt they needed considerable resilience to live at the coast, without air conditioning, refrigeration and other modern conveniences. In the 1920s and early 30s few European women lived in Mombasa as the climate was considered unsuitable and conditions too severe. There was virtually no white settlement at the Coast, unlike the areas around Nairobi, where the temperate climate had attracted many settlers. The Coast Province known as the 'Sloth Belt' was Kenya's depressed area sunk in lethargy starved of funds, staff and hope. The problems of the Coast, said the *Native Affairs Report* for 1923, were "inveterate apathy and ineradicable improvidence."[80] Attitudes only began to change in the mid-1930s when development of Mombasa and the Coast slowly began. The Mombasa the Fannins knew was still relatively unchanged from the earliest pioneering days of the 1890s and so her reminiscences of the period provide a uniquely valuable record.

The Coastal Strip of Kenya, which stretched from Kismayu in the North to Vanga in the South and extended a distance of ten miles inland, nominally still belonged to the Sultan of Zanzibar – its former ruler – although the British administered it. Seyyideh Province, as the Coastal Province was called, was not a British colony, like the rest of Kenya, but a Protectorate leased by the British from the Sultan of Zanzibar on a rental agreement. The Sultan retained the right to appoint his representatives or Liwalis at the major towns and, though their powers were very limited, they were much respected. They upheld the Muslim religion and looked after the interests of the Sultan's former subjects. Only the Sultan's plain red flag could fly from a flagpole directly fixed in the ground. The Union Jack or other flags could only be flown when attached to a building. Muslim holidays and festivals were honoured and Muslim law, Sharia, was still practised in civil cases, although criminal cases came under the British Courts.

In one of her letters Katharine described the famous tea party of 1930, hosted by the chief of the Sultan's representatives, the Liwali of the Coast, Sir Ali bin Salim, in honour of the retiring Governor, Sir Edward Grigg. "Most of the Coast went," Katharine wrote. "All the Arabs and Swahili Twelve Tribes were there, looking very picturesque in their long robes with curly silver swords stuck in their belts. There was one really magnificent old pirate, Feraj bin Shaman, head of the Washihiri Community, big gold earrings, henna coloured beard and bright green shawl. Probably the biggest scoundrel on the Coast, but he has the most perfect manners and looks magnificent. At this particular party we all sat around and were entertained by Arab dancers – mainly lots of noise and precious little dancing, really just a wriggle. Ali himself is a pleasant old rogue, who admits to having kept slaves. He has a splendid palace[81] on a small headland and one has tea under the Mango trees with the sea on three sides."[82]

From her Broadcast Series comes this impression of Mombasa Town:

> "The really important shopping centre was the bazaar in the Old Town - a fascinating if rather smelly jumble of narrow lanes and tall old Arab-style buildings, with latticed balconies and purdah-shuttered windows and dark shops open to the streets. You could turn over bolts of exquisite Chinese and Indian satins, silks and cotton prints; see piles of elephant tusks; if you were a mariner, buy at a ships chandlers anything from a full sized anchor to a brass eyelet; in dark little dens get vellum flasks of oriental scents - henna and jasmine and one pungent variety I'm afraid we called 'Sheikh's Breath.' Messrs Edward St Rose, long established, upheld western pharmacy, but a few doors along Indian and other herbalists compounded their pills and potions and love-philtres. You could pick up curved Arab daggers in silver sheaths, heavy armlets and silver anklets, which have since become museum specimens. When the Indian shopkeeper knew you personally, a visit was the sign for little bowls of bitter black coffee or sweet sherbet or rosewater to be brought out and you sat down there and then for a friendly leisurely gossip, typical of the unhurried friendliness and good manners, legacy of centuries of Arab tradition. Everywhere one saw the sturdy hamals pushing their heavily loaded carts around - no lorries or cars in the Bazaar then, as

> there were hardly any roads they could use. Scores of huts and houses were pulled down to make way even for the few, now pitifully inadequate thirty foot roads, which government at great expense pushed through the congested Bazaar in the face of furious opposition by many property owners. In those earlier times the big European firms kept their head offices in picturesque Vasco da Gama Street (now Mbarak Hinawy Road) which runs down to the Old Customs."[83]

In July 1930 she went on a cruise to Zanzibar on the Italian liner *Francesco Crispi.* "Zanzibar is utterly fascinating," she wrote, "and one of the cheapest places in the world as there are no customs duties. The Sultan is a magnificent old gentleman of the very best Arab kind - perfect manners and dignity that hits one. He used to be driven about in a horse palanquin with runners clearing the way with whips, now he has a carriage and pair with very decorative coachmen and footmen and outriders all in scarlet and fezzes. The runners beat the crowd out of the way with horse hair flywhisks. We saw him bowing very sedately - all the Europeans raise their hats."[84] She admired the Beit-al-Ajaib, (the Sultan's palace on the waterfront), with its famous carved wooden doors painted bright green and gilded with texts from the Koran and the sweeping staircase with enormous silver knobs on the newel posts. The town was spotlessly clean and filled with exotic wares of every kind - chests, old swords, Persian rugs, bottles of clove oil, native pottery and nameless other items, laid out on the pavements and hung out on the walls of the houses to catch your eye. Katharine bought herself a pair of silk pyjamas and Chinese embroidered crepe-de-chine underclothes and proclaimed the place "a perfect paradise." Later she went on a drive through the clove and nutmeg plantations. "I consider Zanzibar a paradise on earth, glorious natural avenues of mango trees and Zebra palm - cloves filling the whole place with scent and seaviews everywhere you go."[85]

The next day they steamed on to Dar es Salaam. Here she admired the way the Germans had laid out the town with double avenues of lovely shade and flowering trees, though she considered it not a patch on Mombasa, which in turn could not compare with Zanzibar. She found the land locked harbour unpleasantly stuffy.

At Tanga, they heard of a recent diplomatic incident involving a German warship the *Karlsruhe*.[86] Apparently the German Captain with excessive zeal had paraded his men and those from a visiting German trading vessel through the streets of the town doing the goosestep to the tune of Deutschland über Alles. The authorities wisely looked the other way but at the public banquet, with the British District Commissioner present, when the German captain got to his feet and proposed a toast – "Here's to the day when the German flag shall fly in Tanga and the territory of Tanganyika is restored to us from whom it was stolen," they could no longer ignore such deliberate provocation. The DC refused to drink to such a toast and walked out. An urgent telegraph was sent to the British Governor of Tanganyika, who ordered the immediate departure of the *Karlsruhe* and forbade its entry into Dar es Salaam. For some days it was the talk of the town and there was much speculation whether British East Africa should close its ports to all German shipping in protest. However, as Katharine reported, no one in Tanganyika took it as a serious threat, so the matter was dropped. This interesting little interlude provides a foretaste of events leading up to World War II and clearly illustrated British attitudes of the period. In 1930 Germany was already beginning to rearm itself and flex its muscles. According to Katharine the German visit did not succeed in provoking a pro-German response in Tanganyika and after this visit Germany made no further move to reclaim its former possession in Eastern Africa.[87]

By 1931 after more than four years in East Africa without a break, Katharine longed for leave in England. She had told her uncle to plant six extra rows of beans and peas and lay in plenty of soft fruit, especially blackberries of which she was particularly fond. She asked him to make sure he had a good supply of fresh farm eggs, large and brown with yellow yolks.[88] They had booked a passage on the *Langithly Castle*, newest of the East Africa Castle Line ships, sailing from Mombasa on May 20th via Cape Town and Tenerife – and due to arrive in London on June 29th. On the way down the coast the liner was to call in at Beira, Durban, Lourenco Marques, Delagoa Bay and Port Elizabeth, all places she was eager to see. They were booked to return to East Africa in December and planned to visit Charles' parents in Natal on the way back.

Before going on leave, Katharine received yet another set-back to her financial expectations. In a long letter of March 1931, she rails against the terrible injustice of her stepmother's will. Ethel Maud Trood had died in India in 1929 and had left £10,000 (a substantial sum of money in those days) to nieces and nephews, while the entire residue of her personal estate went to a sister. Neither of her step-children received anything. Katharine who had been disappointed in her earlier fruitless attempt to contest her father's will felt exceptionally bitter that nothing of her father's estate came to his children, but all went to relatives of the second wife, to whom he had been married only briefly.[89] She wrote with feeling: "I see now that legislation is before the House, whereby a man is bound to make adequate provision for his children," and swore that if she ever came into a fortune, she would overturn the will on principle. Geoffrey had once more proved to be a broken reed and failed entirely to salvage anything from his father's estate – much to his sister's disgust. She vowed on her return at least to wrest some silver back, which she claimed was hers by right! [90]

CHAPTER FIVE
Good works in Mombasa 1932-1936

After her return from home leave in early 1932 Katharine Fannin exuded a new maturity and seriousness of purpose. Her correspondence with her dearest Runcle became less frequent and the letters no longer showed the girlish enthusiasm and zest for life that made the earlier ones so readable. Instead her letters listed people of importance she had met and her new preoccupation with social welfare.

Promotion and a pay rise for Charles[91] meant she did not need to supplement the family income by working in an office as a typist and had time to turn her considerable energies to good works. Her husband was busy developing a town plan for Mombasa Island and laying out a network of roads. She, not to be out done, determined to make a contribution as well.

It is not certain when her interest in the League of Mercy started. Perhaps Bishop Heywood, an active patron, introduced her to this society that provided help for destitute settlers. There was a great need for such a society in Kenya, as not all would-be settlers prospered. Pioneering life was hard and farming could prove disastrous for the inexperienced, while accident and disease left many distressed orphans and widows. The League of Mercy often provided fares for widows and children and indeed whole families, who wished to return to England, having failed to make a new life in Kenya. Karen Blixen's famous account of her struggle to grow coffee at Ngong[92] was a familiar tale and many pioneer farmers suffered similar experiences. For those without extra finances to fall back on, the results could be devastating and many settler families in the 20s and 30s lost their entire savings. Only the most fortunate and resilient succeeded. In 1932 Katharine Fannin was appointed the League of Mercy's representative in Mombasa. Since few white colonialists settled at the Coast,[93] her chief duty was to make sure the distressed settlers and their dependents made the sea passage they had been booked on.

The League of Mercy, in those days, extended its help only to European settlers, but Katharine felt strongly that something more should be done to assist the distressed of all races, whatever their colour or creed. The Indian communities were well organised, yet she could not help but notice the utter misery of the scores of poor, disabled and elderly Africans, who thronged the streets of Mombasa. Katharine felt the Colonial Government needed to become more involved with the welfare of its subjects. The only organisation providing direct help to the needy in Mombasa was the Social Services League, which had been started in 1921 and was run entirely on voluntary contributions given mainly by Asian merchants. In 1930 Lady Grigg had opened a clinic for the Social Services League in a house donated by Sir Ali bin Salim.[94]

Mombasa in the 1920s and 30s had a particularly severe problem following the abolition of slavery. Many people who might otherwise have been cared for in sickness and old age were simply left to fend for themselves. The way of life that had been operating for thousands of years on the Coast had been abruptly dismantled with the arrival of the British and their anti-slavery laws. The changeover from a feudal system that depended on patronage and slave labour to a modern society, which relied on the monetary system and a wage earning labour force was a revolutionary upheaval that caused hardships in the interim period. Not only were the former slave-owners – Arabs and Swahilis – severely impoverished, but their erstwhile slaves often suffered as well. Under Islamic law, masters had been obliged to care for their slaves even when they could no longer work. This was essential as a slave uprooted from his home, often living in a foreign country, had no one else to turn to. But the British had come along and said it was bad to be a slave and even worse to own one. The IBEACo (Imperial British East Africa Company, which had governed Mombasa 1888-95) had a policy of purchasing slaves from Arabs and then turning them on the streets as liberated men.

The abolition of slavery, begun in 1873 with the closure of the slave markets, had been hastened along by the legislation of 1889 and 1890, whereby persons entering the Sultan's dominions after November 1, 1889, were automatically free. Another important piece of legislation was the decree that all children of slaves born after January 1, 1890, were free citizens and that slaves of owners who died also gained instant freedom. In 1897 slave owning was declared illegal in Zanzibar and Pemba, but this did not apply to the Coastal Strip, where laws against slave owning were not enforced until the early years of the 20th century. Some of the more fortunate freed slaves ended up at Mission Stations, where the missionaries taught them to read and write and follow a craft. There was a big freed slave settlement on the north mainland just outside Mombasa called Freretown, where thousands of ex-slaves were cared for.[95] But many ex-slaves had to survive as best they could. Coming originally perhaps from a tribe somewhere in central Africa, they could not return home. They had lost the extended family or tribal network that in Africa works in lieu of a welfare state. So when sickness struck or they became enfeebled by old age, they simply died in the street or slowly starved to death. The Muslim habit of alms-giving tended to exacerbate the problem, encouraging the practise of begging. In 1932 many beggars and ex-slaves lived in misery on the streets of Mombasa.

Katharine had no doubt been aware of the situation in Mombasa for some time, but the desperate plight of Mombasa's poor did not strike home until one day in May 1932. Katharine discovered a poor old Swahili lady, starved and nearly at death's door, who had laid herself down in the Fannin's garden to breathe her last. Katharine rushed her to the hospital in time to save her life. This personal experience of the misery suffered convinced Katharine that something should be done to assist the most desperate cases and provide basic shelter for the aged and destitute in Mombasa.

Katharine wrote: "I at once went to the PC (Provincial Commissioner) Mr Field-Jones, the DC (District Commissioner) and Liwali - I also wrote to the League of Mercy asking them to help finance a home for aged and destitute natives, if I could get such a thing established. I then went back to the PC, DC, Town Clerk and Bishop Hefferman of the White Fathers, the Liwali and certain Indians. By that time the slump was on and money was scarce and nobody seemed to be able to do much. In the meantime I personally was keeping about half a dozen indigent old natives in food, clothing and lodging. Realizing very soon what a big thing it was turning into - quite beyond my means - I went at my own expense to Zanzibar to see the Sultan and the Wakf Commissioners there to try and get a grant from them. Zanzibar had no money to spare as they contributed to their immense model almshouses and leper's home at Welezo. So on my return the new DC, Mr Boulderson, arranged a special meeting of the Wakf Commissioners in Mombasa at which I put before them a complete almshouse scheme - with plans kindly drawn up by Mr McIntyre, finances worked out to a farthing - and land suggested for its site. (This was in December 1932) The Wakf received the scheme very favourably until they heard the Almshouse was to be staffed by nuns - when they (the Wakf Commissioners) backed out because they said they feared proselytising by the Catholics. A very feeble excuse!

"I was in despair and then tried to get a government grant from the Native Betterment Fund. Finally a new ADC (Assistant District Commissioner) Mr Foster came to Mombasa, who listened with great sympathy to my troubles and to him must be given the credit of taking a native house in Majengo, where we put our old people." [96]

From a letter sent in September 1933 to her dearest Runcle, we hear she is "completely swamped in good works" and spends most of her entire day "haranguing venerable Arab gentlemen trying to make them cough up about £5000 for my scheme ......Young Foster (the ADC here) and I have for the past three months rented an eight roomed native house and we've taken a dozen of the most appalling cases and are simply keeping them housed and fed out of our own pockets as an object lesson to Government and the Wakf Commissioners. I drive out to see our poor old creatures practically every day. I am definitely doing this because I think your duty is primarily to give a hand to those nearest you, whatever their colour."[97] Later at a dinner party at Government House, Mombasa, she buttonholed Mr Monke Mason Moore, (the Acting Governor), who promised to do what he could.[98]

But funds proved hard to find despite all her efforts. The Wakf Commissioners, a Muslim body, which looked after some of the mosques, met her appeals with polite equivocation.[99] They had already backed out of any obligation they might have had on religious grounds. In some ways one can sympathise with their reluctance. Why should the Arabs be expected now to look after the very slaves they had been forced to set free, much against their wishes? Under the old system no such need would have arisen and in any case they already did all that the Koran required them to do, in the form of alms-giving. Under the circumstances it is not surprising that Katharine's requests were met by delaying and procrastinating tactics designed to avoid confrontation especially with a woman.

Katharine received two memorable letters from Mohamed bin Ali, Liwali of Mombasa and chairman of the Wakf Commission. The first sought clarification over the exact time of a proposed meeting: "Our arrangement is for tomorrow 8 O'Clock. Did you mean 8 of Kiswahili, which means afternoon, or 8 morning? Please tell me. I am a bit confused lest I mistake the time." (Swahili time, counted from dawn, is six hours adrift from western time, which is counted from midnight. The discrepancy between the two systems caused endless confusion and was often used as a convenient excuse). The following day the Liwali sent a second letter pleading sickness of one of the Commissioners.[100] Katharine Fannin was not deceived nor was she amused. She speaks scathingly of those "rich Arabs who never considered that a blind or paralysed or otherwise incapacitated pauper should do anything but beg or be left to starve to death."[101] It is unfortunate that no records of the Wakf Commission in Mombasa survive pre-1936, so there is only Katharine's version of the story and she was not renowned for seeing any point of view except her own.

Her determined and domineering manner not only caused a falling out with the ultra-conservative Wakf Commissioners, but by May 1934 she had also quarrelled with her chief supporter, P F Foster, who now accused her of taking all the credit for the scheme herself and running it as if it were her private concern.[102] From 1933-1934 the temporary Majengo home had been kept going by voluntary work and charitable donations. Medical help and provisions were given free and philanthropic Asian merchants donated blankets. Sir Ali Bin Salim, chief representative of the Sultan of Zanzibar and Liwali of the Coast, gave £25 a month out of his own pocket, a generous and regular contribution that just about covered running costs. Katharine supervised the delivery of food and clothing, oversaw the administration and visited the inmates nearly every day. Unfortunately it appears that her personality made her unpopular and aroused jealousies. In May 1934 Foster and the representative of the Liwali, Bahamadi, formed an almshouse committee, making the pointed decision that no woman be asked to join.

Understandably Katharine found this exclusion very hurtful. Her health, always precarious, collapsed and for nearly a month she was seriously unwell. At the end of June she wrote a rather pitiful letter to her uncle suggesting he come out for a visit – no mention was made of good works, instead she was immersed in gardening.[103]

However, this was not the end of her connection with the Mombasa Almshouses. Her energetic petitioning in government circles did bear fruit. P F Foster left Mombasa in late 1935 and another Almshouse Committee was formed, headed by the District Commissioner, W Boulderson (Bouldy), which this time included Katharine Fannin. The Municipal Board of Mombasa was now directed to make the setting up of a Government Almshouse a top priority. Formal application was made to build the almshouse on the land Katharine had suggested in the original proposal of 1932. The plot was in Makupa close to where the White Sisters ran a Mission school. From the beginning these nuns had promised to help run the almshouse. This arrangement copied the Zanzibar example, where sisters of St Joseph's Mission staffed the government-sponsored almshouse complex at Welezo under the supervision of the Director of Medical and Sanitary Services. Sir Ali bin Salim and the Wakf Commission rejected the Makupa site and withdrew their support. They wanted the almshouse located in Likoni, away from Christian influence.

Money for the almshouse now came in thick and fast. The Canteen fund of the Municipal Board raised a substantial sum, private firms donated £150, and his Highness the Aga Khan, visiting Mombasa in January 1936, gave £100 in cash to J D McKean, the District Commissioner, (who had succeeded Boulderson) towards construction costs.[104] Just when Katharine's almshouse scheme was at last succeeding, she and her husband were posted to Nairobi. Katharine left Mombasa in March 1936, and, to her disappointment, she was not personally involved in the final completion of the almshouse. However, that year she was awarded the George Vth Silver Jubilee Medal for her contribution to social work – a mark of appreciation for all the effort she had put in and an honour of which she was very proud.

For many people this would have been enough to assuage any feelings of resentment. But bitter controversy flared once more, when, in September 1937, the Colonial Governor Sir Robert Brooke-Popham officially opened the Mombasa Almshouse.[105] Katharine Fannin was neither invited to the opening ceremony, nor was she, in her opinion, properly acknowledged as the initiator of the project. Instead, they gave credit to Foster, who had returned to Mombasa. This enraged her when she read the newspaper coverage.[106] She wrote stiff letters of complaint both to the Governor Sir Robert Brooke-Popham and to J D McKean, DC Mombasa, who had given the unfortunate speech that had been reported in the national press.

There is no doubt that Katharine Fannin was not an easy person to work with. Her steamroller approach had certainly upset the delicate sensibilities of the Wakf Commissioners and her unseemly quarrel with Foster, over who should take the credit for the almshouse scheme, leaves a most unsavoury after-taste. But despite her involvement in petty rivalries and personality clashes, no one disputed her genuine sympathy for the homeless and destitute and she did help achieve a lasting benefit for the elderly and poor of Mombasa. The almshouse scheme continued to be funded by the Municipality with major extensions and additions in 1953 and in 1961.[107] Both P F Foster, who later became the first mayor of Mombasa, and Katharine, when she was elected to the Municipal Council, continued to take a keen interest in the project they had initiated. The complex consisting of the Municipal almshouses and the Children's home at Makupa still operates under the Social Services Department of the Municipal Council of Mombasa.

Katharine also worked for another charity at this period called the Society for the Overseas Settlement of British Women (SOSBW). Affiliated to the League of Mercy, it had started sending single women to Kenya from 1930. Lady Grigg held the position of the patroness in Kenya and the chairman in London was the Dowager Viscountess Harcourt. It acted as the women's branch of the Overseas Settlement Department and gave many young British women, caught in the economic depression of the 20s and 30s, the chance of a better opportunity in Kenya. The Kenya branch was notably successful and the young women who came out to work as nurses, teachers and governesses often did very well, ending up married to farmers and District Commissioners. Katharine provided invaluable service to the Organisation. Between 1932-1935 she met every ship that came into Mombasa and chaperoned the girls as they disembarked, making sure they got through customs without mishap and got on the train to Nairobi.[108] She provided them with addresses of contacts and instructions for meeting up with their new employers. In addition she would take them to tea at her house and give them good advice about all the do's and don'ts in Kenya. Her own arrival and the difficulties she would have encountered had it not been for the kindness of certain people remained fresh in her memory. The young women sent out by the SOSBW to Kenya were mainly middle class and well educated but with no prospects in England, caught in very much the same situation as Katharine had found herself. Her only escape route then had been through marriage and her change of heart, partner and destination mid-voyage had raised a few eyebrows. The new breed of independent young women who came out to Kenya through the SOSBW had no need to resort to such subterfuge or desperate measures, a move that met with Katharine's wholehearted support.

An interview with Katharine Fannin for the *East African Standard* newspaper soon after her arrival in Nairobi entitled "Social Work at the Coast," shows a picture of her as she appeared at this period.[109] A plump and homely face with large chin and worried expression is topped with a jaunty little hat, while in the approved fashion of the time a fox fur stole is draped casually over one shoulder. She had gained quite a reputation for her social work by this time, but according to the article her chief love remained the League of Mercy. "Just being there to try to help anyone in any sort of trouble," gave her the keenest sense of fulfilment. The article also mentions that Katharine was a founder member of the Coast Branch of the East African Society for the Protection of Cruelty to Animals, and a member of the Mombasa Cathedral Council and the choir. The article noted all the books she had brought with her from England, valuable antiquarian collectors' items, which must have suffered most horribly with white ants and the climate, but gave her immense pleasure, along with a collection of old fans and stamps. Among her books, she had a seventeenth century Bible and prayer book and a "volume printed 120 years ago of a voyage all round Africa and into the interior of Abyssinia." This last book was Henry Salt's **Abyssinian Travels**, published in 1814. The book would soon play an extraordinary role in her life.

CHAPTER SIX

Pre-war years: Nairobi 1937-1938

To Katharine travel provided solace to the troubled spirit. From May to November 1935 she had been on leave. In January 1936, Charles was posted to Nairobi and undertook a major survey, which kept him in the field until September of that year. Katharine joined her husband in April, after she had recovered from a virulent attack of tick typhus, and lived in a tent under safari conditions for nearly five months. During this period her sole companions, other than Charles, were a farmer called Bartlett who drove a rather unreliable lorry (it used to break down every 40 miles), her dog Bunny and between 25-33 porters.[110] But by November 1936 they were back in civilisation temporarily housed in a small bungalow fronting the cricket grounds of the Nairobi Club as Charles waited to take over from the Surveyor General, who was retiring at the end of the year. From 1937-1938 Charles Fannin was Acting Surveyor General for Kenya. For some reason he was never given the full appointment.

Her leave followed by the long camping safari had served to revitalise Katharine. Now as the wife of the Acting Surveyor General, she entered Nairobi society with renewed optimism and vigour, determined to involve herself and make her mark. Though she avoided initiating any more major welfare schemes, she was an active member of several committees and concentrated on organising social entertainments and fund raising for worthy causes. She sat on the Nairobi committee for the Society for the Settlement of British Women Overseas and from December 1936 was a member of the Executive Committee for Girl Guides. She was also active in the Kenya Society for the Prevention of Cruelty to Animals.[111]

In October 1938 she helped organise a Girl Guides' Exhibition and sale of work opened by the Governor, Sir Robert Brooke-Popham, followed by a Girl Guide Ball, which she also organised. This event, according to the East African Standard, "turned out to be the most successful and amusing affair." Mrs Fannin, we are told, "wore an extremely effective and brilliant dress of gleaming silver lamé and was indeed indefatigable throughout the evening." There was a cabaret and an ankle competition at midnight won by Mrs Bilborough "who wore a becoming pale blue chiffon dress with a spray of freesias." Among those present, Lady Brooke-Popham looked very elegant in a bottle green gown with two diamond clips. Mrs Stoyle in purple velvet was accompanied by her daughter, while Lady Assheton-Smith "striking with her mane of tawny hair and wearing a jade green ostrich feather cape over her black gown was with Mr Alan Delap." The description of the guests and party covers two columns and gives some idea of the elaborate social occasions held in Nairobi in those heady pre-war days.[112]

Also in 1938 Katharine travelled to the Congo and Uganda with Charles, his two sisters and a Polish Count. In what was to be her last letter to her Uncle John,[113] Katharine described a trip by launch up the Victoria Nile to the Murchison Falls and the hot and gruelling climb to the top for the magnificent view. Charles' sisters were somewhat incongruously attired in white gloves, blue dust-coats, scarves and were carrying bright red sunshades. Aged over sixty, these intrepid spinsters were en-route from South Africa to England to visit their nephew. After meeting up with Charles and Katharine they continued northwards by Nile boat from Butiaba on Lake Albert, accompanied by the Polish Count.

Besides her active involvement in committee work, Katharine was learning Italian, German and Spanish.[114] She kept up a strict routine and studied one language every day for two hours. Languages came easily to her and she already spoke French and Swahili, but taking on three languages at once was ambitious. This, however, was typical of Katharine Fannin, who always wanted to do more and be better at it than anyone else. This trait is remembered by Edward Rodwell, who recalls a dinner-party he attended in Mombasa given by her in the 1950s, when no fewer than sixty side dishes were provided to go with the curry![115]

Charles Fannin in his position as Acting Director of Surveys in Kenya was now asked to investigate the potential of air surveys.

Experiments were being carried out to see if the tiresomely slow foot-slogging and painstaking mapping procedures could be replaced by photographs taken from the air. Tanganyika was trying out this new photographic method in their survey of Pemba Island. In March 1938 Charles went along to see how it was done. Apart from an incident when a startled cow charged the light survey aircraft he was travelling in, he was impressed with the island's survey and registration office and the new photographic unit. Flying in a small six-seater twin engine Dragonfly was an exciting new experience for the seasoned surveyor, who had previously only worked on foot.[116]

Aircraft and their possibilities, both civil and military, moved to the fore in Kenya in 1938. Sir Robert Brooke-Popham, besides being Governor also held the rank of Air Vice-Marshal in the Royal Air Force (RAF). An RAF squadron was stationed at the civil aerodrome at Eastleigh close to the Fannin's new home. This house, a large wood and iron bungalow brought over in sections from India when the railway was being constructed, stood on the rocky edge of a low escarpment. It commanded a grandstand view from the wide verandah where the Fannins could watch the pilots flying and practising stunts in their war-planes, reaching speeds of up to 220 mph, training for the conflict that increasingly seemed inevitable[117]. Rumblings of impending war abounded. Rumours of gun running into Tanganyika via the Rufiji Delta caused a few flutters of alarm, while the unscheduled visit of General Balba of Libya, who touched down in Nairobi in his personal aeroplane on his way to Somalia, also gave rise to wild speculation. According to Katharine Fannin "the Italians with Hitler sitting on the Brenner Pass have got such wind-up now, they don't know what to do." She was worried about the British Prime-Minister, Chamberlain, and his Foreign Secretary, Lord Halifax, who she felt had lost direction and were unconvincing in their leadership. She disliked their appeasement policies but said: "I suppose we still have to play for time."[118]

Home leave came round once more but Charles, hoping for a new posting early in 1939, planned to delay his trip until then. Disappointed in his bid for the job of Commissioner for Lands and Settlement and with the official post of Surveyor General for Kenya eventually given elsewhere, he had applied for a transfer and waited for a suitable position to fall vacant. Nairobi proved a costly place to live and by the end of 1938 the Fannins were in debt. Katharine was extravagant, though she had little interest in clothes and jewels, besides the basics needed to keep up appearances. But she liked attending and giving lavish parties. Sumptuous entertaining and charity work were expensive pastimes. The Fannins found themselves living beyond their means, caught on a merry-go-round of social and financial commitments they could not afford. The most painless and discreet solution to this predicament was a new posting, preferably somewhere with a less demanding social life, while finances were repaired.

But events did not turn out as planned. Sometime during the Autumn of 1938 Uncle John died. His health had been failing for about a year, but Katharine had hoped to see him before he died. His death was a heavy blow and she decided to return to England at once. Cheated of her inheritance twice, this time she would not trust relatives to look after her interests, but go herself. Despite Charles' level-headed warnings that she must not expect much, she seems to have been confident that Uncle John's will would solve their financial problems.

The quickest sea-passage to England from Mombasa was through the Suez Canal via Mogadishu - Aden - Massawa. Katharine had taken this route in 1935 hoping to go ashore to explore what is now Somalia and Ethiopia, but she had to postpone her plans because of a particularly unpleasant war between the Ethiopians and the Italians.

In 1934 the Italians, under the Fascist leadership of Mussolini, had revived their claim on Abyssinia. The Italians had never forgotten the shame of the Battle of Adua in 1896, when a modern trained Italian army had been defeated by the Ethiopians. Mussolini stirred up Italian nationalist pride and revived their imperialist dreams. A clash on the Somali border provided the pretext for a colonial war.[119] Both Eritrea and Somalia were Italian colonies at this time,[120] but Abyssinia under the young Emperor, Haile Selassie had retained its independence. The Italian troops advanced through both Somalia and Eritrea and slowly fought their way into Abyssinia despite fierce resistance. Haile Selassie appealed to the British and to the League of Nations[121] to protect his kingdom from the unprovoked and illegal act of aggression by the Italians. Abyssinia, as it was usually called in those days, had been a member of the League of Nations since 1923 and the Italians had signed a treaty of non-aggression and co-operation in 1928 when Mussolini had recognised Abyssinia as a sovereign and independent state. Haile Selassie had right on his side, but the British lobby vacillated and prevaricated as they wished above all to placate Mussolini and prevent him from allying himself with Hitler. The double dealing and manoeuvring that followed was one of the more shameful episodes of European foreign policy. Both Sir Samuel Hoare the British Foreign Secretary and Pierre Laval the influential French minister had no compunction in paying the Abyssinian price in return for Italian friendship.[122] While outwardly supporting the League's mandate for collective security, they secretly offered territorial sweeteners to Mussolini to restore peace.[123] Slowly and deliberately the Italian invasion continued, confident that other nations would only make half-hearted attempts to avert the war. The League of Nations condemned Mussolini and tried to end the war by applying sanctions.[124] These proved ineffective as oil sanctions would only have worked if the British had agreed to a naval blockade of the Mediterranean, but the British backed down. They were concerned over the safety of their fleet at Malta and did not wish to disrupt trade. Keeping the sea routes open and protecting the Suez Canal was always a major plank in British Foreign Policy and the fate of Abyssinia, a desperately poor, ethnically riven, slave owning and corrupt tribal oligarchy, seemed of lesser importance. To assuage their consciences, some suggested lifting the arms embargo on Abyssinia, but the League overruled this. The British government adopted the pathetic French compromise that arms should be prohibited to both belligerents. As the Italians had no need of French or British arms and the Abyssinians were virtually defenceless, the cynicism of this compromise spoke for itself. In November 1935 came the Hoare Laval Pact, by which the Province of Tigre would be ceded to the Italians in return for peace. The storm of public anger over this complete sell-out to Mussolini, forced the resignations of the British Foreign Secretary, Hoare, and the French Minister, Laval, the authors of the suggested peace plan. After this complete breakdown of diplomacy, the Italians stepped up their campaign.

In December 1935 the Italian General Badoglio ordered planes to drop mustard gas on the Abyssinian army and, not wanting international observers, bombed the Red Cross Camp. Finally in February the Italians annihilated the Ethiopian army at Amba Aradon and the Italians occupied the capital Addis Ababa in May 1936. For three days there was a frightful massacre as the Commander-in-Chief, General Rudolfo Graziani, struggled to gain control of the town. He is reputed to have said: "The Duce shall have Ethiopia with or without the Ethiopians, as he pleases." The spectacle of Italian troops butchering their way into Abyssinia and acting with such savagery against a poverty stricken and ill armed African nation shocked the world and aroused public condemnation of Mussolini's imperialistic ambitions. After 1936 the formally neutral Italians became inextricably linked with Germany. The British and French handling of the Abyssinian crisis had been a complete disaster, which had far reaching effects. The bungled diplomacy pushed Italy into the arms of Germany, destroyed the trust between Britain and France and dealt a blow to British prestige abroad showing them before the world's eyes as dubious allies and inconsiderable enemies. Most significantly it marked the start of a policy of appeasement that that led up to the Second World War.

It is ironic that in Haile Selassie, the diminutive absolute monarch from Abyssinia, anti-Fascism found its first hero, but that was in the future. Meanwhile General Graziani was appointed Governor General in Addis Ababa and he held this post until February 1937, when a bomb attack severely wounded him. In revenge for this attempted assassination, and to prevent a full scale uprising, the General reacted fiercely and carried out systematic executions in Addis Ababa. The public outcry about the brutality of the killings forced General Graziani's recall. The Duke of Aosta replaced him and he tried to rule Ethiopia by more humane methods.

In 1938, two years after the declaration of the Italian occupation of Abyssinia, outsiders knew virtually nothing about conditions in the country. There were no up-to-date maps and the ruling military dictatorship allowed no civilian travel or sightseeing. At the end of 1938, Anglo/Italian relationships suddenly improved. Seriously alarmed and on the brink of war after the German occupation of Austria and Bohemia (Czechoslovakia), Chamberlain met Hitler at Munich in September. At this historic meeting Hitler promised not to expand his borders again, but remain content with what he had. "Peace in our time," was Chamberlain's jubilant call. War had been averted by gentlemen's agreement. The sceptics could not think Germany had any intention of curbing its territorial expansion, especially after such an easy victory. Nevertheless, there was a general feeling of relief on both sides. At the same time an Anglo/Italian agreement of non-aggression was reached and diplomatic relations were restored. The British formally recognised the Italian King, Victor Emmanuel, as the new Emperor of Ethiopia. This eased the tension in East Africa, where the chief threat to peace came from the Italians and not the Germans.

At this exact time Katharine wanted to return to England and, for once, events conspired in her favour. Suddenly her postponed trip through Ethiopia was possible. Ever bold and adventurous, she proposed to get off the boat at Mogadishu, cut across the Horn of Africa by land and rejoin the fast boat to Naples at Massawa. Being told this was impossible, far too dangerous and no one would insure either her or her luggage, made her even more determined.[125] At some point news of her planned trip reached the Governor, Sir Robert Brooke-Popham, and also military intelligence of the Kenyan African Rifles. Katharine Fannin's preposterous travel arrangements assumed new possibilities. Capable and energetic, with a talent for languages and a knowledge of surveys and maps, she seemed just the right candidate for some fast footwork in the field of intelligence. The Governor called her in for an interview. With his dual post as Air Vice-Marshall of the RAF, Sir Robert Brooke-Popham understood the imminent danger of war and the importance of obtaining accurate information and reconnaissance of enemy territory. So Katharine Fannin 'the spy' was born.

In no time at all, obstacles were pushed aside and Katharine's previously impossible journey was organised. It's not known exactly what was said to the Royal Italian Consul General in Nairobi, Italo Zappoli, to give Katharine VIP treatment and an immediate invitation as an honoured guest of the Italian government in Ethiopia. But whatever was said achieved electrifying results. The Italians wanted their position recognised in East Africa, particularly by the British, the dominant colonial power. Anglo-Egyptian Sudan and the British Colony and Protectorate of Kenya stood on either side of Italian East Africa, making the Italians feel vulnerable in the event of war, when they could be invaded on several fronts.[126] It was in their interest to develop friendly relations and Katharine's proposed visit seemed an excellent opportunity to make a start toward a better understanding, which might soften British policy toward the Italian colonies. Still smarting under the press reports of brutality and repression, the Italians would show Katharine Fannin, the wife of a high ranking colonial official, how effectively the Italians governed their colonial possessions in East Africa and how civilised and beneficial Italian rule was to the whole region. They would subject Katharine Fannin to an extraordinary degree of propaganda and personal attention, escorting her at all times so she would see only what suited their purpose.

Katharine's exact instructions from the British remain largely conjecture, but one letter does survive among the Fannin papers, from Joe Powell, intelligence officer of the Kenyan African Rifles, Northern Brigade, enclosing a list of points he wished her to investigate.[127] He asked her to pay particular attention to garrisons at Mogadishu, Kismayu, Belet Uen, Addis Ababa and Neghelli, to count aircraft and lorries and to notice gun emplacements and batteries. She was asked to closely observe the officials she met, estimate the number of Italian troops deployed, the transport available and the general morale, and anything else she picked up in conversation. In the end her most valuable contribution was the reconnaissance she carried out of the main routes into Ethiopia. She bought herself, without Charles' knowledge, an expensive ciné camera and took films and photographs of bridges and scenic landscapes and of her unsuspecting driver posed in front of oil drums and fortifications. Whatever she saw of possible intelligence value had to be carefully memorised for she dare not write anything down as all her letters were opened and read before being sent. This indicates the Italians were probably well aware of her hidden agenda.

Katharine Fannin never forgot her eighteen days in 1938 driving through Italian Somaliland, Ethiopia and Eritrea. She had a chance to live out the adventures of Kim and Francis Younghusband, the heroes of her lonely childhood, to become a player in the 'Great Game' as she had always dreamed. Katharine must have known the allure and the dangers of her mission. In Kipling's **Kim**, E23, the government agent, told Kim: "We of the game are beyond protection. If we die, we die. Our names are blotted from the book. That is all." The bravado needed to carry off her act as an intrepid explorer, special envoy and undercover agent heightened the excitement of an extraordinary journey, while the near royal treatment she received exceeded her wildest imaginings.

Waiting at Kilindini harbour aboard the Italian Ship *SS Piave*, Katharine wrote a last letter to her husband Charles, in which she told him she had made her will and left everything to him.[128] Equipped with her fur coat, silver lamé dress and Henry Salt's **Abyssinian Travels**, Katharine started off on the greatest adventure of her life.

CHAPTER SEVEN
Ethiopia Part 1: November 1938

Nearly one-third of the Fannin papers relate to Katharine's Ethiopian travels. She visited the country twice, once between November 6 - 23, 1938, on her way to London and the second time on her return to Kenya between February 5 and March 20, 1939. She made both trips as an undercover agent for the British Government and it is ironic that she travelled freely on both occasions as a favoured guest of the Italians, who, it seemed, hoped to use her for favourable publicity. Her arrangements with the British were very low key and she was never officially on secret government service. She carried out her "spying" as a freelance adventurer and there is never any mention of remuneration. It was all done in a deliberately vague way, presumably so that if she was unsuccessful, she could be disowned. However, as a result of these trips she sold her story to the weekly Nairobi newspaper *The Sunday Post* in seven instalments, made broadcasts about conditions in Ethiopia and sold two reels of film to the Italians for the princely sum of nearly £200.

Her intelligence work for the British is contained in three reports. One dated January 3, 1939, was made in London for the Foreign Office after her first journey.[129] She made a second report for the Foreign Office after her return to Kenya, dated April 6, 1939.[130] She wrote a third report in Accra in May 1940 for military intelligence just before the start of the Abyssinian Campaign, which was a combination of the previous two reports. Her remarkable memory and eye for detail, combined with her social aplomb in ingratiating herself with important officials, made her a most useful agent for the British. Her reports giving a breakdown of military hardware, personnel and deployment, and including an assessment of the political situation and descriptions of the chief personalities, were read with interest by the Foreign Secretaries, Lord Halifax and Sir Anthony Eden, and Sir Robert Vansittart, head of MI6. The intelligence report she compiled for the army, which involved maps and photographs not used in the previous two reports, proved of great assistance during the war in Italian East Africa, when the British gained an easy victory over the Italians.

A series of letters, mostly written in pencil on scraps of paper to her husband during her first trip in November 1938, survive. These, read in conjunction with the reports, broadcasts and newspaper articles, give a very clear picture of that first journey. It is extraordinary that these letters, although opened and read by the Italian censor, all eventually arrived at their destination. The single letter sent to her by her husband was also opened and read, but did reach her in Addis Ababa. According to her first report, her luggage was searched twice. She fully expected this and neither her letters nor her luggage contained any incriminating evidence.

She arrived at Mogadishu on November 6, 1938, quite uncertain how she would be received. She carried a personal letter of introduction from the Governor of Kenya to the British Resident in Aden,[131] a letter from the Italian Consul in Nairobi[132] to the Governor of Italian Somaliland and an invitation from the Viceroy to be his guest in Addis Ababa. The Port Captain met her and brought her ashore by private motor launch without the usual formalities of Customs. She was escorted to the Croce del Sud, the main hotel in Mogadishu, and given a private suite. She stayed in the hotel for two nights and when she came to pay her bill they told her that as a guest of the Viceroy she would not be allowed to pay for anything. During her time in Mogadishu Cavaliere Pittraluga, chief of the General Secretariat, looked after her and she took the opportunity of sending two maps, one to Sir Robert Brook-Popham and one to her husband, marking her itinerary. The Italians loaned her a car with a Kiswahili-speaking Somali, who acted as mechanic, guide and interpreter and drove her around Mogadishu. This allowed her to make a fairly detailed report on Mogadishu's fortifications. As the Governor Francesco Caroselli was away, his mother, Donna Paula Caroselli,[133] invited Katharine to lunch at Government House, an immense white Arab palace filled with old coastal furniture, which reminded her of Zanzibar. Lunch consisted of ten courses all highly spiced and washed down with four sorts of wine and followed by strong black coffee stiff with sugar. She met rows of Cavalieres and communicated in ungrammatical French. She mentioned the odd working hours; 8 - 12 and then 4 - 7, and then how they all played organised sport from 8 - midnight. The Italians played tennis on floodlit courts and the Somalis played football on soccer grounds illuminated by spotlights. No one, she said, either black or white, seemed to go to bed before 1 or 2 am. She wrote that she was the only English person in Italian Somaliland.[134]

On November 9, she set off with her Somali Sergeant driver on the estimated four-day drive to Harar. They took turns at the wheel and to begin with the road was excellent. She planned on reaching Harar to pick up another vehicle sent by the Viceroy to take her on to Addis Ababa. She posted her first letter from Belet Uen, a small garrison town on the way to Harar. Remembering the instructions from Captain Powell, she did her best to take a mental note of its military capabilities.

The roads in Italian East Africa filled her with admiration as they were far better than anything the British had built in Kenya. The dead straight main road, which took them as far as Fer Fer, was called Via Graziani after Mussolini's general who had massacred and conquered the Ethiopians in 1936-1937. She noticed the Italians had made road building their first priority as the quickest and cheapest method of opening up and pacifying the country. Everything was carried by lorry and the transport of petrol alone for the thousands of lorries was, she commented, a Herculean task. She saw endless convoys of trucks carrying essential supplies, guarded by escorts of armed police and Italian soldiers. The immensely hardwearing, all-weather roads and stone and concrete bridges were designed to support a minimum of 26 tons and were being built by Italian troops and Sudanese labour. Highly trained Italian engineers supervised road building gangs who worked day and night. In her first article for *The Sunday Post*,[135] she described the Italian road programme at length. She wrote that the Italians were under direct orders to complete the arterial road system in the shortest possible time, whatever the cost, and well known private engineering firms along with the public works department were working flat out to do just that. Already at the end of 1938 nearly 3,000 miles of roads had been completed in barely two years. These were not substandard or shoddy affairs, but best quality indestructible "old Roman road-building with a vengeance."[136] She described how the tarmac highways were roughly 30 feet wide, with solid stone foundations, sometimes as much as two metres in depth and buttressed on either side. An infill of stone chips and rubble was finished off on top with a hand laid mosaic of small flattish stones. This was finally sealed and waterproofed with a five-inch coat of bitumen. Dozens of bridges were being built in the same enduring manner, massive stone arches set on equally massive stone pillars. This extraordinary road system was Italy's most lasting legacy to her former colonies – besides a taste for spaghetti – and impressed many later visitors as well as Katharine Fannin.

Katharine wrote her next letter from The Residency, Dagabur, Italian Somaliland.[137] After leaving Belet Uen the tarmac had petered out and for 200 miles she drove over a partially constructed road of rough stones, arriving at Gorrahai well after nightfall. Here an anxious District Officer met her. He had expected her further up the road at Gabbre Dharre some hours earlier. With a security curfew in operation, no civilian traffic could move after 6 pm. He escorted her for the last 16 miles into Gabbre Dharre. Although she did not know it at the time, a solitary vehicle had been shot at and ambushed a few miles up the road that very day and the Ogaden was a notoriously dangerous area. They put her up at the District Headquarters, which consisted of an enormous tent with four 20-foot-square rooms all in a row. The porcelain bath and hand basin impressed Katharine and she thought the degree of comfort managed by Italian officials far exceeded that of their British counterparts living under similar conditions.

The previous day's drive had been so exhausting that she spent a couple of days with her host, Goffredo Romagna, to recover. In charge of this desolate outstation in the arid Ogaden region, he enjoyed the rare opportunity of female companionship and gave her a personal tour of his district. He showed her the Abyssinian fortresses and trenches where the Habash (Ethiopian soldiers) had put up a particularly fierce resistance and took her to Gorrahai to see the military airfield and Graziani's hut from where he had conducted Italian operations during the invasion of Ethiopia.

Gorrahei was originally the headquarters of Gerazmatch Afework, Emperor Haile Selassie's most charismatic and efficient general. He had made it into a military stronghold digging a network of trenches and building fortresses to protect the southern flank of Ethiopia from the Italians. In 1935 he had two machine guns and about 7,000 troops equipped with rifles ranged against the 50,000 Italian and native troops available to General Rodolfo Graziani. The Italians had modern weaponry and thousands of lorries, scores of artillery batteries, tanks, aeroplanes and almost unlimited ammunition and supplies to back them. Mussolini had spent two billion lire and wanted a lot of territory in return. He chose Graziani for the task. Despite the mismatch, it took the Italians the best part of a year to defeat the Ethiopians.

The Italian Ethiopian campaign began in earnest in October 1935 when six Caproni CA133 bombers attacked the outpost round Mullah's Fort at Gorrahei. On November 4, the Ethiopian general Afework was fatally wounded. With their forts battered by continuous air attack, the Ethiopians retreated towards Dagabur, the next garrison post up the road. The waiting Italians sent a token column in pursuit of the retreating Ethiopians, but the rest dug in at Gorrahei, from where Graziani conducted a slow unrelenting war of attrition on the southern front. He sent bombers from these air fields armed with mustard gas, inflicting horrible wounds on the Ethiopians round Harar in December 1935, eventually terrorising the whole region into submission. For this and other crimes against humanity he would earn the title 'Butcher' Graziani and the Italo-Abyssinian War would go down in history as one of the most cruel and vicious in modern times.

Katharine had read about the war in the newspapers written from a British point of view, denouncing Italian atrocities. Now the other side gave her a guided tour. She heard how fierce the Ethiopian fighters were, how no quarter or prisoners were taken and how the Italians feared them. She saw for herself the planes of the Regia Aeronautica Italiana. She smiled and exclaimed pretending ignorance, not quite able to flatter the bravery of the Italian troops or the exploits of their finc planes, while keeping a mental note of how many aircraft she saw, what type and the approximate strength of the military installations. It was tiring work and she was grateful for the luxuries of the tent at the end of the day. She dared not write down anything, but repeated the numbers to herself again and again before going to sleep, fearful of forgetting anything.

Later she wrote a very favourable dossier on Romagna, whom she considered to be anti-fascist and pro-British.[138]

Continuing on her way to Harar, she met Governor Francesco Caroselli returning to Mogadishu in state, surrounded by a large and glittering staff and a cavalcade of vehicles. He invited her to take lunch with him by the roadside. Afflicted with an appalling squint and nicknamed 'The Fox,' Katharine found his true character difficult to assess and was curiously non-committal in her report on him.[139]

She arrived eventually at the frontier station of Dagabur on November 13, in the midst of a military column of lorries. The elderly Major Molinari, the District Officer, or Residente as he was called in Italian colonies, looked after Katharine.[140] He was a straightforward military man, unlike the smooth talking career political servants she had met so far. They spent the evening looking at his family photographs.

In her letters, which she knew the Italian authorities opened and read, she wrote how she was quite overcome by the attention she was receiving and suggested it could only be because she was a novelty. A white woman travelling alone in Africa was considered quite unthinkable in Italian society. She was flattered to be called original and daring and enjoyed a number of mildly flirtatious encounters with the officers she met, who, generally starved of female companionship, no doubt made the most of what was on offer.

Katharine wrote her next letter November 15, from Harar. After leaving Dagabur, she proceeded to Jijiga where she lunched with Commissioner Count Bestagno and his wife. Here she met Signor Aldo Garboli, the official interpeter for British/Italian border conversation, who accompanied her on the drive to Harar. He took her by way of a scenic route to view the Valley of Marvels. She was deeply impressed by the fantastic rock formations, most especially the balancing rock of Dakata, and later was to write that the gigantic stones precariously piled up were like a 'pantomime council of petrified ogres' or a 'cohort of giants' and that the wildly scenic views reminded her of Henry Salt's illustrations (although in fact he never visited this part of Ethiopia). She carried his book with her as it contained a description of Ethiopia and, though written nearly 150 years previously, much of the general information about the geography, customs and people remained unchanged. Her cumbersome antiquarian travel guide aroused considerable interest, because at this date there was no tourist information available about Ethiopia.[141]

Henry Salt (1780-1827) was a key figure in early 19th century travel, Egyptology and diplomacy. He was celebrated for his extraordinary expeditions to Abyssinia, which rivalled those of James Bruce. As a young man he trained as an artist under John Hoppner and then joined Viscount Valentia on his four-year voyage to India, Ceylon and Egypt to record the views and scenes.

He first visited Abyssinia in 1805, under the auspices of Viscount Valentia, when he managed to meet with the Ras of Tigre in Chelicot and bring back letters of friendship addressed to George III. As a result of this successful visit, Henry Salt was then sent as an early freelance envoy by the British Government in 1809/10 to investigate the area and assess the possibilities for opening up trade and diplomatic relations with the Abyssinians. Though this first British mission did not achieve any lasting benefit, Salt managed to meet Ras Welled Selassie at Chelicut and exchange gifts. The lions he was given died on the journey back, but an Abyssinian mare survived, which he presented to the Prince Regent, later George IV. The book he wrote of his adventures, **A Voyage to Abyssinia**, was published in 1814 and became a classic. He was rewarded by being appointed British Consul General in Cairo, a post he held until his death in 1827. He was also famous as a collector and connoisseur of Egyptian antiquities, some of which were bought by Sir John Soane, and can be seen today in the Soane Museum, London.[142]

On arrival at Harar, Katharine was immediately taken to see the governor, General Nasi. She got on well with General Nasi, and stayed in a villa in the grounds of his residence, waited on by magnificently attired tall *askaris* at the meals she took with him and his staff. General Nasi was an old-fashioned cavalryman who rode around Harar on a large white horse wearing jodhpurs, leather boots, a khaki jacket and heavy peaked hat thick with braid. He also sported large dark sunglasses to protect his eyes from the glare of the African sun. Katharine found him to be a martinet and a strict disciplinarian. Conversation with him was stilted as his manner was brusque, and she found his habit of allowing no more than twenty minutes for a meal distressing in the extreme. Nevertheless, in her report she wrote that he was the most able of all the Italian governors and the one who commanded the most respect.[143]

The old walled city of Harar with its thick-buttressed walls and fortified gates is the spiritual heart of Ethiopia's Muslim community and the capital of the Ogaden region. In the 17th and 18th centuries it had been an important centre for Muslim learning and only Muslims were allowed to enter its walls. The first European to visit the city was the British explorer Richard Burton in 1854. Ras Mkonnen, the father of the former Emperor Haile Selassie, was made Christian Governor of Harar in 1887 by the Emperor Menelik II, to keep the Muslims in line and loyal to the Ethiopian Emperor. Tourists are still shown the house where Haile Selassie lived as a boy. Another famous 19th century visitor was the French poet Rimbaud, who lived there from 1880 until 1891. He called himself a trader but seems to have done little except lead a debauched life and eventually died a drug addict.

Harar's importance as a commercial centre diminished after 1902 when the Djbouti railway line was built, with the station at Dire Dawa, but Katharine still found Harar to be a large and populous town. The old white washed buildings of the walled city were secretive and secluded in the maze of narrow winding streets. The mosques, with their stunted minarets, had enclosures and small hidden entrances known only to the followers of Islam. At dusk the gates were closed and no one was allowed in or out.

The Italians had built a modern town on the outskirts of the walled city with a bank, post office, telecommunications and a smart piazza. Streets had been widened in part of the old town allowing a car to drive through the main gates to the market place and out again. Governor General Nasi's residence was in the modern Italian town.

It was here that Katharine met the newly arrived British Consul, Mr Ellison, a keen entomologist who the Italians thought to be completely mad but harmless. A familiar sight with his butterfly net, he was, judging from his subsequent intelligence reports in the Foreign Office Correspondence files, also an astute diplomat.[144]

Still closely attended by the interpreter Garboli, who fed her gossip and information about the government personalities in Harar and Addis Ababa, a chauffeur drove her on to Addis Ababa. Her new car, a gleaming Fiat from the Viceroy's private fleet, had Governo Generale 20 written in large letters on the number-plate. She travelled through Dire Dawa, over the spectacular 9,000 foot pass and into the capital Addis Ababa, which stands at 8,000 feet above sea level. Katharine saw the mean daub and wattle dwellings of the poorer inhabitants. The dusty irregular streets twisted behind and the brown of the thatched roofs blended into the pale dusty brown of the landscape. Eucalyptus trees clustered round a domed church in the surrounding hills. In the centre of the town stood western style buildings, some built by Haile Selassie and some more recently by the Italians. Constructed of concrete, they had classical clean lines and yellow paint. The wide roads with pavements for pedestrians were laid out with logical precision, with piazzas and green squares. She saw shop fronts with Italian goods and cafes and restaurants, large office blocks and a petrol station near the impressive railway station. Garboli told her that two residential complexes for the exclusive use of Italians were being built to the south and east, one for the workers and one for the officials, while Ethiopians were restricted to the western sector. As in Kenya, a colour bar was in operation and the high class aristocratic officials kept a distance from the ordinary soldiers and other Italians.

In Addis they lodged Katharine in the guesthouse of the Vice-Regal Palace, Villa D'Italia, and Marchese Catalano Gonzaga took on the job of chaperone. A dashing Neapolitan and Chief of the Press and Propaganda Bureau, she'd met his kind before, and was not taken in![145] He wined and dined her at the Imperial Hotel and kept a close eye on her during her three-day stay in Addis Ababa. The next day she met Donna Elena Medici, the English wife of the Deputy Governor, Don Canero Medici, and had lunch with Stonehewer Bird, the British Consul General.

On November 19, the day Katharine was scheduled to meet the Duke of Aosta, her front tooth fell out! Donna Elena Medici and her husband, the Deputy Governor, came to her rescue and immediately took Katharine to a dentist for a false tooth to be fitted. She had her smile intact later that day when she finally met the Viceroy, Prince Amedeo of Savoy, Duca D'Aosta, Vice Roi and Governo Generale of Africa Orientale Italiano, to give him his full title. The Italians' fondness for titles suited Katharine down to the ground. They often addressed her as Lady Fannin, which no doubt gave her enormous pleasure. The Duke of Aosta, who stood nearly 6 feet 6 inches in his socks, was a strange and quixotic character, who had led a very varied career. Educated at a British preparatory school in Reigate, then at Eton and Oxford University, he had worked in a soap factory in the Belgian Congo under a pseudonym, been with the Camel Corps in Libya and came out to East Africa with his uncle the Duc D'Abruzzi to start the settlement scheme Villagio D'Abruzzi just outside Mogadishu. Now aged forty, he still nurtured idealistic dreams of a new Roman Empire in Africa, and seemed a sad but imposing figure. Katharine was perfectly thrilled to be seated at his right hand at the lunch party at Villa D'Italia and to be completely surrounded by Italian aristocrats, Marchese this and Contessa that. That same evening she was taken to a very grand concert at the Villagio Savoia, where she wore her silver dress and long white gloves and sat in the front row with the viceregal party on gilded chairs. Behind her sat the Consular Corps en masse and in her rapturous description, "the hall was brilliant with jewels and orders sparkling and the whole place stiff with glittering uniforms." [146] After the show she was whisked on to a series of "marvellous and noisy parties," where she discovered her feat of driving alone and unescorted from Mogadishu was considered a most brave and sportive act and she was quite a celebrity. She danced the night away, ate midnight snacks of spiced chicken and savoury spaghetti and finally at 4 am drove up an alarming road to see a famous view.

During her time in Addis, she showed her copy of Henry Salt's book to the Duke of Aosta and he admired it so much, she felt obliged to present the book to him for his newly formed national library collection. He gallantly promised it would be listed number one in the catalogue.

Katharine Fannin wrote her final letter on board the *SS Sandro*, which set sail from Massawa on November 24, 1938. The letter describes her four-day journey from Addis Ababa down to the Coast. She still had the use of the Viceroy's Fiat and his driver. "On leaving Addis, which is a scattered town situated in very lumpy mountains with fertile valleys in between, one does about 70 miles of climbing highlands through a wild forest covered country full of wheat and flowing rivers until one reaches Debra Sina, a pass of 14,000 feet. Here the landscape abruptly changes into sharp pointed mountain ranges with deep valleys containing village after village of odd conical huts each fortified with its stone wall and here and there a medieval Ras' castle."[147] This area, she was told, was renowned for its warlike people and in Haile Selassie's time every village warred with its neighbour and every Ras (Abyssinian chief or baron) lived by theft and rapine. She could well believe it as the entirely fortified nature of the country bore this out.

Katharine had been issued with a special pass signed by General

Volpini, the Viceroy's Chief of Staff, requesting that all civil and military authorities assist her in every way possible. She stopped at Dessie, Macalle and Asmara and was lavishly entertained at each stop. She was particularly taken with the Governor of Eritrea, who had his headquarters at Asmara. Dr Daodiace gave a special dinner party in her honour at the governor's residence, which she greatly enjoyed being the only woman among seven men. She gave him as a present another of the antiquarian books she carried with her, a 16th century edition of **La Reppublica di Venezia**. As a scholarly bibliophile and a Venetian, this generous gift quite won him over. He told her the sad story of his life until 1.00 am and explained how lonely he was surrounded by pomp and ceremony. His fiancée had been killed in an aircrash and the shock of the news had turned his hair white.[148] This appears to have been the beginning of a sincere friendship as there are several letters from Daodiace in the Fannin papers and she kept in contact with him after the war. The next morning he sent his ADC as a personal escort for the final hair-raising descent to Massawa.

The road to Massawa proved so steep and twisty that Katharine had to stop half way and have a brandy as the rapid descent left her deaf and feeling horribly sick. The 8,000-foot drop in forty miles of hairpin bends, though a remarkable feat of road engineering, did not agree with her constitution. Nevertheless she arrived in time to board the waiting ship with the minimum of fuss. Her escort efficiently took care of her luggage and all formalities. She wrote that the whole trip had been "like a fairy tale come true."[149]

CHAPTER EIGHT

Christmas in London 1938-1939

Katharine's feet did not touch ground until her arrival in London. Her VIP treatment lasted until Naples. They gave her the best cabin and she sat at the Captain's table with a military doctor and two colonels of the Bersaglieri and Alpini regiments. She was one of only three women on board in a ship carrying mainly Italian troops returning home. She befriended the colonel of Alpini, who showed her his gruesome collection of chains and shackles and leg irons, taken by himself off the wretched slaves whom his battalion liberated when they completed operations against a certain Ras. He regaled her with horrid tales of the Italian war in Abyssinia, describing how he had found rows of Ethiopians chained in caves and starving to death. He told her the tortures inflicted on prisoners of war were so horrific that the Italian soldiery were issued with poison in case they fell into the hands of the Abyssinians. Captured Italian soldiers were eviscerated and castrated and then left to die slowly and the Alpini colonel told her how, on one occasion, some of his troops had come across the still conscious remains of a couple of their colleagues and were so enraged that at the next engagement they went berserk and massacred their prisoners, men, women and children.[150]

Katharine's fame had gone before her and on arrival in Naples on December 2, 1938, reporters besieged her and she eventually consented to an interview. Unflatteringly photographed with the Captain against a background of Naples harbour, she appeared dressed in her famous fur coat, clutching a large hold-all, on the third page of the Italian newspaper *Corriera della Sera*.[151] Dramatically headed "Sola in auto" – Alone by car, from one side of Ethiopia to the other! – the long article, taking up three full columns, described the route she took and recorded her praise for the hospitality and kindness shown her by the host nation. It also included a very favourable view of the hospitals, roads and housing being built in Ethiopia by the Italians and her stated opinion of its great potential as a colony. The Italians expended enormous sums of money in East Africa, with apparently no return, and this encouraging report from an "unbiased" traveller was good publicity for Mussolini and the Italian government, which had authorised the heavy taxation that paid for the opening up of Italy's newest and most controversial colony. One cannot help but suspect that Gonzaga, the dashing propaganda minister in Addis Ababa, was somehow involved. Someone certainly had tipped off the reporters.

Giuseppe Bertoni of the Rome newspaper *Il Piccolo*, interviewed Katharine and his article appeared on the front page, together with a much more flattering picture of her, under the heading "Lady Mary Fannin" tells readers of *Il Piccolo* all about her car journey across Ethiopia.[152] In fact, the article dwelt chiefly on the remarkable achievements of the Fascist Government in transforming the savage land of Ethiopia in barely two years into an oasis of Italian civilisation. It was an overtly biased piece of government propaganda.

Katharine had an uneventful train journey back to England through France, but she saw the hundreds of Jewish families crossing by ferry into England. She arrived in London in freezing fog on December 7. One of the first things she did was repay a kindness to Donna Elena Medici, by visiting her small son Nick at boarding school in East Grinstead. The Deputy Governor of Addis Ababa and his English wife had been exceptionally helpful to Katharine when her front tooth had fallen out.

The day after her arrival in London she went to her Barclays Bank, saw the manager and said she had some confidential typing to do. He lent her a private office and a typewriter and she sat down and typed out her preliminary report. She deposited one copy in the bank and took the other round to the Foreign Office. At the Foreign Office Lord Halifax's personal secretary, Harold Caccia, saw her and then passed her over to Victor Cavendish Bentinck in charge of the Africa desk. Her report obviously caused quite a stir in both the Foreign and Colonial Offices and they called her in for further interviews. She described how she would start telling her story only to be interrupted by "this is extremely valuable – please will you wait while we get in Mr X as it affects his department."[153] A messenger would be sent to fetch Mr X and in the end Katharine found herself with six or seven people in the room interviewing her. Even the non-committal and worldly-wise foreign office staff were surprised by her enterprise and her remarkable journey. No English person, let alone a woman, had travelled as she had done through Italian Somaliland, Ethiopia and Eritrea, since before 1935. She was able to give a first hand, up-to-date account of a stretch of country that had been largely out-of-bounds for the British for the last three years. She gave them new information of Italian plans for boundary adjustments and told them the Italian position in Abyssinia was more secure than the British had been led to believe.

The British political line was pro-Abyssinian and anti-Italian, so Katharine's report, which did not mention any signs of serious unrest or obvious scenes of oppression, gave a rather different picture from the British agents residing in Djibouti and Egypt who had been sending back wildly exaggerated reports of imminent rebellion. The former Emperor of Ethiopia, Haile Selassie was living in exile in England and British Opinion supported the Abyssinians, who were seen as the innocent victims of the cruel Italian aggressors. Katharine Fannin, having seen the region herself, felt overall that the Italian occupation was beneficial. She had seen the Italian efforts in road building, farming and construction of public amenities. The infrastructure she saw being put in place and the modern methods of administration were in her opinion an improvement on the previous regime when the Emperor had ruled as a medieval monarch under feudal conditions. Prior to the Italians, the corrupt Church and overmighty Rases had kept the population in abject poverty and submission. Slavery in Ethiopia had been officially abolished in 1924, but despite praiseworthy attempts at modernisation, the Emperor had been unable to control his rebellious barons who continued to rule and do as they pleased. The Italian occupation had at least broken the power of the Church and the Rases, who were now obliged to act within the law. Everywhere she went Katharine had seen Abyssinia being dragged by its bootstraps into the modern era and she could not join with the total condemnation of Italian rule considered politically correct in England. She was thus out of step with the majority in England and much of what she said must have been contrary to the views held in the Foreign Office.

For two weeks she stayed at a small hotel in central London and every day went into the Foreign Office to dictate her report. She was not impressed by Foreign Office working hours – eleven to one and three to six, but enjoyed the social encounters and lunches with the smooth and charming Oxford graduates, who, according to her, made up the bulk of personnel.

As usual finances were a problem for Katharine. Her trip to Ethiopia had proved rather expensive as she had felt obliged to give lavish tips and presents to those who had helped her. In London she "buzzed a tenner" on a new outfit, when invited out to lunch at the Carlton Grill with Cavendish Bentinck.[154] However, she hoped to recoup her losses by writing articles and selling the films she had taken. She had already been asked to make a broadcast by the BBC.

Katharine Fannin's first report did generate considerable interest and it can be seen in the Public Record Office, London, in the Foreign Office Correspondence Files for Ethiopia, 1938, which were opened in 1990.[155] The green heading for her file indicated that this is indeed an intelligence report. Seven copies were made, which were circulated to the relevant departments. Major Miller of the War Office and Major Neate of the Air Ministry found the information of particular value.

Katharine had to explain a delicate matter to Charles in her first long letter sent from London by diplomatic bag.[156] Henry Salt's antiquarian guide book had caught the imagination of the Italians and now the Foreign Office had suggested she bend the facts a little and claim the famous traveller as an ancestor of hers. They thought this "polite fiction" would be accepted by the Italians as a good reason for her continuing interest in Ethiopia and provide cover for her return journey, when she hoped to tour the Amhara and Tigre regions.[157] She had been instructed to take back another copy of Henry Salt and play the family tradition with discretion. The BBC broadcast she eventually gave on January 3, 1939, and entitled "To Talk of Many Things" made use of this "white lie." The broadcast was carried throughout the Empire and Katharine did not want Charles to be publicly surprised or blow her cover!

Immense care was taken over the script for this broadcast talk to make it entirely impartial and neutral so as not to jeopardise the success of her return journey. The Foreign Office had warned her she needed a plausible reason; they also advised her that war could break out as early as spring 1939, so she could not afford to delay her return.

However, she had one item of important family business to attend to. Her original reason for her journey to London had been given a back seat with all the excitement of Ethiopia. Uncle John's will had been a disappointment after all. The £500 she thought had been promised her, was left instead to brother Geoffrey who had persuaded the old man to change his will just before his death. Katharine was left a mere £50. She was furious with her brother, whom she called a dirty dog and a crook, when she met him in a pub at Budleigh Salterton, looking smug and prosperous. They quarrelled and she told him she wished never to see or hear of him again. Later she visited Eastcliff and spoke to the gardener. She collected a bundle of her letters, carefully saved by her uncle John and an old Jacobean chest that belonged to her.[158]

Eastcliff, after the death of Uncle John, had been dismantled and stripped. She could not stay there and accepted the invitation of Major Hankey, who had married one of Charles' many sisters and had a house in Totnes, Devon. Christmas at Totnes was enlivened by the company of her nephew by marriage, Jack Hankey, who like his father was also in the army and at age 37, was almost her exact contemporary. After a pleasant Christmas she spent another week in London finalising the Foreign Office report and giving her broadcast talk on Abyssinia. This talk caused a few problems as she did not see eye to eye with the producer, a Miss Wace, who was extremely anti-Fascist and pro-Abyssinian. She tried to alter the script at the last minute and wanted to cut out anything that put the Italians in a favourable light. Katharine strongly objected to having her carefully prepared and previously agreed text interfered with to suit Miss Wace's political stance. They had quite an argument, but eventually reached a compromise. After it was all over, they paid her fee plus expenses, and she rushed out and "blew" half of it on a silver cigarette case as a present for Charles. This she had engraved "Charles Fannin from Kaffrine BBC 3:1:39."[159]

In the same letter, which described the broadcast saga and the disappointment over Uncle John's will, she also mentioned an interesting tea party she attended in St James's. Here she met Wing-Commander Clinton Wells of the Air Ministry, but tantalizingly refused to say more. A letter from Clinton Wells turns up in her papers dated December 30,

1938, in which interest is shown in the petrol supplies and fuel stocks she had noticed and asked for fuller information. She collected her films, which had come out well, and met up with her cousin, Leonard Atkinson, who was a senior curator at the Public Records Office.

By the second week of January, with the report and broadcast behind her, she began to feel rather bored at Totnes, with only the company of kindly retired Major Hankey, as she waited to finalise her return to Ethiopia. The Duke of Aosta had already given her permission to stay in Addis Ababa and she was waiting for news of the travel arrangements from the Italians. Understandably, she found the inactivity and suspense hard to bear. She described the tedious and pathetic life style of poor Major Hankey, who went nowhere and saw no one for months on end, living for news of his glamorous son and his friends. "Breakfast at 9 – household orders at 10, short walk 11-11.45 – a potter round the house and garden – lunch at 1, sleep from 2-3.30, walk 3.30-4, tea at 4, more time wasting until 6, then the wireless news – change at 7, dinner at 7.30, wireless again at 8.15-9 or so – reading the newspaper until 9.45 and then bed. So on every day." She found the house perishingly cold and complained that she could not get warm unless actually crouching over the drawing-room fire.[160]

Finally the news came through that she had a passage from Naples to Massawa, leaving on January 26, 1939. She had arranged that most of her private letters, particularly those from the Foreign Office and Lord Halifax, who wrote to thank her for her information, be deposited in the bank. She did not want to have any Foreign Office letters on her person while travelling. She spent the rest of her money from the broadcast on old books and maps of Ethiopia to take with her. She planned to present them to the Viceroy for his library to give further authenticity to the part she had to play – a harmless and eccentric traveller, interested in old books and antiquities, who was sympathetic towards the Italians and what they were achieving in Ethiopia.[161] She eventually left England on January 22 on the Newhaven to Dieppe ferry.

Katharine sent long affectionate letters to her husband during this period, full of endearments and their private coded language. She called herself 'fat pussu' or 'fat girl' or even just signed herself with a circle. Charles is addressed as 'tizzles' or 'jaiboy' or even 'dearest lambkin.' Her effusiveness over her 'darling little doggies' and occasional lapses into coy baby language have to be seen in perspective. At that time such expressions were not considered as affectedly sentimental as they are today. However, even so, the letters she wrote to Charles from Abyssinia and London were exaggeratedly fond. They seem to have been written by someone who felt guilty about something and hoped to be forgiven. She obviously felt guilty about her overspending and about having an exciting time while he worked hard in Nairobi trying to repay their debts. He stood in as Commissioner for Lands and Settlement instead of taking leave before another posting.

But there may have been additional reasons for the tone of her letters: she may have been unfaithful, and there are one or two oblique references to a certain "Roberto." She certainly enjoyed flirtations with the attractive Italian officials she met, and travelling quite alone in areas where no white woman ever went, there must have been several opportunities for extra-marital activity. She was aged nearly 36, in her prime, while Charles, quiet and staid, was nearly 50. Her letters had an undertone of anxiety, as if she was not at all certain about Charles' reaction. It seemed he had also been kept in the dark about the full scope of her intelligence activities in Ethiopia and the information that his wife was doing a bit of spying on the side might have come as something of a shock. Katharine became very worried just before Christmas, when she had not heard from him, but was reassured when letters arrived at last. It is impossible to guess what Charles felt as none of his letters survive from this period. However, their marriage did not break up and perhaps the temporary separation helped them both get over a difficult period in their relationship.

CHAPTER NINE

Ethiopia Part 2: February-March 1939

Katharine's return journey through Italian East Africa occurred at a providentially auspicious moment. In January 1939, Chamberlain and Lord Halifax had met with Dino Grandi, Count Ciano and Il Duce Mussolini in Rome and the Italo/British accord was strengthened and both parties reaffirmed their mutual desire for peace in Europe.[162] The Italian position in Ethiopia was fully recognised by the British and the Italian King re-acknowledged as Emperor of Ethiopia. Nevertheless, despite the soothing words of the diplomats, the thunderclouds of war rumbled ever closer and any journey across potentially enemy territory was still a risky venture. Although Italy did not officially enter the Second World War as Hitler's ally until June 10, 1940, Katharine Fannin couldn't know that. In February 1939, war was generally considered imminent. None of her letters survived from this leg of her journey and the information for this chapter is taken from her second report written for the Foreign Office in Nairobi,[163] from her articles in *The Sunday Post*[164] and from the brief entries of her pocket diary for 1939. The other important source is her second copy of Henry Salt's **A Voyage to Abyssinia**, which she carried and asked every official she met to sign and date, both as a personal memento and as an aide memoire to the dossier she would later write on each one of them for British Intelligence.

On her way through Rome she briefly met with Achille Starace, Mussolini's colourful and controversial right hand man, who served as the Party Secretary of the PNF (Partito Nazionale Fascista). As Party Secretary, Starace staged massive parades and marches, proposed anti-Semitic racial segregation and expanded Musssolini's cult of personality.

Starace had played an important role in conquering the Northern part of Ethiopia during the Italian invasion in 1936, largely due to his idea of using his soldiers to build roads as they progressed and his use of trucks for transportation over rough terrain. In March 1936, as Starace and his truck column prepared to advance over rough tracks to seize Gondar, 'The Panther Man,' as he was called, gave the following memorable speech to his men:

"Soldiers this is the most risky, most difficult and most important venture of the campaign. Don't waste a shot. We are carrying all the ammunition we are going to have on this trip. This column must be like an electric live wire. Death to the touch! Truck drivers must learn to keep to the right of the road under pain of severe penalties…Britain is a rich country, Italy is a poor country but the people of poor countries have hard muscles. The only way to explain the action of the English is that they thought they had only to mass a war fleet in the Mediterranean and Mussolini would take off his hat and bow in submission. Instead he reared up like a thoroughbred horse and sent his soldiers into Africa."

The road building skills of Starace's men was as important as their combat prowess. On April 1, 1936, Starace and his column entered Gondar in triumph and two days later reached Lake Tana securing the border region with British Sudan. The East African Fast Column (Colonna Celere de Africa Orientale) had covered approximately 75 miles in three days.

Starace had later taken a prominent part in promoting road construction in Italian colonies and he must have been delighted by Katherine's sincere admiration of the new road network being put in place in Italian East Africa.

From Rome Katharine travelled to Naples, where she joined a cargo ship transporting 88 newly qualified doctors, part of a batch of 300, being sent out to Italian East Africa. This was a government ploy to improve relations with the Ethiopians; they hoped to win their hearts by providing free medical treatment.

Katharine arrived in Massawa on February 5, 1939. At Massawa she attended the ceremonies given for General Attilio Teruzzi, the Italian Undersecretary of State for the Colonies and Commander of the 5th Blackshirt Division, Ethiopia, as he completed an official tour of Italian East Africa. An old friend of Mussolini, short in stature and renowned for his hot temper, he was popularly known as "the pocket Vesuvius." Katharine thought him ill-mannered and conceited and disliked the way he flaunted himself, all gold braid and medals, on the dance floor with his Cuban mistress.[165]

Katharine must have taken a long look at the Massawa port, memorising the lay out and photographing a general view showing the large cranes and main jetty with railway lines running onto the quayside. The Italians had made Massawa their chief port in East Africa as it had a much better natural harbour and deep water anchorage than either Assab or Mogadishu. Its position at the entrance to the Red Sea was also closer to Italy and more favourably placed for international trade. In the early months of 1939 it was a bustling modern port, importing diesel engines from Germany and spare parts for the Fiat trucks that were the workhorses of the Italian Colonies. Huge amounts of construction materials and machinery were also being brought in to service the ambitious programmes of the Fascist Government, even as the old dhow trade between Yemen and Saudi Arabia continued uninterrupted.

A number of outlying islands protect the coastline and entrance to Massawa, which is situated on the inner side of one of two small islands directly facing the mainland. Katherine recalled that when her purported ancestor, Henry Salt, first visited the area in the early 19th century, the port of Massawa was ruled by a Governor, or Nayib, appointed by the Ottoman Pashas in Egypt. He based himself on the island and the old coral houses and narrow streets of the Muslim quarter remained much the same as they had in Salt's time.

The Italians had built a new modern town on the other island, and had constructed three causeways joining the islands together and to the mainland. A railway line linked Massawa to Asmara, the capital of Eritrea. The smart Italian official buildings were clustered together along a broad palm-lined highway running down to the sea front.

Katharine travelled on to Asmara. During the 1930s Italy had transformed Eritrea into one of the most industrialised and modern colonies of all Africa and Asmara, the capital, became its showcase. Italian professionals and artisans had flooded into Asmara, built shoe factories, plazas, hotels, a railway, clubs and cinemas for the Italians as well as churches and grand official buildings. Here they built using the most daring and extreme art deco architecture, such as the ultra modern

Impero Cinema, the famous Bar Zilli and the palm-studded main Harnet Avenue. The Fiat Tagliero gas station designed by Giuseppe Pettazzi looked like a giant aeroplane with 90-foot unsupported concrete wings!

In Asmara Katharine stayed as the guest of the Governor, her old friend Dr Daodiace. Here Katharine met a dubious character, an American called Ruth Williams Ricci, a former nurse and reputed mistress of the first Italian military governor of Ethiopia, General Graziani. Ruth told Katharine she was a journalist, writing articles for an American newspaper about the Italian colonies in East Africa. She suggested to Katharine they travel together. It seems probable Ruth Ricci was a plant, detailed to keep an eye on Katharine and her activities. She was a devoted Fascist and pro-Nazi and Katharine immediately suspected she was an Italian spy.[166] Ruth Ricci and Katharine Fannin struck up a friendship and they travelled together first on a day trip to Keren on the road to Agordat, where Katharine filmed the gun emplacements, and then for ten days on a visit to Tigre Province and Gondar, where Ethiopian resistance still troubled the Italians.[167] Ruth Ricci was extremely anti-British, but excellent company and Katharine wrote an extensive report on her for the British authorities – as no doubt Mrs Ricci did about Mrs Fannin for the Italian authorities.

They passed through Adi Ugri where the Duke of Aosta's young cousin, the Duke of Ancona, was the Commissario, then visited Adua, the scene of Italy's shaming defeat of 1896, where stood a war memorial and a new military hospital. They stopped at Axum and Katharine took photographs of "some disordered monoliths standing in a nearby field."[168] These were the stelae of the Aksumite emperors, who had ruled in pre-Christian times and were just beginning to arouse archaeological interest. The Ethiopian Church kept some of its holiest relics and church treasures at Axum and the Ethiopian High Priest, the Abuna, brought some out into the courtyard of the historic church of St Mary to show Katharine, as women were not allowed inside the Sanctuary.[169] She saw the Gold Book of Amhara filled with brightly coloured pictures of the saints, gold and jewelled three-decker crowns, worn on state occasions, valuable icons and crosses and beautiful embroidered robes.[170] Katharine, with her love of glitter, was fascinated and impressed by the overt wealth and power of the Ethiopian Church. It is significant that the only Ethiopian she sees fit to include in her report is the Coptic Bishop of Eritrea, who she met in Asmara.[171] She noted the influence of the Ethiopian Church, which the Italians encouraged.

Crossing the River Tacazze over the new bridge – Ponte Mussolini – they entered the dangerous province of Tigre, where they joined an armed convoy, which went twice daily over the Ualchefit Pass. The new road, which had just been completed, was another amazing feat of Italian road engineering. Blasted out of a sheer precipice and carried to the top on walls in a series of long zig-zags, it opened up Gondar and the Lake Tana region, which previously had been isolated by the 10,000 ft barrier of the Tigre escarpment. Here Katharine saw Italian soldiers working on the road armed with rifles slung over their backs, while others stood on guard. Resistance fighters lurked in the Semien mountains, waiting for ambush opportunities, but the military road driven through by 15,000 Italian troops, harassed all the way by Ethiopian sharpshooters, had greatly improved security, or so Katharine was told. [172]

The two ladies crossed over without incident into the fertile plain that stretches all the way to Lake Tana. Near Gondar they visited an ambitious settlement scheme for ex-Italian soldiers and their families. The wives and children had not yet arrived, but the husbands lived in long communal barracks and spent all day breaking new land, ploughing and planting grain. They assured Katharine that as soon as houses had been built, the families would follow. On this family settlement scheme each family came out for a two-year probation period. They received a small labour-saving stone house and each family was expected to cultivate about 100 acres. Large machinery like tractors, all social welfare and marketing of produce was to be done on a co-operative basis. At the end of the probationary period the family had the choice of either leaving or taking up the option to buy the house and land.

A similar type of scheme already operated in the Italian colony of Libya and the Italians hoped to settle Ethiopia in this way. The scheme would provide an outlet for Italy's swarming population and increase Italian self-sufficiency by cultivating food crops for export. Katharine was told the settlement programme was proving popular in Italy, where conditions were increasingly difficult under Fascist rule, and the organisers had already received more applications than they could cope with. She heard a similar settlement at Bischioftu outside Addis Ababa was already self-supporting and that another had just been started at Olleta.[173]

Both these farming settlements were situated in the fertile highlands of Galla Sidamo, where there were other large Italian experimental farms. Katharine thought the Gondar settlement very isolated, but could not help admiring the hard working Italians.[174]

She noticed the concept behind the settlement programmes was entirely different from British East Africa, where the settlers had employed native labour to do most of the manual work. In Italian East Africa Italians did all the work and in the capital, Addis Ababa, all the waiters, servants, drivers, etc., were Italian. This system grandly called "demographic colonisation" by the Fascist author Carlo Giglio,[175] had one drawback, which caused the Italians grave concern. It posed the problem of a possible decline of European prestige in "native eyes." However, the author declared: "We cannot allow ourselves the luxury of doing it the English way, that is to live and get rich at the expense of others. We must take to our Empire our own peasants, our own workers and our own artisans. It is necessary to abandon the old concept that the European in Africa must only command and substitute for it the Fascist concept of the prestige of the white race as creators of great works." Even Katharine with her admiration for the hardworking Italians, could not help expressing doubts as to whether this concept was entirely practical and questioned whether it was wise to exclude the Abyssinians so entirely from the new order.

In the third article of her series in *The Sunday Post*[176] Katharine further explained how the opportunities for settlement and investment were exclusively reserved for Italians, at the discretion of the Government in Addis Ababa. Even the Italians themselves criticised this investment policy, she said, as it allowed certain favoured individuals and companies to operate monopolies and act as quasi-governmental bodies making vast profits at the expense of the home government, without regard to cost or efficiency and discouraged genuine private enterprise. The chief culprits were of course in the construction and transportation businesses. Katharine also noticed that only Roman Catholic missionaries were allowed to proselytise. Catholicism, the Ethiopian Church and Islam were the three religions granted freedom of worship in the new Roman Empire of Eastern Africa.

After touring the Portuguese castles at Gondar, Katharine visited the tomb of the murdered British Consul, Plowden, and the ruins of the town where the brilliant but unstable King Theodore had had his headquarters. King Theodore or Tewodros, who ruled 1831-1868, had been one of the pioneers of modern Ethiopia and had tried unsuccessfully to forge the area into a kingdom with a centralised authority. However, his imprisonment of British missionaries and the envoy of Queen Victoria, led him into conflict. Lord Napier defeated him at the battle of Magdala, when, rather than fall into the hands of the British, he committed suicide. From Gondar Katharine and Ruth Ricci travelled to Gorgora on Lake Tana[177] and after relaxing at a small hotel on the lake, the two ladies returned to Asmara, where they parted company.

On her return to Asmara, Katharine was introduced to a German former Naval Officer, Count Felix Von Luckner, a fellow guest of the Governor. She suspected he was a roving German intelligence agent. He was travelling around the Italian colonies with his glamorous Swedish wife and, like her, was on his way to Addis Ababa. Katharine noticed he was treated with a great deal of respect and was very popular with the German community.[178] She estimated that at this time there were about 1,000 Germans in Massawa and Asmara, mainly businessmen on government contracts, supplying German machinery and diesel engines to the Italians, as well as consumer goods. Katharine also mentioned meeting an English woman, Melissa Reed, at the palace in Asmara.[179]

Katharine drove on to the capital, where she stayed once more at the guesthouse attached to the Governor General's residence, Villa D'Italia. At Addis Ababa she found her friend Canero Medici had been transferred to Tripoli and reported that the Duke's new deputy was an unpleasant individual called Enrico Cerulli,[180] who reported to Mussolini directly. Practically every other official in Italian East Africa belonged to the Italian minor aristocracy[181] and one significant change Katharine saw on her return was fewer pictures of Il Duce and more posters prominently displayed of the Viceroy with slogans such as Viva Il Re Imperatore and Viva La Casa Savoia. The royalists were suspected of being only luke-warm Fascists and were known to dislike the Rome-Berlin Axis that Mussolini had joined.[182]

In Addis Ababa the British Consul General, Hugh Stonehewer Bird, who had now had time to settle in, told Katharine he thought Ethiopian resistance was stiffening and in the event of war, the Ethiopians would need very little encouragement to rise of their own accord to throw the Italians out of Ethiopia. Katharine disagreed with him. According to her personal observations, Ethiopian resistance was confined to small pockets with no organisation or unity. And in her opinion the Italians were more entrenched than the British had been led to believe by partisan informers.[183] (Interestingly, just over a year later in April 1940 General Arconovaldo Bonacorsi, Inspector General of the Blackshirts, was sent from Italy to assess the situation in Ethiopia. He wrote a most damning report of the Governor General, Duke of Aosta, whom he accused of being too lenient towards the Abyssinians and allowing security in the region to deteriorate. He recommended a complete military crackdown. "A people such as we have found in Africa must be treated with bread and a whip; any other method is fatal." It is interesting how he echoed Stonehewer Bird's view, when he wrote: "If from any of our frontiers a single British or French unit marches resolutely into our territory with its flag flying it will not need armed men because the greater part of the Abyssinian people will join them to fight against us and turn us out. I do not know if we will be able, in case of emergency, to face up to what may happen in view of the unprepared and abandoned state of our army." Written in support of the common soldier and the military, Bonacorsi wrote scathingly of the Government officials and the bosses of the parastatal monopolies, who lived a life of ease and luxury, while the Italian soldiers and workmen dressed in rags and tatters as they laboured on the roads and building public amenities for the Abyssinians, who merely looked on with scorn. "Let the truth be known: Our troops are in rags, barefooted, torn and naked, in such a lamentable state of absolute inferiority compared with the Abyssinians that they call them mosquin, beggars." [184]

On this occasion Katharine had several private talks with the Viceroy. The Duke expressed support for Mussolini, but had reservations about the increasing German influence. He told Katharine how he wanted above all to give Italians a chance for a better life and improve Italy's status as a nation. The vexed Djibouti question came up several times in conversation. The French at Djibouti, in French Somaliland, controlled land-locked Ethiopia's nearest and most convenient outlet to the sea. But so far all negotiations for free passage of goods and favourable terms for Italian shipping and transportation had fallen on deaf ears. The French also owned the railway that ran between Djibouti and Addis Ababa and relations had become very strained as they refused to sell this to the Italians. The Viceroy considered the French stupidly obstinate and in event of war intended immediately to strike and take Djibouti. Only fear of reprisals held the Italians back as they could not afford to ignore British superiority in East Africa. They had got away with Ethiopia but Djibouti, they knew, would be another matter.

In order to circumvent the difficult French, the Italians had built a road at vast cost and at enormous speed across the Danakil Desert to the port of Assab. This port was not as well appointed nor as convenient as Djibouti but much nearer than Massawa. It took at least four days drive from Addis Ababa to reach Massawa, while they hoped a lorry could reach Assab in about 24 hours on the new road. Developing reliable transportation arteries and a good supply system for Ethiopia seemed at this stage to be the Viceroy's chief concern.

The Viceroy suggested Katharine try out the new road, which was nearly completed. He also gave her a set of 14 1/1000,000 maps covering the whole of Italian East Africa on which all the new roads had been marked by hand and exactly coloured to show the most recent state of communications to take back to Sir Robert Brooke-Popham, the Governor of Kenya. Nine of the sheets were marked "Instituto Geografico e Militare - Edizione 1934, 1935, 1936" but five sheets were marked "Commando Superiore delle Forze Armate Dell A.O.I." and included the most recent map of the capital, dated November 1938. These maps were handed over immediately to the Commander of the Northern Brigade in Kenya and not sent to the Foreign Office and London with her report.

A gift of a set of the most up-to-date maps of one's territory to a potential adversary is an unusual gesture, under most circumstances. But the Italians had everything to gain by friendship with the British in Kenya and possibly the Duke thought Katharine Fannin a more influential envoy than she really was. He also wanted to give something in exchange for the antiquarian books and maps she had presented to him for the library. This cousin of the King of Italy was kind and humane, but not a strong character. Lonely without his wife – the Princess Anna of France – and delighted to have someone with whom he could speak English, he may have succumbed to Katharine's blandishments and obvious respect for his rank. He may have given her the maps without proper forethought as they happened to be handy. However, it is more likely that the Duke, who had no personal grudge against the British, hoped in the event of war to hand over Ethiopia with as little damage and bloodshed as possible. Perhaps he thought by putting the most recent map of the capital in the hands of the British Governor in Kenya, it might help save the thousands of Italian civilians living there from being massacred by avenging Ethiopians. Certainly the Italians would far prefer capture by the British than the Ethiopians, whose brutality towards prisoners was well known. The British in Kenya were likely to be more sympathetic to fellow settlers and colonials. As nothing appears in writing, this supposition must remain conjecture, but certainly there was little resistance, when the British did finally invade. The only fierce fighting took place in Eritrea, where there was a considerable German presence, and the main strategic Axis port of Massawa.

Both the Duke of Aosta's and Stonehewer Bird's signatures appear prominently on the flyleaves of Katharine's copy of Henry Salt's **A Voyage to Abyssinia**. Stonehewer Bird's neat signature appears dead centre surrounded by many others, while the Duke signs boldly and alone across the empty page immediately preceding the title-page: "Amadeo de Savoia - Vice Roy & Gov. Gen. - Addis Abeba 1939 XVII." Daodiace, Governor of Eritrea, is the first signature on the first page and one of the few that is clearly legible. Katharine collected more that a hundred signatures in all, which continue on to the end papers. One illegible one from Gondar includes a row of kisses, while a couple written in green ink have faded badly. There is a string of names from a dinner party held on March 4, 1939, which includes the bold black signature of Catalano Gonzaga, the Propaganda Minister. Nowadays it is difficult to imagine carrying such a heavy book on your travels and producing it at every social occasion attended. But that is what Katharine did and every official she met in the remotest district and under whatever conditions, was persuaded to place his name on the flyleafs of her book.

Katharine's drive across the Danakil Desert gave her great personal satisfaction. She set off on February 26 and returned March 3, staying one day at Assab, where the Italians were building a new port. The first Englishman ever to cross the Danakil Desert was called Nesbitt and his journey in 1928 had been written up and became a travel classic. Katharine claimed to be the second English person and the first English woman ever to see the arid landscape of this inhospitable mainly lava desert. The road of course made it much more accessible. Nesbitt went across by camel, when there was no road, but still the seventeen-and-a-half hour drive was the most arduous Katharine had ever experienced, and she travelled in the cool season when temperatures did not reach the 70°C common between May and September but stayed around 50° C. Katharine stayed one night at the road camp at Tendaho and spoke to the engineer in charge. He told her the road was being built by 3,000 Italians and a native workforce of 24,000, 11,000 of whom were indentured labour from the Sudan. Between May and September it was too hot to work by day so they worked only at night by flares. As the wife of a civil engineer and road-building expert, she could not help but admire the enterprise in undertaking such a venture and described the landscape of the Danakil as resembling nothing but telescopic photographs of the moon, a "veritable abomination of desolation."[185]

She visited the important market at Batie, where the Danakil tribesmen come with their salt and camels to trade with the Abyssinians for cotton, grain and hides. While there, an Italian Court was dispensing justice under a tree in the market place. Katharine was shocked to witness a public flogging of three Abyssinians, who were made to lie face down and receive 40 or 50 lashes from a hippo hide whip. When she queried this, she was told that compared to the former Abyssinian habit of public hangings and chaining and amputation, this punishment was mild. Her Italian hosts said the Abyssinians were so used to cruelty they did not understand leniency or civilised treatment. This incident, where she saw Italian brutality with her own eyes, was one of the very few bad impressions she received.[186]

Katharine concentrated so hard on memorising information for British Intelligence it seems she had little time to notice anything else. However, she does describe the colourful procession of an important chief, Ras Hailu,[187] who she saw just outside Addis Ababa at the Teramber Pass.

> "He was a grave distinguished looking person wrapped about in a long shiny black silk coat all embroidered and collared in gold, and spread as formally over himself and his pony as a guardsman's cape. The pony was even grander, its harness all scarlet and silver and brass. Before the Ras danced a picturesque rabble of soldiery, leaping wildly about and

firing off their antique matchlocks, which from the look of them must have dated from Portuguese times. A retainer lead a riderless white mule in front of the Ras, a custom invariably followed by the 'quality' in Abyssinia, and more soldiers and an orchestra brought up the rear. I felt I had stepped straight back into the Middle Ages. Stout Cortes never gazed in half such wild surmise as I did, when showers of pebbles from the arquebuses started to rain down in a most untutored manner."[188]

She also went to several markets in Addis Ababa and admired the silver ornaments and the brightly coloured paintings on parchment of saints and St George and the Dragon, which were everywhere until an order came one day that painters had to have licenses. The paintings disappeared overnight.[189]

Katharine left Addis Ababa on March 8, and started her long drive back through Italian Somaliland to the Coast to catch her ship. While in Addis Ababa she received a telegram from Charles telling her that his posting to Accra, as Assistant Director of Surveys Gold Coast, had come through. The time had come for her return to Nairobi, before the rains came and made the roads impassable. She drove through the province of Galla Sidamo, past the chain of lakes, Lake Zuai, Lake Abiata, Lake Langana, Lake Sciala and Lake Marguerita towards the Kenyan frontier. She turned east to Lugh Ferrandi on the Juba River. Here on March 13, she slipped across the border at Mandera through the barbed wire fence to have lunch with the District Officer, R Tatton-Brown, wire her husband and hear news from England.[190] She then continued on to the Coast. Originally she had intended to follow the Juba River direct to Kismayu, but she was advised the road was impassable so she had to take the longer route via Ischia Baidoa to Mogadishu, and then along the Coast via Merca, Brava and Giumbo to Kismayu. Little is known about this part of her journey as her report only briefly indicated the main towns and military posts she passed through.

Katharine barely caught her ship, the *SS Tripolitana*, which arrived a day earlier than scheduled, and was not able to look around the port as she had intended. She noted curtly in her report that she was not impressed with Kismayu or the Commissario, who, though charming, she found to be slack and untidy.[191] Hurriedly she produced her last fiver and bought a ticket to Mombasa. Katharine had her final view of Italian East Africa from a chair on which she and her luggage were carried, rather precariously, by native porters splashing through the shallow sea out to the ship's tender.

CHAPTER TEN
The return of the prodigal traveller 1939

Katharine Fannin arrived in Mombasa on March 22, 1939. She had succeeded in bringing back an important set of maps, had spoken personally and at length with the Viceroy and many of his senior officials and had seen at first hand conditions in Italian East Africa. Her return warranted a front page interview by *The Sunday Post* 'East Africa's Cheerful Weekly'[192] in which the intrepid lady traveller described her most compelling impressions of her unique journey. This included a flattering description of the roads, her pioneering Danakil trip and a favourable mention of the Duke of Aosta and all he was doing to make the Italian colonisation of Ethiopia successful and peaceful.

The report she made for the Foreign Office, dated April 6, 1939,[193] contained more details than her first report made in London. She compiled it in ten days. Katharine divided her report into four sections: an account of the roads and places she had visited on the motor journeys she made between February 5 and March 20, 1939, through Italian East Africa; notes on the general Military Situation; notes on the general Political Situation; notes on the Italians she had met and sketch maps of the ports of Massawa and Assab.

In her notes on the General Military Situation, she estimated there were only 100,000 native troops, mainly Somalis, and 20,000 regular Italian troops in the whole of Italian East Africa. However, there were also 100,000 Italian workmen, ex-soldiers, working on the roads and farms. She noted most of the regular soldiery worked on the roads as well. The entire Italian population she estimated at 330,000, which meant approximately 210,000 civilians lived in Italian East Africa as well. She thought there were approximately 400 aircraft, 40,000 lorries and an unspecified number of armoured cars. In addition, every Italian male was issued with and required to carry a service rifle with 50 rounds of ammunition.[194]

Apart from a few specified regions, she had found the country peaceful. Because the Italians allowed her to travel alone where she wished, over more than 7,000 miles of roads and tracks, proved to her the Italian conquest of Ethiopia was complete. The Viceroy himself had openly admitted there were about 10,000 rebels still disaffected – out of a population of 15 million. He pointed out the that these rebels moved about in small bands, sniping and stealing cattle and escaping into the canyons and hills, making them almost impossible to catch and giving them greater notoriety than they deserved. The Duke of Aosta had told Katharine that he hoped by conciliation, free pardons and generous treatment of those who submitted, to have the whole of Abyssinia in sufficiently good order to allow the King of Italy to come on a state visit in March 1941.[195] According to Katharine, the area most affected with insecurity was the Gojjam area and near Lake Sciano, where an unfortunate recent incident, when a Ras's two sons were shot dead, had caused unrest to flare up again.

From her own observations Katharine advised the Foreign Office: "If we are hoping for a spontaneous Abyssinian rebellion in the event of Italy having to face external trouble, we are deluding ourselves." She castigated the pro-Ethiopian pressure group 'The Abyssinian Association' as "gentlemen who sit in armchairs in London and Cairo and invent stories, which they hope will wring the hearts of sympathisers and thus keep up a steady flow of contributions from woolly-minded sentimentalists."[196]

She predicted that in event of war the Italians would strike at French Somaliland and Sudan as priorities, rather than Kenya, which they considered less important strategically and militarily. However, she thought the border station at Moyale would be put out of action early on as a precautionary measure to disrupt communications. She commented on the shabby appearance of the Italian troops, who were employed as road-builders rather than a fighting force and pointed out that only a very small minority were blackshirts, the dedicated fascist militia. She had found nearly everyone extremely friendly to the British and was favourably impressed by the easy relations that prevailed on both the Sudanese and Kenyan borders.

Katharine Fannin, as an ardent colonialist, firmly believed Africa as a whole was better off under western rule – be it British, Italian, or even French. She did not wish to see Haile Selassie reinstated. The roads, the houses, the hospitals she saw being built convinced her the ordinary Ethiopian was benefiting from Italian rule. She saw the Italians developing and modernising a country that had been suspended in a time warp somewhere in the 15th century. Nearly everything she observed was an improvement and the people going about their everyday life did not look to her more downtrodden or unhappy than previously. The Chiefs or Rases, who previously had ruled as medieval barons, now had to act within the law and could no longer terrorise and enslave their people.

Unfortunately, however fair-minded Katharine's views were, they ran counter to the political line in Britain. Her championing of the Italian cause felt like a betrayal to many. They did not understand her fine-line distinction between royalist personnel operating in Ethiopia, who were only lukewarm Fascists at best, and the full blown Fascism of Mussolini. Britain was on the brink of war, about to sacrifice everything in the fight against Fascism and Nazism and it could not afford dissenting or confusing voices in the ranks. Italy and Germany were the enemies. It is therefore understandable that Katharine Fannin's pro-Italian bias was not well received although her secret information was enormously helpful. *The Sunday Post* curtailed her series of articles as the subject matter became increasingly controversial and her viewpoint increasingly politically unacceptable.[197] Mussolini, following Hitler's example, invaded the small defenceless kingdom of Albania in April, 1939, forcing King Zog, his young queen and newborn son to flee. The civilised world loudly condemned the Italians and the certainty of war grew ever closer.

However, Katharine's outspoken support for the Anglo-Italian Accord was balm to the heart of the Italian Consul General in Kenya, Italo Zappoli, who wrote her a special letter of praise and thanks.[198] Her exploits reported fully in the Italian press also gave her quite a reputation in Italy. Katharine received several letters from Ruth Williams Ricci, written from Rome, fulsomely complimentary and openly trying to convert her to Hitler's cause. One letter makes a mysterious reference to the loss of Katharine's green glasses at Gondar. Katharine Fannin was notoriously short-sighted without her glasses. Had this been a clumsy attempt at sabotage by one spy to another? In the separate report written on Ruth Ricci, Katharine remarked: "I am quite sure she is working for Italian Intelligence under cover of her American citizenship. Should we go to war with Italy I would not be surprised if she tried, as an American, to enter this country (England). Nobody can help liking her personally."

Discreetly, the British Government acknowledged their appreciation of Mrs Fannin's efforts: First came a letter from the Governor of Kenya, Sir Robert Brooke-Popham, dated April 12, 1939.

"I am sending four copies of your report to England and also the letters you want sent on. I am just in the middle of your report, which I find most interesting and I am sure will be very valuable. I am full of admiration for your wonderful memory and still more for the enterprise and initiative you showed in undertaking this expedition. I wish again to thank you for the services you have rendered to this country and the Empire."

Lord Halifax, The Foreign Secretary, sent a note via H A Caccia his private secretary, May 30, and in June a formal acknowledgement came from the Colonial Office.

SECRET

"The Undersecretary of State for the Colonies presents his compliments to the Private Secretary to the Governor of Kenya and, with reference to his of the 11th April, begs to request that an expression of appreciation may be conveyed to Mrs Fannin for the report which she has furnished on her recent journey through Italian East Africa to Kenya."[199]

The Maps of Massawa and Assab Ports in her report she marked: "for Squadron Leader Paynter, Air Ministry." They were roughly drawn because, as she explained, it had been too dangerous to make notes or drawings. It is almost certain MI6 were in touch with her, although she was probably not an accredited agent. There is an empty file marked MI6 stuffed haphazardly amongst her Ethiopian papers.

Katharine's second report generated considerably less enthusiasm at the Foreign Office than the first and it was criticised for being too long and verbose. However, there are 78 pages in the Foreign Office Correspondence File of letters and comments relating to her report. By this time she was considered politically unsound and her opinions about security in Abyssinia were largely discounted because, as Cavendish Bentinck wrote in his official cover note accompanying the report to other departments, "greater precautions were taken for Mrs. Fannin's safety than she realised and every effort was made to cause her to believe that security was complete throughout the Empire."[200]

Cavendish Bentinck's earlier dismissive remarks, after first reading her report, set the tone:

"The Italians would have been very stupid if they had not done their utmost to turn Mrs Fannin into a first class honorary Propaganda Agent. After her first trip through Abyssinia she was fairly well balanced and not so ecstatic. Latin flattery has a powerful effect on Anglo-Saxon females and I suspect that compliments from and interest on the part of HRH the Duke of Aosta have thrown Mrs Fannin completely off her balance."[201]

The British Consul General, Stonehewer Bird, had already sent in March this report from Addis Ababa:

"English visitors, not a feature hitherto, have been descending thick and fast. The Lennox-Boyds were followed by Mrs Fannin, of whom we have seen and heard quite a bit and yesterday out of the blue descended Mrs Emmet and Lady William Percy.[202] Mrs Fannin is regarded by the Duke as a bit of a joke but good value. She must have cost vast sums in petrol and wear and tear of cars. Since her arrival in Italian East Africa about a month ago, she has been taken from Massawa to Gondar, round Lake Tana and back to Massawa. Thence to Addis Ababa, whence after a few days she was driven to Assab and back. She stayed here three days and this morning left for Kismayu by road (a small matter of 2,000 kms). She is writing a monster memorandum on all she has seen and heard, of which, she tells me, you are to receive a copy, so I am not attempting to pass to you all or nearly all she has told me."[203]

Stonehewer Bird had found Mrs Fannin a tiring visitor and did not enjoy her forthright style. He was also, it seems, slightly envious of the attention she was receiving. But, although her outspoken political opinions and copious verbosity did not suit the diplomats, her general information of facts, figures and maps could not be faulted and were most helpful to the 'service' departments, as the Foreign office condescendingly referred to the Admiralty, War Office and Air Ministry to whom the report was duly circulated.

Charles and Katharine packed up and left Nairobi and Kenya on July 19, 1939. Charles headed for Accra, while Katharine travelled to England first. In a letter to Leonard Atkinson, her cousin, she mentioned how she sold all she could before leaving Kenya, because, as usual, she was short of cash. Her ambitious schemes for making a financial killing out of her Ethiopian trip did not materialise. It appears she made two broadcasts on Kenyan radio, but like the articles for *The Sunday Post*, these were discontinued. She gave a talk in Italian to the Italian community in Nairobi, but she never wrote the book she planned and the public acclaim she hoped for was not forthcoming. Instead, she became involved in acrimonious exchanges with other journalists who opposed her views and belittled her journey.

G L Steer, who wrote for the *Daily Telegraph* and *Morning Post* got short shrift when he suggested the Italian Government "takes pro-Italian visitors down the garden path and shows them just what it wants them to see: the best roads, the latest improvements and the most docile natives."

"How does Steer have the cheek to write about Abyssinia? He hardly went ashore for an hour or two, while the ship picked up cargo," asked a short piece entitled "Truth in the News,"[204] which bore the unmistakeable stamp of Katharine Fannin's pen.

G L Steer held strongly anti-Italian views and got most of his information about Ethiopia from Ethiopian émigrés in Djibouti. Even the Foreign Office considered his articles exaggerated.[205]

Katharine's most serious clash came with Sylvia Pankhurst who in her paper *New Times and Ethiopia*, founded in 1936, had been printing violently anti-Fascist articles and illustrations showing Italian atrocities in Ethiopia. Sylvia Pankhurst at this stage had never visited Ethiopia, or indeed Africa, but nevertheless she dedicated herself to the public defence of the Ethiopian cause and made herself a self-appointed authority on Ethiopian affairs. Initially the Abyssinian Association led by Professor Stanley Jevons, funded her paper, but she soon fell out with the more conservative members of the Society and she then worked directly for Haile Selassie.

A former suffragette, champion of women's rights, militant left-wing agitator and anti-colonialist, Pankhurst appealed to the emotions and did not care whether the material she published was factually correct or not as long as it furthered her cause.[206] This cavalier treatment of the truth upset Katharine Fannin and led her to challenge Sylvia Pankhurst to put the record straight.

In a lengthy letter addressed to the editor of the *Manchester Guardian* entitled "Conditions in Abyssinia: An Englishwoman's Tour of Observation," dated July 9, 1939, Katharine Fannin attacked Sylvia Pankhurst.[207] She pointed out that contrary to the Pankhurst reports, the native labourers working on the roads were happy and well paid, the ordinary Ethiopian not sullen and depressed but better off than ever before and the country organised and peaceful, not in a state of barely suppressed rebellion. She finished with these words:

"I am shortly returning to England and hope I may perhaps have a chance of meeting Miss Pankhurst. I have always had a great respect for her stout championship of those she considers oppressed, but I fear that in regard to Abyssinia and the fate of the Abyssinians and the actual condition of the enormous majority of the fifteen million natives now under a foreign administration, she, in company with a large number of others has been sadly misinformed.

Yours &c Katharine Fannin"

This provoked a sharp retort: "A Comment on Mrs Fannin's Journey" by Mr Beaufort-Palmer, Honorary Secretary of the Abyssinian Society and a strongly worded letter from Sylvia Pankhurst headed: "A Favourable Report Discounted"[208]' In this article Sylvia Pankhurst casts doubt on Katharine's journey and refuses to believe what she saw.

"Mrs Fannin states that she motored alone through the greater part of Abyssinia on a tour of investigation. One wonders how she was permitted by the Italian authorities to do this. An Administration that has totally expelled the foreign press does not lightly admit visitors to investigate what is happening under its authority. Judging from her account of the route she took and what she has to say about Abyssinia, I am driven to the conclusion that Mrs Fannin saw very little of the country and still less of the people."

Katharine's fierce rebuttal accused Miss Pankhurst, Mr Beaufort-Palmer and the Abyssinian Association of relying on out-of-date, second-hand and inaccurate information.[209] She took particular exception to Mr Beaufort-Palmer's use of an article by the New York journalist R G Woolbert, "Ethiopia in Revolt," who she says was writing from hearsay and was deliberately trying to distort the true picture of conditions in Italian East Africa. However, the full denouement of this battle of words was cut short by the outbreak of the Second World War on September 3,

1939, when British newspapers turned their attention to more momentous matters than whether or not the Italians had full control in Ethiopia and were employing Sudanese legally or illegally on their roads.

The start of war delayed Katharine's departure to Accra to join her husband and she tried to find employment with the newly formed Ministry of Information, but with no success. Her money-making scheme to sell her two 16mm reels of colour film of Abyssinia to the British government also did not succeed, but in February 1940, just as she was preparing to leave England, an offer came from the Italians. G Paresce, from the Chancery Department of the Italian Embassy in London, approached Katharine on behalf of the Ministry of Popular Culture and offered £200 for the films. First she cleared this with the War Office in London, who had no objections provided an exact copy was retained and she cut out anything that might be used against the British.

Katharine had an interview with Mr Maclaren, Room 373A MI3, about the films. He recommended her to Cecil Cattermoul of Cattermoul Film Service, who undertook work of this nature. Cattermoul agreed to doctor the original, make the required copy and conduct the transaction with the Italians (for a fee of 10%).[210] The copy was to be placed in the vault of Barclays Bank and Katharine left for Accra on February 16, 1940.[211]

Amongst Katharine Fannin's private papers are four letters from Amadeo de Savoia, Duke of Aosta, three of which are personal notes in his own distinctive spikey handwriting. These letters and a photograph taken of herself with the Duke were found among her most treasured possessions at her death. Expressed in perfect English the Duke wrote with affectionate friendship to say how much he appreciated her visit and her donation of rare books and prints of Ethiopia. In one of the letters dated April 24, 1939, he wrote: "I will consider the opportunity of making the forced labour optional with the flogging - perhaps you may be right." This was in response to Katharine's complaint about the cruel treatment of Abyssinian offenders she had witnessed at Batie on the Danakil Road to Assab. Another letter is dated August 31, 1939, and the last, dated March 28, 1940, contains these words:

"I quite agree with all you say and hope that all will turn out well somehow in this great muddle in which the world is in - that you will be able in future to motor from the Gold Coast to Addis Ababa."

CHAPTER ELEVEN
The Abyssinian Campaign 1940-1941

Katharine Fannin had an exciting time during the war, although at the beginning she found it frustrating not to be in East Africa, where the action was, but in Accra on the other side of the African continent. On Katharine's arrival in Accra, Major Fisher, the Intelligence Officer for the Gold Coast Regiment, asked her to write another report, her third on Italian East Africa.[212] She handed over this report, marked 'strictly confidential' to Brigadier Richards, the commanding officer, together with copies of her two former reports, her photographs and 95 maps.[213] As it became increasingly evident Mussolini would enter the war as Hitler's ally, secret plans for an Abyssinian campaign had begun. The Gold Coast Regiment was posted to Kenya in May 1940 and before they left, Katharine briefed the soldiers about conditions in Italian East Africa and supplied the command with a detailed description of the main transport routes of that part of Italian East Africa bordering on Kenya. She minutely described the main southern road to the Coast: Addis Ababa via the central lakes – Neghelli – Lugh Ferrandi – Ischia Baidoa – Mogadishu – Brava – Gelib – Kismayu, as well as the route going from Mogadishu to Jijiga via Belet Uen – Fer Fer – Gorrahei – Gabbre Darre – Dagabur. She carefully labelled a set of her photographs showing those roads and the chief landmarks to accompany her reports and made sketch maps of each town. She did all this in great haste as she only arrived in Accra in mid-March.

After June 10, 1940, when Italy declared war on Britain and France, the Italians, as Katharine had predicted,[214] immediately made strikes on the Northern Frontier District of Kenya,[215] and on the Sudanese border. They also invaded and captured British Somaliland and its port of Berbera and dropped a few bombs on Malindi. Edward Rodwell remembers manning the guns in Mombasa on the waterfront, but fortunately never had to fire in earnest as the expected air attack never came.[216] The Italian strikes caught the British troops in Kenya and Sudan unprepared. They were far outnumbered by the Italians and at first could only put up a spirited defence.

The most crucial front was on the border of Anglo-Egyptian Sudan, which if lost could have endangered the Suez Canal – a vital supply route for the Allies – and left Egypt unprotected. The frontier posts of Kassala and Gallabat fell to the Italians on July 4, 1940, but the British managed to stop the Italians at the border. The planned Italian advance to Atbara did not materialise due to the resourcefulness of the small Sudanese Defence Force and their 'motor machine gun companies,' which kept the Italians fully occupied. Major General Platt, the Chief-of-Command in the Sudan, succeeded in bluffing the Italians into thinking his forces were far stronger than they were and a stalemate situation ensued.

On July 3, 1940, the exiled Ethiopian Emperor Haile Selassie and a small suite arrived in Khartoum. He was eager to lead an army into Ethiopia against the Italians as soon as possible, but the British wanted him to wait and act as part of a coordinated campaign, the timing of which had to fall in with the general Middle East strategy. They reached a compromise to foment an Ethiopian guerrilla rebellion with the help of a small British military mission, led initially by Brigadier Daniel Sandford and then by Major Orde Wingate, who arrived in Khartoum in November 1940.[217]

The Emperor's presence in Sudan caused nervousness among the Italians as many Abyssinians rallied to the side of their former ruler or joined the resistance fighters. The British supplied arms and ammunition, which they smuggled over the Sudanese border, encouraging the Ethiopian patriot fighters to step up their activities and stir up a revolt against the Italians. The fear of internal rebellion kept a sizeable part of the Italian army occupied in maintaining security and made life increasingly difficult for the Italians. Katharine Fannin disapproved of this type of warfare and thought it very dirty and dangerous tactics to incite guerrilla fighters to kill Italian civilians in this way. She felt so strongly about it that she wrote a long letter to Sir Anthony Eden, who had replaced Lord Halifax as Foreign Secretary. Her letter is dated January 12, 1941.[218]

"If our B.B.C. wireless news is to be believed, we - a white race - are deliberately arming black tribesmen and inciting them to murder men, women and children of a fellow white race in Africa; for that, stated crudely, is what our support of the Abyssinians in Abyssinia really is. The utter inhumanity, shortsightedness and criminal folly of such an act should be self-evident. The matter far transcends any present local consideration of military expediency, or diplomatic or political gain. It is one of colour; and I assure you that if H.M. Government persists in this unchristian and inhuman folly it is we ourselves, and all other whites in native countries who will eventually pay the price of this ignoble act which is dishonouring our Great Empire. The African is an acute observer and an apt pupil. So surely as we for our present ends incite black to rebel against and murder whites, so surely will we pay a terrible and deserved price. I cannot remain silent about this, for I look ahead and have the ultimate good of our country, and the lasting good relations between all black and all white races in this black continent, very much at heart, and these races if they are to live together in peace and friendship, must respect themselves and each other.

"In the hateful necessity of war it may be permissible for white troops to fight cleanly in co-operation with black troops against similar opposing forces, though whether it is ever advisable is a debatable question. But for any white race to incite a black 5th column to harry, betray and murder other whites and inevitably other blacks - for who in their senses thinks that natives in Abyssinia will not be equal sufferers in civil war? - is an affront to God and man.

"Another point. H.M. Government must be aware that in Italian East Africa cut off from all hope from their native land with no friendly war ships or planes to rescue them and no friendly country to which they can flee in their terrible predicament are at least

20,000 defenceless white women and children being deliberately exposed by us to the danger of native revolt engineered by us. What in God's name are we about - to have sunk so low? What would we think of any foreign government that so exposed British women and children?"

The letter went on for several more pages praising the Duke of Aosta's regime and pointing out that the previous rule of the Negus (the Abyssinian term for Emperor) had not been without its grave faults.

> "One can understand and sympathise with the very natural wish of the Negus to regain Abyssinia. But that should not blind objective judgement to the fact that they lost their country by their own incompetence and misgovernment, by the rapacity of a corrupt Coptic priesthood and by the misrule of dozens of warring petty chiefs. Abyssinia torn by internal dissension, riddled with treachery, a prey to national and international self-seekers was betrayed and sold by Abyssinians prior to the arrival of a foreign invader. Its governors were not fit to govern, so Abyssinia fell and a brief and utterly disgraceful Fascist reign of terror under a Blackshirt sadist resulted. But mercifully this interlude was brief; put an end to by the attempt on Graziani's life."

The views put forward in this letter clearly indicated Katharine's deep concern for the Italian civilian population in Ethiopia. Much of what she said sounds old-fashioned to our ears, but it reflected the way many people thought at that time, and the idea of maintaining a united front of racial superiority was an important, if usually unspoken, tenet of British imperialist belief and colonial rule. The British in general thought the Italians very unsatisfactory as colonial rulers, who let the side down badly. But there was a fear that if the Italians totally went to pieces, and there was chaos and bloodshed in Ethiopia, then it could cause dangerous precedents for insurrection and insecurity in the neighbouring regions, which could hamper the entire Allied war effort in North Africa.

Sir Anthony Eden read her letter and replied to it, but unfortunately it cannot be seen in the Public Record Office as, although her correspondence is listed,[219] the file is not available and the letter she received from Sir Anthony Eden is not among her papers. Her forcible remonstrations may have had some effect as on February 21, 1941, Sir Anthony Eden visited Cairo and discussed the Ethiopian situation with General Sir John Dill and Sir Philip Mitchell, who had been earmarked to head the political administration of an interim military occupation of Ethiopia. Among the points that came up was the evacuation of Italian civilians and the importance of maintaining law and order once the Italians were defeated.[220] The agreed British line on Ethiopia was that they would recognise the claim of the Emperor Haile Selassie and would welcome the re-establishment of an independent Ethiopian State.

Major Orde Wingate,[221] the mastermind behind the Gideon Force, as the Ethiopian special army mission was called, was an uncouth and unpleasant individual, but an expert on this type of irregular warfare. He and the more likeable Sandford were made responsible for bringing the Emperor and his army into liberated Addis Ababa and for orchestrating the Ethiopian operation to coincide with the Allied Campaign. On January 18, 1941, Haile Selassie crossed over the Ethiopian border at the head of an army of 5,000 men. They set up a secure base at Mount Belaya in Gojjam, where Wingate and Colonel Hugh Boustead, commander of a detachment of Sudan Defence Forces, made their headquarters and worked out a plan of battle.

They intended to cut the road that linked Addis Ababa to Gondar, which was guarded by four towns – Bahr Dar, Dangila, Ingebara and Burie – each one garrisoned by Italian troops. They would then fight their way towards the capital via Dembecha and Debra Markos. It is clear from contemporary descriptions that the Ethiopian Patriot leaders, though brave and fearless, were difficult to work with and on occasion could be treacherous, disobeying orders and even allowing Italian troops to escape when it suited them. At the capture of Agibur, Major Thesiger, one of the British officers who went with the Gideon Force, admitted his main task was to prevent his Abyssinian Patriots from looting and massacring the prisoners. He described how he had two looters thrashed at the Fort Gateway as an example to the rest. For his role at Agibur he was awarded the DSO (Distinguished Service Order).[222] The official British account of the Abyssinian campaign makes little mention of the exact role of the patriot guerrilla fighters, so perhaps there was a slight misgiving about admitting too close an involvement with some of the methods and agents employed.[223]

The main Abyssinian Campaign had started in November 1940, when after the defeat of the Italian 10th army in Libya, General Wavell ordered the 4th Indian Division transferred to Sudan and South African regiments were sent to reinforce Kenya. The plan was to attack Italian East Africa simultaneously on two fronts, through Sudan and Kenya, with the Emperor's army as the third arm of a pincer movement converging on the capital, Addis Ababa. Eritrea was invaded in January through Kassala. Agordat, the next town, fell easily, but the Allies met stiff resistance at the mountain range outside Keren guarding the approach to Asmara, the administrative centre and seat of the Italian Governor of Eritrea. General Frusci's brave defence made this area, where Katharine had been filming less than two years earlier, the scene of the fiercest fighting of the entire campaign. But finally on March 26, 1941, Punjabi and British troops stormed the fortress stronghold of Dologorodoc. The town of Keren was then quickly taken and the way to Asmara was laid open to the Allies. Allied forces occupied Asmara on April 1, before pushing on to Massawa, the main Italian port and naval base in the Red Sea. Here Admiral Bonetti barely had time to scuttle his ships and blow up the port. He was found sitting rather moodily in a deck chair at the side of the harbour. He had tried to break his sword across his knee, but it only bent, so he threw it into the water.[224]

Katharine felt a keen interest in the battles taking place where she had so recently visited and made intelligence reports. She once again offered her films – free this time[225] – and was in close touch with her local Intelligence Officer, Lieutenant Colonel Gibson of Achimota, the Headquarters of the Military Forces in West Africa. He liaised with Brigadier Shearer, Department of Intelligence, Middle East Command, Cairo, from where all Allied operations in Africa were co-ordinated. On March 23, in response to urgent telegrams, she sent extra photographs of the guns at Keren and of the town and notes on the main road into Asmara. On March 29, a further request came for notes and photographs of the road between Keren and Asmara and Harar and Addis Ababa. She had already sent Brigadier Shearer a full personal set of her reports on Italian East Africa.

During the height of the Abyssinian Campaign, Katharine broadcast talks from Accra about Italian East Africa on March 5, 26 and 28, and on April 28. In her broadcasts she described the countryside and towns and tried to give a general picture of where the main fighting was taking place and what progress was being made.

The military arm of the pincer invading from Kenya, commanded by General Alan Cunningham, met with even more spectacular success. The main army drove via Garissa through to Mogadishu, and once the border stronghold of El Wak had been taken and the Italian line fell behind the Juba River, they encountered virtually no resistance. Kismayu fell on February 13, 1941, Gelib on February 22, and on February 25, British troops marched unopposed into Mogadishu, which had been deserted by the fleeing Italians. They had left in such haste, nothing had been sabotaged. The port and all its equipment remained untouched together with vast stores of ammunition, petrol, weapons and enough rations to feed 10,000 men for six months.[226]

The Allied army turned north up the main tarmac road to Jijiga, passing abandoned lorries and fuel dumps. They arrived at Jijiga on March 17. They met slight resistance outside Harar at the Marda Pass but by March 25, the South African infantry had entered Harar, and the Italian governor had surrendered. They dashed on to the capital and General Cunningham reached Addis Ababa on April 4, 1941. It had been the fastest recorded advance through enemy territory in military history.[227]

The Duke of Aosta made his final stand on the Massawa Road at Dessie. Here, trapped between General Platt, who had entered Massawa on April 8, and General Cunningham who had taken Addis Ababa, General Frusci and the remnants of his Savoia Grenadiers fought a last desperate battle. The Duke of Aosta with 18,000 Italian troops surrendered on the peaks of the mountain range at Amba Alagi on May 18, 1941. On May 16, the Duke had sent General Volpini, his chief of staff, to negotiate terms, but he was murdered by the Abyssinians and this shameful incident slightly delayed the surrender.[228]

After the main campaign ended, General Sir Alan Cunningham wrote to acknowledge the help Katharine Fannin had given. This letter written to her on his behalf by the Assistant Military Secretary (A.M.S.), Lord Francis Scott, gave Katharine particular pleasure and she said: "made me as proud as if I'd been mentioned in despatches."

"I have been instructed by the G.O.C. (General of Command) to write and inform you that your excellent reports have been invaluable assistance to the troops, whilst operating in the Juba area and up the road Neghelli - Addis Ababa.The G.O.C. thought you would like to know how much your work has been appreciated."[229]

Although the Abyssinian Campaign ended in May 1941, scattered remnants of the Italian army refused to surrender. Some Italian southern forces under General Gazzera were trapped in the Galla Sidamo area of the Lakes and these were flushed out mainly by contingents of the Kings African Rifles and the Patriots. The last pocket of Italian resistance was at Gondar, where the tough old former Governor of Harar, General Nasi held on until the end of November 1941.

It is evident Katharine felt personally involved in the fighting. She followed the course of the campaign as closely as she could from Accra and agonised over the fate of her friends. As a patriotic Englishwoman she had felt it her duty to spy and betray the Italians. As an ardent colonialist she hoped that having conquered Abyssinia, the British would stay and administer it, thus adding to the areas of pink already colouring the map of Africa. But by an ironic twist of fate she found she had rendered a valuable service not to the British Empire but to the Abyssinians whom she distrusted and thought unfit to rule. Ethiopia, as it became known under Haile Selassie, did not become another British colony. Instead it was eventually handed back to its legitimate ruler as an independent country.

However, to begin with Ethiopia was placed under British Military Occupation. Haile Selassie was not welcomed back by all his former subjects and some of the chieftains who had prospered under Italian rule might have caused trouble had it not been for the British presence, which ensured a peaceful transition. General Platt was made General of Command in Ethiopia and Sir Philip Mitchell was appointed Chief Political Officer, with the responsibility of negotiating an agreement on behalf of the British Government with the Emperor.

The Anglo-Ethiopian Agreement, signed on January 31, 1942, recognised Ethiopia as an independent state, but specified that imperial appointments could only be made with British consent and that all major appointments had to be British subjects. A further military convention placed Addis Ababa and all the main cities under the authority of the

British police forces. The Emperor heartily disliked this agreement. He had hoped to take up the reins of government immediately, without British interference. There was considerable friction between the Foreign Office, who wanted to placate the Emperor, and the Colonial and War Offices, whose chief concern was to maintain security in the region.

Finally a second Anglo-Ethiopian Agreement, signed in 1944, granted complete freedom to most of Ethiopia, but with Britain still retaining control of the Reserved Area and the Haud. These regions were kept back because they had never been securely under Ethiopian rule and it was felt their ultimate fate would have to form part of a broader reorganisation of the Horn of Africa – comprising Eritrea, French, British and Italian Somaliland. Eritrea and Italian Somaliland were also for the meantime kept under British Occupation until a decision was reached as to whether they should be returned to Italy, placed under a new colonial master or given independence.

Ethiopia and Italian Somaliland had fallen almost with no resistance, as if the Italians had no wish to fight, preferring to surrender the country to the British with as little damage as possible. It seems the Italians hoped that their colonies would be restored once the war was over and the Duke of Aosta in particular trusted in an amicable arrangement. However, he sadly miscalculated. Although he had friends in Kenya, the policy makers in London had other plans.

Katharine Fannin rarely talked about her Abyssinian adventure in later life or how she had collected information for British Intelligence. She must have been bitterly disappointed with the political outcome and have felt dismayed she had in the end helped reinstate an administration she personally disapproved of. It greatly distressed Katharine when the Duke of Aosta died as a British prisoner-of-war in Kenya on March 3, 1942. Held at Naivasha, he died of complications of malaria and tuberculosis in the Maia Carberry Nursing Home, Nairobi. He died a broken man, whose vision of a new Roman Empire in Africa had ended in humiliating defeat and whose efforts in colonialism and settlement had been overturned by the British whom he had trusted and emulated. The Duke found it hard to forget the cruel and senseless murder of his loyal colleague General Volpini by the Ethiopians and, despite being accorded the best of treatment under the circumstances, his health went into terminal decline.

Many other Italian prisoners-of-war were interned in Kenya. There was a camp at Bergeret near Nanyuki, another near Taveta[230] and one in Mombasa. The Italian prisoners-of-war in Kenya were treated well, many helped on the farms and assisted in building roads and houses and when the war was over a considerable number decided to stay on and make a new life in Kenya.

When Haile Selassie had entered his liberated capital, Addis Ababa, on May 5, 1941, it contained 40,000 Italian civilians,[231] mostly old people, women and children in a state of near panic on account of the reprisals they feared from the Abyssinians.[232] He issued the so called 'Golden Proclamation' in which he assured the Italians that the Ethiopians were not seeking revenge for Italian atrocities and told them they could remain and continue with the development and modernisation schemes already started. A few did stay, but thousands of women and children were repatriated by the Red Cross and religious organisations and many were evacuated to Kenya.

The reason for Katharine's Abyssinian journeys of 1938-1939 became clear in 1941. Armies travelled along the exact routes she had taken and fierce battles were fought in the mountain passes she had traversed. With the assistance of her reports, maps and photographs, her former hosts were killed or taken prisoner and Italian East Africa became no more. Her immediate reaction was one of pride that her efforts had borne fruit and that she had been instrumental in ensuring such a decisive and swift British victory. It was only later as the political map unrolled that disillusionment set in. But that is jumping ahead somewhat. In the spring of 1941 Katharine was in optimistic mood. The campaign in Abyssinia was hailed a resounding success and the news of victory in far off Africa lifted the spirits of the British people who now stood alone in Europe against Hitler's might. Germany had already overrun France, Belgium and The Netherlands and only Britain remained undefeated and still able to fight back.

Although in the main context of World War II the Abyssinian Campaign was a very minor sideshow, the victory occurred at a psychologically important moment. Let down by his Italian allies, who were supposed to be securing the Mediterranean, Hitler changed his plans. He shelved the invasion of Britain and instead sent German troops to North Africa and the Balkans, thus fatally extending his area of operations. What had begun as a European contest gradually drew in the remaining world.

CHAPTER TWELVE

Accra 1940-1941

Katharine Fannin arrived in Accra in March 1940 and stayed until December 1941. During this period her husband held the position of Assistant Director of Surveys, Gold Coast. Life in wartime Accra was spartan, with no imported goods, few expatriates and non-existent amenities. Vichy France was the chief threat to peace in West Africa and the British colony, the Gold Coast (now Ghana), was surrounded by French colonies, which after the fall of France came under German influence. In November 1940, they seriously considered evacuating all foreign women and children from the Gold Coast. Fortunately Katharine Fannin flourished in times of emergency and danger and the wartime situation in Accra provided her with new opportunities to exercise her varied talents.

Besides her involvement in the Abyssinian Campaign, Katharine organised the Accra branch of The British Women's Emergency Organisation, worked as Assistant Censor of Foreign Correspondence – Italian, French and Spanish – and ran a private monitoring service of enemy broadcasts. She also continued in her role as self-appointed spy and intelligence agent, informing British authorities on conversations overheard while having her hair waved. Her hairdresser, a French Swiss, was apparently an indiscreet Vichy sympathiser.

Nevertheless she missed Kenya desperately and tried on several occasions to get permission to return there. This was not to be, as civilian travel during the war period was severely disrupted and restricted. Even her appeals to the new Governor of Kenya, Sir Henry Monck Mason Moore, met with a firmly negative reply.[233] For her, the west of Africa could not compare with the east and in a letter to Lord Francis Scott[234] describes and gives her general opinion of the part of Africa, where she now found herself.

> "This colony is one of most interesting contrasts to people like ourselves, who have spent 15 and 20 years in E. Africa and have seen how things are done in Kenya, Uganda, Tanganyika, Zanzibar and to a certain extent in the Belgian Congo. The Gold Coast is fantastically rich; it is quite literally a Gold coast, and with the additional riches of other essential and valuable minerals and vegetable oils has every prospect of remaining rich, war or no war. This affluence has two odd effects: in one way to make the country twenty years ahead of E. Africa, in others to keep it unbelievably primitive. We have wonderful hospitals, schools, good roads, and so on, but the ordinary amenities of civilised life - as one normally understands the word are lacking to an unbelievable extent. No decent hotel in the whole Colony, third rate shops and precious few of them, no newspaper of any standing, no clubs to touch Muthaiga or Gymkhana, or Mombasa, no good library, a twice weekly cinema with museum specimen films (except for the war news films which are excellent) no attempt by anyone to cater for educated tastes and needs. I think the very short tour (15-18 months Government, 12-15 months mining, commercial and business) and the brief sea voyage from England have in the past made people out here live in England, and rather "camp out" here (for instance the "Cocoa-kings" and other fabulous beings spend six months in large and beautiful houses here, and the rest of the year at home). I notice this attitude of mind in the repeated expression of people here both in Government service and business: "Oh, we don't bring our good stuff out etc., entirely different from the E. African attitude where we (in Government service and private life) tried to make pleasant homes, and looked on them as such.

"I think too it is fair to take into account climatic and health considerations: Accra and the coastal strip are wonderfully good climatically; vastly less trying than Zanzibar for instance, and positively cold between April and September: but the whole Colony is more or less on a dead level, the country itself is either magnificent but gloomy forest or plains rather like the Ngong area, and inland it is hot, trying, boring to look at, and one can get no delightful local change of height and climate as in Kenya. The white man's grave business is utter rubbish and can be summed up in a few words: too much alcohol and native mistresses, but for all that, owing to the enormous percentage of infected mosquitoes, yellow fever and so on, the Colony is no health resort. But there again, it could be made more healthy by better town planning, drainage schemes, and the provision of recreational centres. Our Coast is as lovely as any in E. Africa: bathing is splendid, but very dangerous for there is no protective reef and huge rollers come crashing in: but in the past no one has worried about improving bathing facilities, and because England was so conveniently near, and shipping regular and easy, done anything about trying to make the country self supporting for a large part of its foodstuffs. For instance I was told I would have to use tinned milk: that seemed unintelligent, so I looked about and finding a herd of native-owned cattle arranged for a daily supply of milk as good as any I got in Kenya, in fact so good I get three bottles a day and make my own butter. This has all been due, I think, to the fact of the country and its inhabitants having (figuratively) money to burn: fresh meat, fish, game, milk and so on used to come out from home in sufficient quantities for people here to live, not too expensively, on English food; the war has stopped that." [235]

In the absence of any other form of amusement, Katharine spent much of her time censoring the letters of foreign nationals written in

French, Spanish and Italian, for the Post Office. For this she was provided with an official censor's stamp and whenever she had a disagreement with the Post Office, which was frequent, she would threaten to return her stamp. However, as not many people in Accra, apparently, had her command of foreign tongues, they always persuaded her to take it back.[236]

After the fall of France and the entry of Italy into the war as Hitler's ally, the Gold Coast began to feel the threat of war approaching. In the summer of 1940 Katharine began to agitate for the formation of a British Women's Emergency Organization in Accra. This voluntary organization had been started first in England and branches were mushrooming throughout the Empire as war spread. Its chief aim was to make full use of women as a work force in case of emergency and to keep a register of every woman, listing what she could do and where she could be located should an invasion or some disaster occur. Katharine wrote to the Colonial Secretary, Gold Coast, asking for permission to start a branch in the Gold Coast.[237] She pointed out that in Kenya a branch of the British Women's Emergency Organization had been set up in 1938 and she was surprised that something similar had not been done in Accra. In Kenya a complete scheme had been worked out whereby every British woman, free and able to take her part in the defence of the country, was assigned her job, and knew exactly on the outbreak of war what she was to do, and where she was to go. All women were accounted for, even if their orders were to remain in their own houses, or on their own farms.

Kenya always had a much greater settler population than Ghana, where, as Katharine had explained, most Europeans tended to live in temporary residence only. Therefore the number of British females available to take part in an organisation of this nature in Ghana would have been minimal. Nevertheless her suggestion was met with enthusiasm, and she set up a committee and drafted a circular and an application form for registration in 'The Gold Coast Emergency Reserve,' which was sent to every British woman in the Colony. The circular said:

> "In a number of Colonies and Dependencies our British countrywomen have formed voluntary organizations to compile records of those who wish to serve their land in any possible way, and to have a complete record of all British women in the territory concerned.

This information has been put at the disposal of the Authorities, who have selected suitable women for special work in emergency while all women - whether to be employed or not - have been informed about what they are to do in any grave emergency.

"War has now come to women in E. Africa, the Sudan and elsewhere, and it has found them organised and ready to play a valuable part in helping the Authorities; each woman detailed for special services has gone to her appointed station; and all are now playing their part - even if it be that of remaining quietly in her home, controlling her staff and showing by quiet and courageous example that attack by land, air or sea is not excuse for panic, or disorderly flight; this will be of particular value in the case of dealings with African staff.

"Here in the Gold Coast some of us who have had experience of these very valuable voluntary Women's Organizations wish to start a similar one here. We are working voluntarily and at present all expenses are being met privately by those of us who have such help for the Empire very much at heart.

"We know that all British women in the Gold Coast Colony wish to help our Empire to the utmost of their ability, and it is with confidence we ask you to fill up and return to us the enclosed form; even if you do not think you are professionally qualified to help; good will and generous service can be directed to valuable channels."

Amongst Katharine's papers can be found her own form duly filled in, and a transcript of a broadcast from the Governor of the Gold Coast and the Director of Medical Services announcing special courses in First Aid and Home nursing for all women throughout the Colony.[238] In the end, war never came to the Gold Coast, but Katharine had made sure the women were prepared. In case of invasion and evacuation of all British subjects, which could have occurred, her efforts would have proved invaluable.

From June 1940, Katharine worked on compiling dossiers for the 30 Italian nationals interned in the Gold Coast. In addition she helped sort out some confidential Italian paperwork for the Commissioner of Police. This was possibly part of the vast mass of official papers captured during the Abyssinian Campaign. There are several mysterious references to the 'Comazzi papers,' presumably documents of some importance as she wrote two reports on them for the Ministry of Information. The CID supplied her with a steel filing cabinet in which to keep her confidential material. Despite recurrent bouts of malaria, Katharine bravely continued her secret work, refusing to be hospitalised.[239]

The Information Department 'Monitoring' Service (Voluntary) set up by Katharine from June, 1941, had six volunteers, who covered French, Spanish, Portuguese, Italian, German, English and Arabic hostile broadcasts. She sent daily reports to MI Achimota (British military headquarters in West Africa), MIHQ Franck Mission, The Free French Mission, and to the information officer for Accra, Tom Barton. At one stage she intercepted the Vichy station at Abidjan (Ivory Coast) broadcasting messages in Morse code and she reported that continuous anti-British propaganda was coming out of Dahomey, Ivory Coast, Senegal and Algeria, all French Colonies controlled by Vichy France.

German broadcasts in English on June 12, 1941, worried Katharine. She reported: "Hostile broadcasts go on day and night from German and some Vichy French stations. The German broadcasts are really dangerous: so intelligently thought out, so entertaining, so well fitted to their audience, that I cannot help feeling some action should be taken to counter their effects on educated and semi-educated native and other opinion in this Colony. I am quite sure that some of the wild exaggerations which spread through the Colony come from German programmes imperfectly heard or maliciously enlarged upon by any disaffected person. I consider myself normally capable of detached judgement upon current events: I assure you that after a solid week of German talks, news, etc in English, I feel both depressed and impressed by the potential danger of such broadcasts." Some of these talks were transmitted by the infamous Lord Haw Haw, whose persuasive anti-British radio propaganda became legendary.[240]

Another aspect of Katharine's wartime efforts in Accra was assisting the Free French cause. With her memories of happy childhood days spent in France, she hated the idea of France defeated and occupied by Nazi Germany and she decided to help.

When France fell to Germany in June 1940, chaos followed. Marshall Henri Philippe Pétain, hero of Verdun, aged 80, was one of the few leaders who did not flee in panic. He stayed at his post and tried to prevent complete collapse. The Germans persuaded him to head a new French government, which sued for peace and signed an armistice with Germany at Compiègne on June 22. Under this agreement Germany occupied Paris and half of France, while Marshall Pétain became head of state of the Unoccupied Zone, governed from the small town of Vichy in the south. The majority in France held his opinion that their best hope lay in accepting defeat and in collaborating with the Germans. But a few did not and General Charles de Gaulle, leader of the dissenting party, escaped to England at the evacuation from Dunkirk with 120,000 French troops. He declared his intention of continuing the fight from London and from France's overseas territories. The British gave him support and helped him set up a national committee of Free French in London and establish missions to recruit resistance fighters, who were armed and equipped from London. The French Resistance movement gained momentum after 1942 and when France was eventually freed from German occupation in 1945, General de Gaulle became France's new president.

Amongst Katharine's closest associates in Accra was Captain G L Ponton, Chief of the Free French Mission in the Gold Coast. She worked with him on several radio broadcasts, which were transmitted in English and French on behalf of the Free French. The first of these was a brief message on July 28, 1940, when Upper Volta and part of French Ivory Coast declared itself in support of General de Gaulle.

"Monsieur Louveau, the Chief Administrator of the French territories of the Upper Ivory Coast and Upper Volta Colony has asked that the following telegram be transmitted to General de Gaulle, who is so splendidly leading all free Frenchmen. This is the telegram: In the upper Ivory Coast and Upper Volta Colony all French subjects, both military and civil, and I, their chief Administrator, Captain of Reserve and president of our ex-servicemen's Association support you heart and soul in keeping aloft, proud and free, the flag of our beloved land."

That was followed on August 8 by a broadcast programme about General de Gaulle – a joint effort by Captain Ponton and Mrs Fannin:

"General de Gaulle, brilliant leader of all free Frenchmen, has taken such a valiant stand that assuredly history will give him a place as one of the world's great figures…When Marshall Pétain's decision to enter into negotiations with the enemies of France and her Allies became known, General de Gaulle left his native land in order to continue to the end an unswerving resistance to the enemy who now has his country under a conqueror's heel."

The French version added the following:

"We British who know and love France and retain our love for all that for which that great nation stood and still stands, salute our gallant allies, Free Frenchmen the world over, and look forward with supreme confidence to the time when France proud and free, shall throw off the foul yoke of this Mechanised Attila, and regain her rightful place as a leader amongst the great free nations of this earth. Citoyens Francais - Vive la France Libre."

Katharine wrote at least two more broadcasts on behalf of the Free French in 1941 and even composed a poem in their honour:[241]

Katharine kept several letters from grateful French residents, who wrote to thank her for her efforts on their behalf. She kept in touch with the gallant Captain Ponton, who was last heard of in Fort-de-France, Martinique, in 1944, when he wrote of the pleasant memories he had of evenings spent in the "Pink and Green House" or in Katharine's delicious cottage in the "cantoonments."[242] Charles Fannin's two-year tour of duty in Accra ended in December 1941, when he was recalled to England. Katharine, however, discovered that owing to the wartime situation, no provision had been made for her passage home. She was expected either patiently to await his return or to follow him when she could. If she managed to get to England, she had no guarantee of passage out again. This did not suit her at all and she decided to try to fly to Cairo, reasonably accessible from Accra, and find voluntary war work there, at least while Charles was in England.

CHAPTER THIRTEEN
Cairo 1942-1943

Cairo in 1942 was the centre for all Allied operations in the Middle East and, unlike Accra, it still boasted every luxury and amenity you could wish for. It was stuffed full of high ranking officials, both military and civilian, refugees and evacuees from all parts of the world, war weary officers on a few days leave and raw recruits straight out from home. For Katharine, fresh from her bungalow in the Cantonments, Accra, it was bliss indeed, sophistication and civilisation in its fullest glory.

Since the successful Allied conquest of Abyssinia in the spring of 1941, the theatre of war had changed dramatically and had shifted from Europe to North Africa. Field Marshall Erwin Rommel's Panzer divisions, which had landed in Tripoli in February 1941, had put new life into the demoralised Italians. Gradually the former Italian defeats in the Western Desert had been reversed. The German and Italian forces, known as the Axis, besieged Tobruk and captured the British General O'Connor. The Axis powers stood dangerously poised on the threshold of Egypt. The deteriorating situation in North Africa cost the British Commander-in-Chief, General Wavell, his command and in July, General Auchinleck replaced him. Someone new was also needed to lead and put heart into the re-grouped Allied Forces, now called the Eighth Army. British Prime Minister Winston Churchill desperately wanted victory in the desert. Until the enemy were driven out of North Africa, the Mediterranean was not safe for Allied shipping and until the Cyrenaica airfields in Libya were in Allied hands, air cover could not be provided for the Malta convoys.

To lead this new offensive they chose General Cunningham, who had been knighted in May for his spectacular success in Abyssinia, and had shown such dash and élan in East Africa. They appointed him General of

Command, Eighth Army, on September 10, 1941, and put him in charge of the battle plan code-named 'Crusader,' which was to relieve Tobruk and force Rommel into a decisive tank battle scheduled for November 18, 1941. Unfortunately for General Cunningham, Field Marshall Rommel was a much stiffer opponent than the Duke of Aosta. Cunningham's easy success in Ethiopia was followed by a string of disasters in North Africa. By November 23, 1941, it was clear the battle plan had failed; the Allied forces were in disarray and defeat was imminent. The Commander-in-Chief, General Auchinleck, hurried to the front and relieved the despairing Cunningham of his command on November 26. Auchinleck ordered the Eighth Army to stand firm, thus avoiding complete collapse.[243] Major-General Neil Ritchie, Auchinleck's deputy chief of General Staff, was appointed as the Eighth Army's new commander. They finally relieved Tobruk, though Crusader did not achieve its original objectives.[244]

At this point Katharine made her way to Cairo to add her contribution to the war effort. With her connections, qualifications and experience she had no difficulty in finding a job at the highest level. On January 18, 1942, she started in the Secret Telegrams room[245] but later on February 17[246] she was appointed Personal Assistant to Sir Arthur Rucker KCMG CB CBE Chief Official of the Office of the Minister of State Cairo and Secretary of the Middle Eastern War Council.

The Ministry of State Cairo had been formed in July 1941, when the War Cabinet sent out Oliver Lyttelton, from the Colonial Office, as Minister of State Resident with cabinet rank, to represent it in Cairo. According to his ponderous official job description: "His main function was to ensure a successful conduct of the operation in the Middle East by relieving the Commander-in-Chief as far as possible of extraneous responsibilities, giving the Command-in-Chief political guidance and settling promptly matters within the policy of His Majesty's Government, more particularly where several local Authorities or Departments were concerned and keeping the war cabinet and ministers generally informed of what was happening in his sphere." He carried out his functions by means of a small office with a branch in Baghdad, and the Middle Eastern War Council, which met rarely. The Ministry of State largely transacted its business through sub-committees and executive action carried out by the local British representatives already in place or by specially created bodies such as the Middle East Supply Centre.

The Ministry of State Cairo represented British Government interests within the enormous Allied administrative headquarters, known as GHQ, a notorious warren teeming with bureaucrats and officials who pushed pieces of paper around and pulled strings rather than actually doing the fighting. To the soldiers in the desert the administrators in the city seemed very far removed from reality and Cairo had a reputation for easy living, where vast numbers of bureaucrats lived off the fat of the land. The Ministry of State was located at number 10 Sharia Tolumbat, Cairo. To illustrate the sheer size and complexity of the Allies' administrative operations, Katharine Fannin's room number was 9037, next door to Sir Arthur Rucker in room number 9036.[247]

By 1942 the Australian R G Casey[248] had replaced Oliver Lyttleton as Minister of State Resident and a deputy minister, Lord Moyne, [249] was appointed in August. Sir Arthur Rucker, the Permanent Secretary, came next in order of seniority and below him came three deputy secretaries, who liaised with the Military, Administrative and Political Divisions of GHQ as well as the Director General of Political Warfare, Sir Walter Monckton, and the infamous and far reaching Ministry of Supplies. All these separate departments employed large numbers of personnel, but such was the secrecy and red-tape of this beehive of civil servants they apparently had little social interraction. Dorothy Kirkman, an exact contemporary of Katharine Fannin, recalled meeting her for the first time in Cairo, where they both worked as secretaries in the Ministry of State. Dorothy however worked for Colonel A T Cornwall-Jones, the deputy secretary for Military Headquarters, and they rarely met because, she explained, they were in different sectors and worked such long hours.[250]

Sir Arthur Rucker, Katharine's superior, had been the deputy secretary in the Ministry of Health before being transferred to Cairo. As a typically discreet civil servant working in an office full of state secrets, it's hard to find exact details of what Sir Arthur Rucker actually did. He held the brief as representative of the Foreign Office and Treasury and was appointed to deal with establishment questions of consulates and missions in the Middle East.[251] But his chief responsibility was to co-ordinate the office and make sure it ran smoothly. He chaired a conference in Cairo on September 23-25 to consider measures for combating inflation, which was running at an alarming level in the Middle East.[252] He also acted as secretary to the Middle East War Council and a photograph from the Fannin papers shows Sir Arthur Rucker seated at the conference table next to Lord Moyne, R G Casey and General 'Jumbo' Wilson, second-in command to General Sir Harold Alexander who had replaced Auchinleck as Commander-in-Chief in August 1942.

Katharine remained entirely silent as to what she actually did during office hours, though she said she found the work interesting and stimulating. She complained in one of her letters to Charles how tired she felt handling intensely personal and confidential matters all the time. "I don't even express opinions now about even the most ordinary things in case (always that fearful in case) I am unwittingly giving a line on something."[253] Katharine worked long hours, nine hours a day, until 8.30 every evening and often worked on Sunday mornings as well.[254] She also accompanied Sir Arthur on his travels in the Middle East. Once her car broke down and she became separated from him in Cyprus and had to commandeer a military supplies vehicle full of potatoes to catch up with him. She also visited Syria and the Lebanon in April 1942,[255] but unfortunately her description of this trip, which she sent to Charles was lost in the post. She met Churchill twice as well as the United States ambassador. No doubt she saw Harold MacMillan, who visited Cairo in March 1943. He described staying in R G Casey's luxurious villa and meeting with Sir Arthur Rucker in his war diaries.

Fed up with paperwork, she wrote in one letter: "I'm so done and tired of paper,paper,paper."[256] She could hardly bring herself to write personal letters in her time off. Certainly three out of the four letters to Charles that survive from this period are very short, most unlike her usual chatty style. Only one, dated Christmas 1942, when she had two weeks leave, approaches her usual expansive manner.

As always, Katharine worried about financial matters. Katharine was spending rather more than she earned in Cairo and Charles felt obliged to help his elderly and ailing sisters in England. When Katharine heard Charles had been posted to Trinidad, instead of returning to Accra, she had the additional concern with what to do with the household effects, which she had left in the Gold Coast. Her original intention had been just to spend a few months in Cairo, while Charles was in England. But her job turned out to be so interesting and worthwhile that she decided to stay in Cairo as long as she was needed.

Katharine's childhood home in the Dooars district of northern India.

Katharine, age 2, on a camping trip with her parents to the Toorsa River in India.

All photographs and images in this section used with the kind permission of the Rodwell family.

Katharine as a child in India being carried in a dhoolie or a simple litter or palanquin. The handwritten caption in the battered photo album reads: *"Being carried in Bandies."*

Katharine's parents on a camping trip in India, for which the elephant provided the transport.

Katharine's parents' horses in India. The label in the album reads: "Kanchee and Honesty, Dalsingpara." One is harnessed to a light carriage, possibly Katharine's mother's. The other is a sturdy hack with docked tail, surely her father's usual mount.

Two of William Trood's "hillmen" from Tibet and Bhutan.

Katharine, at about age 12, in a pony trap in front of Rose Cottage in England.

Charles Fannin on board the *S S Morvada* in 1926. Katharine met Charles on the voyage as she travelled out to East Africa, engaged to marry a doctor in Tanganyika. Katharine decided to call off her engagement and marry Charles Fannin instead.

In her first weeks in Mombasa in 1926, Katharine went swimming at the swimming club off the sandy beach at English Point. She left a description of changing behind the bushes into a long thick dark stockinette bathing dress and sponge bag mob cap.

The DC's house in Kwale, 1926. Charles sent Katharine to this hill top station in the Shimba Hills some 30 miles South West of Mombasa, where she stayed with Bar and Billy Marchant, the District Commissioner (DC) and his wife.

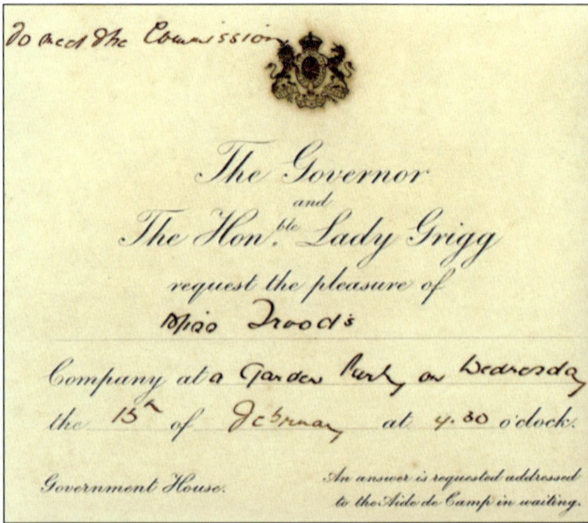

To meet the Commission

The Governor
and
The Hon.ble Lady Grigg
request the pleasure of
Miss Woods
Company at a Garden Party on Wednesday
the 15th of February at 4.30 o'clock.

Government House.

An answer is requested addressed
to the Aide de Camp in waiting.

In March 1927 Katharine shook hands with Governor and Lady Grigg at a Garden Party. Only the cream of Nairobi society were invited to the Governor's Garden Parties and being introduced and shaking hands with the Governor was the ultimate seal of social approval. Katharine Fannin carefully preserved her invitation amongst her personal papers.

Katharine Fannin on the edge of Nairobi about 1927.

After her marriage to Charles Fannin in 1929, the two of them drove to Malindi to spend Christmas with the DC, Mr Brailsford, crossing both Mtwapa Creek and Kilifi Creek on a singing ferry.

Crossing Mtwapa Creek in 1929 on a ferry pulled across by cables.

Christmas sports at Malindi with Charles Fannin, Mr Brailsford and Ali bin Salim, 1923.

During the early years of Katharine's marriage in Mombasa, she kept a pet mongoose to which she was very attached. The mongoose protected them against snakes and it also ate rats and other small rodents.

Ndia Kuu, the main street of Mombasa, as it looked when the Fannins lived there in the early 1930s.

Katharine with her dog at their home in Nairobi about 1938.

Katharine Fannin drove across Italian East Africa, accompanied by various Italian chaperones.

The Duke of Aosta (left) and Cobili Gigli, Director of Public Works, greet the crowd of Ethiopians lining the streets.

The Duke of Aosta (centre leaning back) discusses matters with his staff.

Amadeo de Savoia, Duke of Aosta, Viceroy & Governor General of Italian East Africa.

General Nasi, Governor of Harar, was the most able of the Italian officials Katharine met. Here he is pictured on a white horse in full uniform sporting large dark sunglasses to protect his eyes from the glare of the African sun. He signed and presented this photograph to Katharine, when she stayed at his residence in November 1938.

Katharine Fannin with the Duke of Aosta, who stood six feet six inches tall.

The Viceroy's residence in Addis Ababa, known as Il Piccolo Ghebi.

Italian labourers building a road in Ethiopia. By the end of 1938 they had completed nearly 3,000 miles of roads in barely two years. These were not substandard or shoddy affairs, but best quality indestructible "old Roman road-building with a vengeance."

Katharine visits an Italian road building crew, which included many soldiers.

Katharine saw the Italians had made road building their first priority in opening up the country. They built a road at vast cost and at enormous speed across the Danakil Desert to the port of Assab using Italian troops and Sudanese labour.

...mbre 1938 — Anno XVII 3

SCACCO MATTO AI FALSIFICATORI DI NOTIZI...

Sola in auto

da un capo all'altro dell'Etiopia

Una signora inglese constata da Mogadiscio a Addis Abeba e Massaua l'incivilimento dell'Africa Italiana

La signora Katharine Mary Fannin insieme col comandante del piroscafo «Nazario Sauro» all'arrivo a Napoli (Telefoto)

On Katharine's arrival in Naples on December 2, 1938, reporters besieged her for an interview. This article appeared on the third page of the Italian newspaper Corriera della Sera. Dramatically headed "Sola in auto" – Alone by car, from one side of Ethiopia to the other! – the long article, taking up three full columns, described the route she took and recorded her praise for the hospitality and kindness shown her by the host nation.

Katharine Fannin (left) with the Commissario of Semien (middle) and Ruth Ricci (right).

On her visit to Eritrea in 1939 Katharine filmed the Italian fortifications at Keren. These images of the guns were sent to military headquarters during the allied invasion of Eritrea in 1941, when stiff resistance was met at Keren, guarding the approach to Asmara.

Katharine Fannin (centre) with Ruth Ricci and a collection of Italian officials in Gondar.

Katharine visited Adua, the scene of Italy's shaming defeat of 1896, and had her photo taken in front of the war memorial.

Katharine's map showing her route through Italian East Africa along with her handwritten notes.

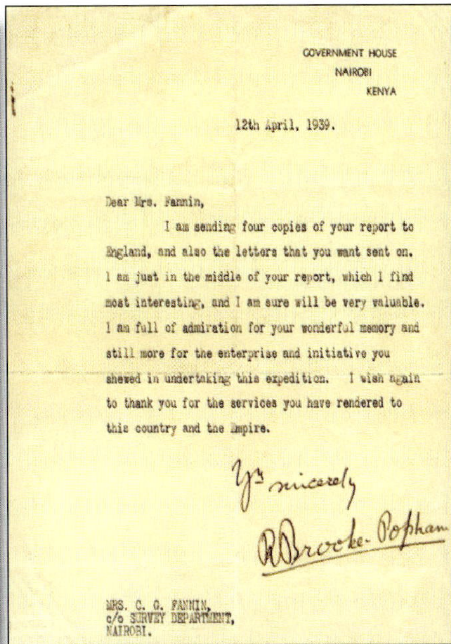

GOVERNMENT HOUSE
NAIROBI
KENYA

12th April, 1939.

Dear Mrs. Fannin,

I am sending four copies of your report to England, and also the letters that you want sent on. I am just in the middle of your report, which I find most interesting, and I am sure will be very valuable. I am full of admiration for your wonderful memory and still more for the enterprise and initiative you shewed in undertaking this expedition. I wish again to thank you for the services you have rendered to this country and the Empire.

Y^s sincerely
R. Brooke-Popham

MRS. C. G. FANNIN,
c/o SURVEY DEPARTMENT,
NAIROBI.

A letter from Sir Robert Brooke-Popham, the Governor of Kenya, commending Katharine for her reports on her journeys through Italian East Africa.

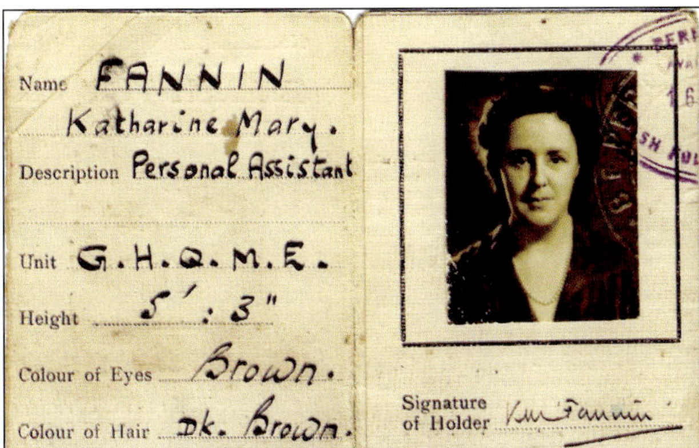

Name FANNIN Katharine Mary.
Description Personal Assistant
Unit G.H.Q.M.E.
Height 5' : 3"
Colour of Eyes Brown.
Colour of Hair Dk. Brown.
Signature of Holder K M Fannin

Katharine Fannin's ID card from when she worked as a personal assistant for Sir Arthur Rucker at the General Headquarters for the Middle East in Cairo.

Council of War.
Sir Arthur Rucker seated at the conference table next to Lord Moyne, R G Casey and General 'Jumbo' Wilson.

Edward Rodwell, well-known Mombasa journalist and historian, knew Katharine Fannin well and the Fannin Papers are still in the possession of his heirs in his archive of historical materials

Dr Rana (right) was a member of the Mombasa Municipal Board and later Mayor of Mombasa during the period when Katharine Fannin, as a journalist, covered the deliberations of the board.

Poor Charles arrived in Trinidad not knowing what had happened to her and didn't receive news of her movements until mid-1942. He found bachelor life in Port of Spain, Trinidad, lonely and his teeth were causing him trouble, but he, like his wife, was involved in important war work. Most of Britain's military equipment had been left behind at Dunkirk. The United States supplied fresh arms and supplies and American destroyers to patrol the sea lanes in exchange for naval and air bases in Britain's Atlantic possessions. Charles Fannin worked on the technical details of the transfer of an important naval base in the Gulf of Paria, to the Americans. To a dyed-in-the-wool British Empire-man, handing over a British strategic possession to the Americans can hardly have been congenial work, so it is not surprising that his letters have a somewhat gloomy tone.[257] Indeed his letters showed stoic forbearance, considering he had been abandoned once more by his errant wife.[258]

Katharine left a couple of interesting glimpses of her life in Cairo. One of these came from her Christmas letter to Charles:

"I am sitting writing to you in my dear little flat. Darling, it has been such a bit of luck finding it - a simply perfect small place for one person on the eighth floor of a brand new building right in the heart of old Egyptian Cairo - and yet the outlook is lovely because the building faces on a big open 'Midan' (square) with trees and so on and I look from a hundred feet up over the whole of miles of Cairo and the desert and the Pyramids. Saladin's Citadel, all minarets and very picturesque, is just behind and the thousand year old El Azhar university not far off."

She described how she used to walk about in the native quarter and explore the maze of small alleys; "the office think this very daring, God help them!" She had moved to this flat from a room in a hotel and although it should have been cheaper, she found it actually cost her more as "my flat is so enchanting that the office rather comes in to lunch and dine with me." She explained how she had become a sort of 'Aunt Confessor' to quite a few of the office, especially the younger unmarried girls and had acquired a 'clientele' of rather senior people in uniform, who liked to come to a pleasant civilised room for a simple meal and to talk or not as they wanted. She went on to say how Sir Arthur, who was very nice, often came to lunch. He called her "Mrs F" in the office. His flashing intellect impressed her and she described how pleasant he was to work for and how much he had come to depend on her. The Minister, R

G Casey, in her opinion was less intelligent, but "frightfully handsome, unassuming and generally liked."

To help her in the flat, she had taken on a Sudanese boy, Abdul, who only spoke Arabic and wore a spotless white robe and white cap with a turban wound round it. She bought him some leather slippers with pointed toes to wear inside the house and he did all the housework and cooking for £5 a month. At just 40, she complained that her hair was starting to go grey and the dry air and sand from the desert had left her face thin and wrinkled.

The other splendidly atmospheric glimpse of life in Cairo is captured in the introduction to an article she wrote for her Saturday column in the *Mombasa Times* entitled 'Rock Bound.'[259]

> "One evening during the war some of us working in the Middle East met to dine together on the roof of the Mohammed Ali Club, a dignified Cairo mansion where at any moment one was liable to run into potentates, Pashas and peripatetic Very Important Personages of the warring nations. Costi, the Club's renowned maitre-d'hotel, a benign imperturbable little Cypriot, whom nothing could dismay, presided over his beautifully appointed tables set in bowers of living greenery hung with garlands of coloured lights and set high above the bustle and confusion of the traffic, and dusty, jabbering, thronging humanity below. It was remarkably pleasant once in a while to be able to sit quietly and comfortably enjoying the passing show which could, and in fact not infrequently did include a brace of Ambassadors suitably ambassadorial, periodic coveys of Balkan Royalty in flight, Generals, Admirals and Air Marshals of the seven nations, cotton kings, contract millionaires, occasional film celebrities 'doing their bit for the boys in the desert' and for good measure a scatter of extremely expensive ladies: lovely, languorous, lusciously gowned and positively incandescent with diamonds earned, whispered the know-alls, by spying for anyone who would pay. As

everyone did, and handsomely, their bread was very satisfactorily buttered on both sides.

"To offset this somewhat exotic company small parties such as ours, in uniform and out, were to be seen here and there taking an evening off to remind themselves that there were still such things as gracious living and good conversation. Our particular half dozen included a cheerful grey-haired civilian from our Embassy in Teheran; and a coldly reckless Polish pilot whose escape from solitary confinement in a German fortress had involved jumping straight down a thirty foot wall, stealing a plane after garrotting a guard, and subsequently a crazy incredible flight in an unfamiliar machine over unknown territory until his petrol gave out and the inevitable forced landing found him by chance, and God's grace, in friendly hands.

"We had come from the four quarters of the earth, and there on that cool, quiet roof sat happily swapping stories of our varied experiences grim, grave, gay and indeed sometimes farcical. And so the evening passed."

In June 1942 Rommel's Afrika Korps were poised before El Alamein, 65 miles from the Nile. Mussolini had arrived in Bardia (Libya) and was waiting to lead the victory procession into Cairo and Alexandria in triumph on his white charger. So certain was he of victory that he had already had Italian campaign medals struck for the occasion. These showed Mussolini and the Pyramids on the front, while the back was stamped with a figure of Victory and the motto: SUMMA VIRTUS ET AUDACIA.

Fear and confusion reigned in Cairo, as the Egyptians secretly negotiated terms of surrender with the Germans and the staff of GHQ put the finishing touches to an evacuation plan for the city. Lieutenant General Bernard Montgomery's eleventh hour stand and great victory at El Alamein in July 1942, which halted the German advance on Cairo, was one of the most famous battles of World War II and marked a turning point in favour of the Allies. But everyone in Cairo knew "it was a close run thing," and it was the war with Russia, which tied up all available German troops and armaments, that really saved the day. [260]

Montgomery took formal command of the Eighth Army on August 15, 1942, and his successes continued during the autumn and winter of 1942 as they pushed the Germans and Italians back through Libya into Tunisia. On May 15, 1943, an allied victory was officially declared as it was clear that the Germans were defeated in North Africa. The theatre of war moved to Europe once more. Katharine stayed on in Cairo until October 1943, when Sir Arthur was recalled to England and resumed his former post at the Ministry of Health. With the office in Cairo much diminished and no longer needing her services, and with the Allied cause set on a favourable course, Katharine travelled to Trinidad to join her husband.

CHAPTER FOURTEEN

Postwar blues: Decolonisation in Eritrea and Somalia

We know absolutely nothing of Katharine's time in Trinidad except the date of her departure, December 1944, and that the Fannins lived in the capital, Port-of-Spain, where Charles was Director of Surveys and Sub-intendant of Crown Lands. Katharine seems never to have quite got over her wartime experiences in Ethiopia and Cairo, where she had rubbed shoulders with the high and mighty and been at the centre of great events. For some time after life seemed tame and provincial and she found it hard to return to the role of a dutiful colonial wife.

After they returned to England one last mention is found of Charles in the Colonial Lists for 1946, when he worked as Principal Computer for the Directorate of Colonial Surveys in London. Katharine also briefly worked for the Colonial Office in London, during 1945.[261] However, they found post-war London, gripped by austerity and rationing, unbelievably miserable and cold. When Charles reached retirement age of 55, the Fannins returned to Kenya and settled in Mombasa, because the cost of living was cheaper at the Coast. To begin with they rented a large house in Cliffe Avenue (now Kaunda Avenue), in the centre of town not far from the Mombasa Club.[262] Katharine indulged her passion for cats and exercised her talents for outspoken journalism and large scale entertaining. Charles set himself up as a freelance surveyor and for the first few years they lived very comfortably.

Katharine wrote a series of letters dating from 1949, entering the political fray and airing her opinions on the vexed question of the future of Eritrea and Somalia. One of the many problems that came up in the aftermath of World War II was what to do with the colonies of the conquered nations and the whole concept of colonialism came under review.

In 1945 ideologies and world politics had shifted dramatically. Both Russia and the USA, who had emerged as the new superpowers of the post-war period, supported anti-imperialist policies. They wished to imprint their own stamp on a new world order, replacing the influence of the old European colonial power blocs by systems beneficial to their interests. One of the conditions in the Atlantic charter drawn up by Roosevelt and Churchill in 1941, when America entered the war on the side of Britain, was that timetables for independence in all British colonies should be drawn up. America, though allied to Britain, was anxious that its support should not be used to shore up the British Empire. Roosevelt as the leader of a nation bred in the tradition of anti-imperialism, believed fervently that any endeavour to dismember the world's empires and end colonial exploitation was morally justified – and it happened to suit American interests.

Russia too had its own reasons for wishing to see the European powers diminished and while paying lip-service to anti-imperialistic polemic she assuaged her own land hunger with vast territorial acquisitions, swallowing them up and placing them behind the Iron Curtain of the Russian Communist Empire, the Union of Soviet Socialist Republics.

The United Nations Organisation, (superseding the old League of Nations) was formed and given new powers and was increasingly called upon to mediate and produce solutions in cases of international territorial dispute. The UN, following the lead of the USA and the USSR, also held strongly anti-imperialistic views. Its charter drawn up in 1945 specifically made self-government the goal of its policies. Within twenty years the destruction of the former colonial European power blocs was almost complete. France, Britain, Italy, Belgium and finally Portugal relinquished control of large tracts of overseas property as one by one the former colonial dominions became independent nations.

But in 1949 this headlong decolonisation programme had only just begun. India was the first to go in 1947, leaving behind it a trail of bitterness and disillusionment as Partition between the Muslim North and the mainly Hindu South left the country weakened and torn by religious and racial differences. In 1950 came the decolonisation of Burma and Ceylon (now Sri Lanka). High on the agenda were the former Italian

East African colonies, still occupied by the British in 1949 as a result of the successful Abyssinian Campaign. In an earlier age these colonies would simply have been handed over to the occupiers as part of the spoils of war, but a new style of consensus politics had arrived. The question of what to do with the former Italian colonies was put to the United Nations Organisation, who appointed a Commission to weigh up all proposals carefully and come up with the best solution. The UN felt immediate self-rule was impossible, as the Horn of Africa, one of the most desolate and underdeveloped parts of the world, was not ready to rule itself in a manner conforming to Western standards. Some kind of compromise had to be reached and a caretaker government put in until the infrastructure for self-administration was in place.

A number of suggestions were put forward. In 1943 Ernest Bevin, British Foreign Secretary, had proposed a greater Somaliland to comprise of Northern Kenya, Italian, French and British Somaliland all under a British trusteeship until the country was ready for self-rule. But this idea did not meet with universal approval. Ethiopia had designs on parts of Somalia, Kenya did not want to hand over any part of its territory, Italy wished to reclaim its former colony of Somaliland, France did not wish to give up Djibouti and the rest of the world did not want to see such a large chunk of Africa under even temporary British control. Already the seeds of Africa's modern predicament had been sown and the second scramble for Africa began, where political compromises reached at international conference tables overrode all considerations of practical reality. The Horn of Africa was left in an unworkable condition, carved up once again to suit the great powers to the great detriment of the inhabitants.

Eritrea fell outside the proposed United Somaliland, but it too had its own share of complications. Eritrea, taking its name from the Latin name for the Red Sea, Mare Erythraeum, had a distinct identity of its own and was the most advanced area in the region having been an Italian colony for over 50 years. Its capital Asmara had been the seat of the Italian Governor since 1900 and was a substantial town. Massawa, its main port, was the chief trading outlet for the area and was on the international shipping route to Europe and India via the Suez Canal. Ethiopia laid claim to it on the grounds that a part of Eritrea had historically been part of the Abyssinian Empire, though in truth the Ethiopians wanted control of the ports of Massawa and Assab for strategic reasons.[263] The Eritreans themselves were divided: the Tigreans, who were Christian, wanted to join Ethiopia, but the Muslim population at the Coast and in the Western lowlands favoured independence. Some solution was needed to diffuse ethnic aspirations and preserve stability.

Katharine Fannin strongly advocated a return to Italian rule. She felt the Italian record in Eritrea had been good and their rule had promoted peace and prosperity in the region and this should be allowed to continue until such time as self-rule was practical. Dr Daodiace, the former Governor, had particularly impressed her in 1938-1939 and now she made an effort to influence the outcome by energetically writing letters on the subject to *The Times* of London and New York.

Her first letter appeared in *The Times* of April 21, 1949:

"The Future of Eritrea"

> "I too would like to express agreement in the main with your views on the future of Eritrea and with Mr. Wise's admirable letter in *The Times* of 7th April. His personal experience of Eritrea is recent; mine of 1938 and 1939 at the height of Italian rule when its peoples were living under the enlightened Vice-Royalty of the late Duke of Aosta and more directly under the Governorship of a singularly able scholarly humanist Dottore Giuseppe Daodiace.
>
> "At that time unquestionably, Eritreans with the possible exceptions of a very few living actually on the western border regarded Ethiopians in general with dislike and contempt; in no circumstance would they have agreed peaceably to being amalgamated with them, even administratively, and the Italians were too realistic to attempt any such move. The traditional enmity to the Ethiopians of the coastal Eritreans including all Muslims, Christians, numerous Copts and the wild tribes of the Danakil country has been maintained for centuries; and even so late as 1939 I saw an example of it in the "neutral" open-air market at Batie, when I crossed the Danakil Desert to Assab…Batie was one historical customary safe limit of Ethiopian descent to the lowlands to trade; and here they still kept to their

side of the big market clearing, and the Danakils to theirs during barter of coastal salt, incense and kohl for plateau grain, hides and cloth. At the end of the day's trading, Ethiopians present mounted their horses and mules and rode back to the hills, the Danakils loaded their camels and returned to their inhospitable desert; there was no fraternization of any kind.

"To contend that the great majority of Eritreans would view with anything but loathing and indignation an attempt to place them under the uneasy alien suzerainty of Ethiopia is to have little regard for fact. It would be equally ill-advised to hope that secession to Ethiopia of Eritrea, or of the port of Massawa would be other than a major disaster for Eritrea and its inhabitants of all races and creeds. It is fair that Ethiopia should have an outlet to the sea; why should not that country enjoy complete freedom of the port of Assab and maintain to it the splendid direct Italian trunk road from Addis Ababa?

"Mr. Wise's statement that the inhabitants of Eritrea might welcome a continuation of British administration is perhaps gratifying to our national pride; but honesty and impartiality impel the view that were the whole truth ascertainable it might prove that most Eritreans would welcome equally the re-institution of Italian rule under which they lived peacefully and contentedly for more than forty years. Common justice seems to indicate that the Italian's excellent past record of administration in Eritrea surely entitles them to an honourable share in its future government."[264]

Another short letter was duly published in *The Times* on July 12 and from her final letter of October 21 come these words:

"I agree that Eritreans in general are insufficiently advanced for the grant of immediate independence. A sincere regard for their welfare must ensure that for some years they benefit by the advice and help of an older and western civilisation; one likely to understand their needs and forward their legitimate aspirations. This being so how in justice can Italy's excellent past record there, and strong moral claim to a tutelary position be ignored? The great powers seem eager enough to return Somaliland to her; perhaps because that country is so barren and unprofitable! How much more honest, realistic and sensible would it be to have done with the present short-sighted potentially disastrous plans for Eritrea and in the best and lasting interests of both Eritrea and of good international relationships in Europe accord a great Christian people - the Italians - a chance to show that they can again, as in the past, administer their oldest colony, wisely, humanely and well, and in future lead its native peoples to stable self-government."[265]

These articles were widely circulated in pro-Italian circles and she received several letters from complete strangers supporting her views. Her old friend Daodiace, living in poverty and obscurity in Rome, wrote expressing his gratitude for her kind words.[266] Professor Romano Romanelli praised her understanding of the delicate situation in Eritrea and asked her to write for the Italian press.[267] She wrote back to him and her letter was published in Italy and in Eritrea.[268] Later she received a letter of congratulations on behalf of the Italian Ministry of Foreign Affairs via the consulate in Nairobi.[269] The Italian Ambassador to the US, her old friend Paresce,[270] urged her to bring her arguments to the attention of the public opinion by writing a letter to the *New York Times*.[271] She did, but the editor refused to publish it.[272] The Italians had few friends in international circles and indeed were held in contempt by most of the Western Nations. Mussolini's policies and wartime activities had brought disgrace upon them. Anti-Italian feeling in the US and in Britain was very powerful in the period immediately post-war, and so Katharine's favourable reporting of the Italian record in Africa was much appreciated by the Italians, while her arguments in favour of returning Eritrea and Somaliland to the Italians were circulated for maximum effect by the small pro-Italian lobby.

Predictably, however, Katharine's pleas fell on deaf ears. The Ethiopia pressure group under Sylvia Pankhurst and Brigadier Stephen

Longrigg[273] triumphed. Sylvia Pankhurst, who was now using her paper *New Times and Ethiopian News* exclusively as propaganda for Ethiopia, fiercely denounced the Italian claim. She was blindly loyal to Haile Selassie and joined him in pressing for a Greater Ethiopia, which would include the whole of Eritrea and Italian and British Somalilands as well. The Labour Government of Britain supported Ethiopian claims in Eritrea but not in Somalia, and in 1950 a General Assembly of the UN recommended Eritrean federation with Ethiopia. This solution linked Ethiopia and Eritrea, but allowed Eritrea certain freedoms. The Ethiopian Government was given control of Foreign Affairs, Defence, Finance, Commerce and Ports, but Eritrea was allowed its own elected government and assembly to deal with local affairs. Eritrea had its own flag and the official languages of Tigrinya and Amharic. Just before the British departed in 1952 elections were held, which resulted in an assembly equally divided between Christians and Muslims. This federated system however was short-lived as slowly and steadily Ethiopian officials consolidated control over the territory and undermined various freedoms. In 1958 Ethiopia discarded the Eritrean flag. In 1959 Ethiopia extended its law code to Eritrea and banned political parties. Finally in 1962 the federation was dissolved and Eritrea, by vote of an Amharic controlled Assembly, became fully part of Ethiopia. (This Ethiopian take over was rejected by much of the population and from 1962-1993 there was civil war in Eritrea, when the Eritrean Liberation Front (ELF) and the Eritrean Labour Party (PLF), fought to free their country from Ethiopian control. In 1993 Eritrea was once more declared independent, but since then there have been several border conflicts and Eritrea still remains a shadow of her former prosperity).

The Reserved Area, Haud and the Ogaden, were given to Ethiopia, while the former British and Italian Somalilands were united in 1955, and granted full independence in 1960. The Somalia solution, also worked out by a UN Commission, gave the former colonial owners, Italy and Britain, a tutelage period of ten years to prepare the way for self-rule in a United Somalia. Like all compromises it was less than perfect and left dangerous potential for conflict. The Somalis felt cheated of their true territories, and still are reminded of their grievances through the five points of the star on their flag, which stand for the Ogaden (Ethiopia), Northern Frontier District (Kenya), and Djibouti as well as the two

Somalilands, which formed independent Somalia. The British and Italian settlers, disgusted with the short-sighted rulings of the UN, pulled out all investment and removed valuable equipment and installations, when they reluctantly departed.

Katharine Fannin neatly summed up her views on the issue of the reorganisation programme in the Horn of Africa in the reply she gave to Professor Robert Gale Woolbert of Denver University, who had written to her following her October article in *The Times* asking for her opinion on the proposals for an independent and united Somalia.[274]

> "I hope you will not think me impertinent if I say we in Africa suffer from somewhat doctrinaire conclusions of honest intelligent research workers like yourself, who take infinite pains to inform themselves upon the purely academic side of African questions and propound what seem perfectly reasonable schemes for the unification, administration and so on of native territories and peoples, but which schemes in fact are utterly unworkable because the academic planner is totally unfamiliar with the people and lands concerned, has either ignored or omitted to make due allowances for human nature, centuries old deeply rooted antipathies, customs, religious differences, nationalist pride, an African or Eastern outlook on all moral and material subjects (as opposed to Western ideas) and so on. By reason of that - often inadvertent ignorance he cannot have an inkling of the inwardness and wide ramifications of the problems whose solution looks so sensible on paper."[275]

Also from the same letter came this brutally frank description of the Somalis, who the UN fondly imagined would rule themselves successfully after a crash course in Western Government from Italy and Britain. This visionary concept of United Somaliland was, she said, "unattainable" and the idea of the Somalis being able to achieve independence in ten years "so absurd as to be laughable - were it not so serious."

> "For myself; my first hand experience of that country is of the time when it was under Italian rule. I can

tell you about that if you wish and of what I saw for myself there. I know a bit about the Somalis (who are much alike wherever you find them) and from what friends tell me they do not seem to have changed in the last ten years. In fact why should they have? Ninety percent are concerned only with two or three basic all important things; grazing for their camels, WATER for themselves and their herds and religious observance, they could not care less who rules them so long as they are left in peace to follow the rains and grass with their beasts and to scratch up enough to keep body and soul together, and occasionally have a pleasurable border raid or do a little enjoyable hut burning. Please do not think this is overdrawn: it is the truth as anyone who has lived out here will agree.

The five percent of sheikhs and elders are also primarily concerned with their sub-tribes' grazing and water rights, the increase of camels, goats and fat-tailed sheep etc, that can be acquired (without regard of course to such little trifles as overstocking, erosion, and destruction of already sparse grazing) and when these matters have been arranged to their satisfaction, they make for the nearest centre large or small - preferably large - where for three or four months they take their gentlemanly ease outside cafés sipping sweet black coffee, devoutly observing all religious duties (praying five times a day etc.) and gossiping with their cronies. The remaining five percent mostly to be found in the suspect, dubiously financed Somali Youth Movement are in the main young workshys...Silly idle fellows ripe for mischief and the wiles of agitators. The frugal nomadic life of their people no longer appeals to them (for which one has a certain sympathy). The white-collar job seems to hold dazzling promise (until it is found that employers strangely expect work and regular hours in return for pay - a most ungentlemanly attitude) and they drift to the towns, there to initiate

> secret societies…In other words, the Somali youths like many of their betters in older civilizations, see in independence and all the stuff they are shouting for: 'jobs for the boys.' They have neither the education nor the ability to govern themselves, they have no glimmer of what disinterested service of any kind means (let alone public service). Though from this please do not think I infer they lack the Mohammedan virtues of hospitality, physical courage and a contempt for the value of their own lives in battle. But they share with all African tribes, (and I speak as one who greatly likes Africans and has returned to this tropical land to spend my life here) a disastrous lack of ability for <u>sustained</u> effort, the capability of seeing a thing through and for coping with emergencies."[276]

It is probable that Professor Woolbert took offence after reading this letter; certainly their correspondence came to an abrupt halt. They had crossed swords once before over an article he had written about Abyssinia in 1939, when his claim that Ethiopia was in a state of rebellion had angered Katharine.[277] She had accused him then of using unreliable source material and exaggerating for political ends, and certainly they had widely divergent views on what was best for the Horn of Africa.

Katharine's forthright views on the subject are a good example of her political writing at this period and with hindsight we can appreciate just how disastrous the UN solutions in the Horn of Africa have been. For nine years after the handover and declaration of Independence, Somalia functioned as a democratic state, but in 1969 the situation deteriorated, when after allegations of poll-rigging and nepotism, the newly elected President Dr Shermaarke was assassinated. In October that same year General Mohamed Siad Barre seized power and established a military dictatorship. The disastrous war with Ethiopia from 1977-1978, devastated the economy and Siad Barre's increasingly brutal and repressive regime alienated his people. In 1990 civil war erupted and after the fall of Siad Barre in 1991 infighting among the various clans continued, leaving the country in ruins.

CHAPTER FIFTEEN
Coast Correspondent: The Settlers' View 1949-1956

In 1947 Arthur Creech-Jones the Labour Government Secretary of State for the Colonies (1946-51) issued an important set of instructions to Governors of all British colonies in Africa. The directive, that a western system of local government be set up in all colonies to provide a training ground for democracy and eventual self-government, was a radical departure from previous Colonial Office policy and marked a crucial step in the process leading to decolonisation. It signalled the end of the method known as 'indirect rule' that had served the British Empire so well, whereby indigenous chiefs and rulers, provided they did as they were told, had been allowed to govern their people through traditional institutions and following established custom, without too much interference. After World War II power was taken away from the old hierarchy and put in the hands of an educated minority, who were now urged to join local government and the civil service and be groomed in the mysteries of the western democratic system. British colonies were promised self-rule once they had mastered the proper procedures of western style administration and government.[278]

The Colonial Office Establishment was outraged but, as government servants, had no option but to comply. In Kenya they consoled themselves with the thought that training and educating Kenyan personnel to the required standard would take many years, perhaps forever. The White Settler community in Kenya, who distrusted Colonial Office policies as a matter of principle, decided to take steps of their own to make sure they retained control. They forced the hand of the Governor, Sir Philip Mitchell (1944-52), by demanding and keeping the largest representation in the Legislative Council (LegCo) that was now re-organised and extended, in line with decolonisation policies, as the eventual parliament for a democratic and nationalist government in Kenya.[279] In 1949 the Settler-dominated LegCo brought out the so-called 'Kenya Plan' in which they demanded that European leadership be recognised as 'paramount' and called for a creation of a new British East African Dominion to consist of a federation of Uganda, Tanganyika and Kenya and to include closer ties with Rhodesia and South Africa.

The Settlers, however, had left out of their calculations the growing political aspirations of the African majority and in particular the increasingly powerful and vocal Kikuyu tribal group. The Kikuyu leader, Jomo Kenyatta, who had returned from England in 1946 and became leader of the Kenya African Union (KAU) party, began campaigning for Kikuyu and African rights.[280] The Kikuyu KAU claimed the colonialists had stolen African lands and the rightful owners had been displaced by the large Settler farms in the fertile temperate zone, just north of Nairobi, known as the 'White Highlands,' which was reserved exclusively for Europeans.

The Africans were further angered by the Soldier Settler Scheme, whereby English soldiers returning from World War II were encouraged to immigrate to Kenya and take up farming. A great many new Settlers escaping the post-war unemployment and depression in the UK came to Kenya in the late 1940s and bought land in the White Highlands. On the other hand 75,000 Kenyan Africans had also fought for the British and were now returning from the war, but they were not offered attractive job opportunities or housing or land at favourable terms.[281] There was land set aside for the Kikuyu but it was not enough, as with prosperity and the health programmes brought in by the colonialists the Kikuyu population had multiplied exceedingly.

In addition many Kikuyu had gone to work on European farms in the White Highlands. The families and dependents of these farm labourers lived on the Settler farms, often in seemingly permanent village-like encampments, and yet the land was not legally theirs. They were regarded as squatters. The other Kikuyu who had not gone to work for the Europeans lived in the Native Reserves and owned their land. With the greatly increased Kikuyu population, it now became apparent there was no room for the squatters and ex-soldiers to own land in the Kikuyu

Reserves. The White Highlands became a battleground as squatters and ex-soldiers joined hands to lay claim to land, which they thought had been denied them by the Settlers.[282]

The Settlers maintained they had not taken land away from the Kikuyus, as much of the White Highlands had been unoccupied when they first arrived and they had been legally allocated plots of land on long lease from the colonial Government. It had been the pioneers' hard work and determination that had turned the area into prosperous farming land, where previously there had been – in European eyes – nothing but bush. Furthermore, the economy of the colony depended on the agricultural produce of the large European farms and ranches, which exported coffee, tea, wheat, hides, vegetables, etc. To begin with the Settlers got their way, their point of view carrying the day almost without dissent. A few members of LegCo warned the Government of the growing seriousness of the unrest, but their voices were drowned by the overwhelming majority.[283]

The failure of the European Settlers and the Colonial Administration to take serious notice of what was going on resulted in the Mau Mau rebellion, primarily involving the Kikuyu tribe, which lasted from 1952-56. The Emergency, a period of extra tight security measures and laws enacted to combat the Mau Mau, declared on October 20, 1952, did not officially end until January 12, 1960. Although there were relatively few Settler deaths inflicted by the guerilla fighters, an extraordinary mystique and aura of terror surrounded the Mau Mau who lived in bands in the forests and were bound together by secret oaths. European farmers lived in a perpetual state of fear, imagining that at any moment they or their families might be bestially murdered by formerly trusted staff, their stock stolen and their fields burnt. In fact, only 32 European and 26 Asian civilians were killed by Mau Mau in the first four years of the Emergency, less than road accidents for one year. This was in contrast to the much greater number of African civilians who were killed, many of them Kikuyu 'loyalists' who lived in the Reserves and supported the government against the Mau Mau fighters.

The Mau Mau movement gathered momentum in 1953, when the Settlers, using security as an excuse, evicted many Kikuyu squatter families from their farms. These evicted squatters, eventually totalling more than 13,000, were sent back to the Reserves. This put pressure on already limited land space, making them unwelcome and forcing many to live as outcasts. As a result many joined the Mau Mau Movement.[284] More Kikuyu supported this fight for independence when the British accused Jomo Kenyatta of fomenting and leading the rebellion and imprisoned him in 1953.[285] The Mau Mau forces, which had started as small groups of disaffected outlaws living in the dense forests of the Aberdare Mountains and Mount Kenya, poorly armed with native knives, spears and homemade guns, now doubled in number and were formed into loosely controlled fighting groups, which raided Settler farms and loyalist villages. A passive wing of supporters helped feed the outlawed freedom fighters and smuggled guns and ammunition to them from a central supply base in Nairobi. The Nairobi base was put out of action in 1954 and active resistance ended two years later with the capture of the notorious Mau Mau leader, Dedan Kimathi, in October 1956.

From the end of 1952 there had been virtual martial law in Kenya. In June 1953 General Erskine had been asked to take control of the situation and deploy British troops to stamp out the Mau Mau rebellion. Military operations were suspended in November 1956, when the army was withdrawn and the police re-assumed full responsibility for law and order. But the cost to the country had been enormous. By the end of 1956, 11,503 Africans had been killed, 2,902 captured, 2,716 surrendered. A total of 27,000 arrests had been made, 1,104 had been executed and an unknown number had died in the forest from disease, or had been murdered by their comrades in arms, or had disappeared. Over 77,000 suspects were detained during the Emergency, and many of those remained in detention camps until after 1960. The cost of all this misery was £56 million sterling pounds – to a country with an average annual revenue of about £43 million sterling pounds.[286]

By employing British troops to help suppress the rebellion, the British Government wrested political control in Kenya from the Settlers. Never again were the Settlers able to bully a British Governor in Nairobi or take control of affairs. By 1956 the Settlers' day was over. The question was no longer whether Kenya would become independent, but when and under what conditions.

The Fannins threw in their hand with the Settler community. Katharine offered her services to Mervyn Hill the outspoken and talented editor of the *Kenya Weekly News* – the Settlers' newspaper, published at

Nakuru and founded in 1928. This weekly paper, specialising in articles of farming interest, also contained political commentary and was a handy digest for busy people who did not have time to read a daily newspaper. Katharine Fannin joined the staff as Correspondent for the Coast in 1949 and sent weekly bulletins of events, political and social, from Mombasa until 1955. There were very few Settler farms at the Coast and although the European population had expanded since the 1920s, most were either retired government servants such as the Fannins or businessmen, who did not put much pressure on available land. The European minority did, however, control Mombasa. They sent representatives to the LegCo in Nairobi and had the majority of seats on the Mombasa Municipal Board. The period 1947-1955 in Kenya was a time when the Settler community was particularly truculent and vociferous and Katharine Fannin wrote for the few Settlers at the Coast and identified herself entirely with their hopes and fears.

The Settlers' view at this period is succinctly expressed in an article published in the South African newspaper *The Cape Times* in June 1951 when Katharine reported on the visit to Kenya and Uganda of the new Labour Secretary of State for the Colonies, James Griffiths.[287] The minister was energetically lobbied by the Settlers who were nervous of Colonial Office policies and wanted clarification that their position was secure. Katharine voiced the feelings of many Settlers of that period when she wrote:

"Settlers and other white people in Kenya feel that one way and another they have had rather a raw deal recently, with precious little credit ever given them by the Powers that Be at home for the cracking hard work that has gone into the past fifty years' effort to bring this bit of Africa out of pure savagery. A part of Africa where before they came, predatory tribes roamed the bush: famine and rinderpest periodically decimated man and beast, and the majority of upcountry natives cowered in their tribal areas, a prey to malnutrition, disease and inter-necine warfare - not to mention the earlier cruel raids of the slave traders. These are facts too easily forgotten or conveniently ignored by long-haired intellectuals and politicians in Britain and elsewhere, and by noisy young African politicians out here."

As far as the Settler community was concerned, Griffiths' visit in 1951 was a success, as they retained their overall control in LegCo. The

Africans were given two more seats, increasing their representation to six. The Indian representation increased by one, giving them six seats, and the Arab representation remained the same at two seats; but the Settlers were given three more seats raising their number to fourteen, which meant that parity was kept, and Settler domination of LegCo was undisturbed .

Katharine Fannin's *Kenya Weekly News* column "Along the Coast" portrayed Mombasa carrying on life entirely unaffected by the Mau Mau disturbances up-country. Her lighthearted breezy style was intended to cheer up the hard-pressed Settler farming community living in fear with revolvers ever handy. Her articles appeared alongside advertisements for Sanatogen, the nerve tonic, and backed onto the satirical column 'Diary of a Colonial Lady,' which poked fun at the accepted norms of would-be 'Really Nice' Colonials and provided endless hilarity with the tortuous wedding preparations of Gordon and Lucinda. Katharine described coastlife in all its variety; colourful local festivities, the arrival of dhows from India and Arabia, migrating birds, the love-life of her cats, anything to give her up-country readers light relief from the troubles around them and assure them of the continuance of normal life in Mombasa.

The ceremony held on the Arab festival of Idd ul Haj, when all of Mombasa's dignitaries turned out in full costume to exchange speeches and niceties with the Sultan of Zanzibar's chief representative, the Liwali, was a colourful spectacle Katharine enjoyed and wrote about.[288]

> "Last Monday the Liwali for the Coast, Sheikh Mbarak bin Ali el Hinawy, held his customary baraza on the occasion of Idd ul Haj. A dignified figure in his magnificent Arab robes, sword in hand, curved silver dagger thrust into an exquisitely fine blue and gold tissue belt and round his neck the bright ribbons and jewels of orders recently conferred upon him, Sheikh Mbarak welcomed His Excellency the Acting Governor, Mr. Henry Potter and many Arab, European and Asian guests, in a charming speech given first in English and then in Ki-swahili. Mr. Potter replied in Ki-swahili only. Amongst other matters he spoke of what pleasure it gave him to be present, and hoped that Sheikh Mbarak whose health has been sadly indifferent

of late would rest as much as he could and soon be quite restored. The Acting Governor said how greatly he had enjoyed his visits to various centres and how truly amazing he found the general progress of the Coast, not only in Mombasa, which had changed remarkably in the past few years, but everywhere he went.

"He mentioned the Institute of Muslim Education and the admirable work it is doing - and paid tribute to Sir Philip Mitchell's support of the project from its inception - and wished well all Muslims, who were away undertaking the pilgrimage to Mecca. After this pleasant speech we were regaled with pink sherbet and little bowls of coffee, and our handkerchiefs were scented with rosewater.

"This friendly occasion was as colourful and picturesque as you could wish. Officials clanked in garnished with swords, medals and other trappings, the majority of Arabs present wore traditional dress (though the younger generation seemed to prefer Western suits) and the handful of European ladies present wore charming gowns and hats. There is an idea going about that these barazas are strictly male affairs. Far from it! - at any rate here."[289]

The 1950s saw great changes in Mombasa when large industries such as the Bamburi Cement Factory and the oil refinery were started and substantial extensions were carried out in Kilindini harbour, making Mombasa the most modern and important port in East Africa. There was frenzied house building as the population increased dramatically and early worries were expressed over parking and traffic congestion. Tourism at the coast benefitted from the insecurity up-country. Countless traumatised up-country dwellers came to relax and get away from it all on the safe and sunny beaches of Mombasa. (There was still the question whether it was good for Europeans to be exposed to tropical rays, but fortunately medical opinion had at last decided yes, in moderation. Felt terais were out and beach holidays were in. However, the general consensus remained firm, that though European children suffered no lasting damage up to the age of 10, living in the unhealthy humid climate of the Coast would leave children between the ages of 12 and 17 feeble and pale and it was imperative to send them to cooler climes.)

Katharine faithfully attended the monthly meetings of the Mombasa Municipal Board and many of the drafts for her articles are typed on the backs of the voluminous Municipal Board minutes. W F Foster, her old friend and rival from Almshouse days, was now Chairman of the Municipal Board. The minutes tell of the new shop-hours ordinance, plans for municipal housing and how Dr Rana was concerned for the preservation of ancient monuments in Mombasa. However, the Board dealt with this item swiftly, deciding there weren't any monuments worth preserving.[290] The meetings, according to Katharine, were uncontroversial affairs, with all members amicably agreeing with each other. This was hardly surprising as the Europeans held a comfortable majority.

In 1951 the Municipal board consisted of 27 members – 15 Europeans, three Arabs, two Africans appointed by the Government, and seven Asians, who were elected on a ward basis. In 1954 the number of African and Arab members were increased by one and the Europeans by three, bringing the board membership up to 32. The Board became a Municipal Council in 1958, and a more equitable elective system brought in. Even then councillors were elected according to ethnic group and the Europeans retained control of Mombasa Council until 1963, although they represented less that 3% of the total population. In 1958 the total European population of Mombasa and outlying districts was 4,000.[291]

The Town Clerk, Arthur Ratcliff, was a European and so were all the main officials who ran the town. Charles Fannin sat on the Municipal Board and was one of its most respected members. He chaired the Housing Committee and the Valuation Court where he gave judgements on objections to Municipal Valuations for rating in Mombasa. In 1953 he was appointed Deputy Board Chairman.

Katharine carefully reported the May 1952 election for coastal representatives to LegCo. Two Europeans, C G Usher for Mombasa and S V Cooke for the Coast, were returned as were two Asians, Dr Hassan for the Muslims and A B Patel for the Hindus. The one Arab member for the Coast was Sheikh Saleh Mackawi. As only a fraction of the population were eligible to vote, voting day was a very decorous affair. Special provisions had to be made so the Muslim ladies could vote in strict seclusion and Katharine supervised the 'Purdah' vote.

Katharine faithfully documented meetings of the Mombasa and Coast Province European Association (MACPEA) meetings, attended usually by between 60 to 70 members and held either at the Nyali Beach Hotel or the Little Theatre Club. The Meat Commission, Nyali Bridge Tolls and the Finger Prints Bill[292] all came up for vigorous discussion, but the really hot topic in 1950 was the proposed Federation with Tanganyika and Uganda. The Coast members voted unanimously against the 'Liberianising' tendencies of the Tanganyika proposals, which suggested African and Asian representation on the East African Central Assembly, which was to be the governing body of the proposed Federation.[293] In October 1953, Major Heath spoke on the dangers of Asian immigration, and a scheme for the settlement of German peasants at Ol Kalou received a determined veto from all Coast members. However, the most controversial meeting was the one held in April 1954. S V Cooke, LegCo's representative for the Coast,[294] attempted to explain how changes to the Constitution had been voted through despite previous assurances that no constitutional changes would take place without prior general consultation and debate. Attached to Katharine's report on this meeting is an anguished note to the editor explaining just how many times she had rewritten her account to try and hide her feelings of bitter disappointment.

This mandate for constitutional change, which Katharine Fannin knew spelt the end of Settler control in Kenya, had been engineered by the Conservative Secretary of State for the Colonies, Oliver Lyttelton, (later Lord Chandos). The Lyttelton Constitution, which was announced in March 1954, contained an important innovation: there were to be Asian and African ministers in the government. Lyttelton had managed to persuade Michael Blundell, leader of the Liberal European voice in LegCo, to support his proposals. Blundell, S V Cooke and a few other European members voted for the Lyttleton Constitution, supplying the needed majority. The die-hards of the Settler community were furious and spoke of treachery and political skulduggery. They were bitterly opposed to sharing ministerial power with Asians and Africans and they claimed the Lyttelton Plan had been imposed on the European elected members as a fait accompli. However, by 1954 moderate opinion realised white minority rule could not last and, supporting Colonial Office policies, held the view that the best way to preserve British socio-economic interests in Kenya was to provide conditions for the emergence of a moderate nationalist African leadership.[295]

The Coastal Settlers, who had not experienced the terrors of Mau Mau, tended to be a rather reactionary lot. They, with Katharine Fannin, could see no reason why white minority rule should not continue and felt badly let down by the British Government and Blundell. They thought the government was mishandling the Mau Mau situation and wanted the country to be run as before. They opposed any kind of change. Many coastal people, particularly the Muslim communities, were also suspicious of the idea of African rule from Nairobi, dominated by the Kikuyu, and could see little benefit in it for them.

In the run up to the 1954 elections Katharine reported on the poor turn out for the political rally held in Mombasa by the newly formed United Country Party, composed of Europeans who asked for cooperation with African and Asian political parties, led by Blundell.[296] According to Katharine, Mombasa was not impressed, indeed the coastal people were totally fed up with up-country politics. She reported much better attendance for the celebration of the 70th birthday of the Aga Khan, which was held at the Diamond Jubilee Hall on August 22, 1954. This gave Katharine the excuse to recall how in 1937 she had witnessed the Aga Khan being weighed in gold:[297]

> "His Highness settled himself in a massive leather armchair attached to one side of a huge pair of scales and his devoted followers then heaped solid gold bars and nuggets on the other tray until amidst excited applause the august weight was lifted and finally trembled in the balance."

In 1954 the Aga Khan was due to be weighed in platinum, but this spectacle never took place as it was felt an exhibition of such conspicuous wealth might cause offence. Most Asians had supported the Lyttelton Constitution and now had two ministers in the Government and they were seen as an increasing threat to European economic and social dominance. In 1958 the Asian population of Mombasa stood at over 26,000, more than six times the European, almost double that of the Arab and was only topped by the African, which stood at 89,000.[298]

The last political event Katharine Fannin covered in her capacity as Coast Correspondent was the dock strike in March 1955, when for six days Mombasa Port remained closed amidst scenes of unprecedented rioting and stone throwing. This shocking disturbance in the heart of peaceful Mombasa was, she said, engineered by Mau Mau and communist influences. Union leader, Tom Mboya, eventually persuaded the dockers to return to work after being awarded a pay increase for shift work.[299] In one of her last articles written for the *Kenya Weekly News* Katharine Fannin lamented the passing of peaceful Mombasa and predicted a gloomy future influenced by the disturbances and divisive politics of up-country Kenya.[300]

> "Since the beginning of the Emergency, our correspondent at Mombasa has frequently reminded us of the pleasant happy relations existing there between the races and of how nice it is to be protected by a cordon sanitaire of desert and bush from up-country Kenya, where men are divided by bloodshed and bitterness. While others in this sunlit haven beside the eastern seaboard joined our correspondent in a chorus of 'Oh! I do like to be beside the seaside,' swift undercurrents were running under the placid surface. Now complacency is swept away, like candy floss machines from the storm lashed pier, by the six-day strike of 6,000 dockers which paralysed Kilindini. Although the strike most certainly was engineered by Mau Mau, it is indicative of the possibility that African nationalism may be taking a fresh turn and that pangas (machetes) will be replaced by pesas (money) in a new agitation of labour troubles and industrial disputes."

For nearly six years the Fannin column 'Along the Coast from our Coast Correspondent' had appeared with praiseworthy regularity keeping readers abreast of events and well informed of Coastal goings on. She struggled to keep her accounts impartial and balanced and wrote apologetic notes to the editor whenever anything of a more serious nature crept in. Over Christmas and New Year of 1954-1955 she took a well-earned holiday and travelled to India, to find her father's grave and revisit childhood haunts. While she was away Edward Rodwell retired from the editorship of the *Mombasa Times*[301] - a moment Mervyn Hill had been waiting for as he had always wanted Rodwell to be the *Kenya Weekly News* Coast correspondent, as he was by far the most experienced and established journalist at the Coast. A few articles written by Katharine appeared in the newspaper in early 1955, but after March they ceased entirely. Edward Rodwell took over with his new column entitled 'Along the Waterfront.' It is evident that by 1955 Katharine's hard line Settler views were becoming embarrassing to a paper now obliged to resign itself to inevitable self-rule in Kenya and she was finding it harder and harder to produce the "strictly accurate, objective and unsensational" accounts required of her.[302]

Katharine's misgivings about the future of Kenya coincided with those of Lord Altrincham, who as Sir Edward Grigg had been Governor of Kenya in the 1920s. He felt so strongly that British post-war policies in Africa were heading towards disaster that he wrote a book in 1955 entitled **Kenya's Opportunity**. Many of the older Settlers, Katharine among them, agreed wholeheartedly with the sentiments expressed in this passage taken from his foreword:[303]

> "We are prone in this country to misunderstand other peoples because we assume that, if they are right minded, they must see things in the same light as we do and that what is good and right for us must accordingly be good and right for them. On this theory we have now apparently convinced ourselves that the democratic progress of the African peoples is best to be secured by breaking up their indigenous type of government and forming them into Parliamentary Nation-States, in the image of this island (England), which is not at all like Africa...We are, however, mistaken if we imagine that the result would in any way resemble what we intend. The result in Africa would not be democratic Parliamentarianism on our model but single party rule of either the Nazi or Communist variety, under which the germs of true democracy would be starved of sustenance and killed.
>
> "Since 1945 we have ignored tribal sentiment in our blind addiction to our insular ideal of Parliamentary Nationalism. There is only just time to reverse the process and revert to the principles, which we pursued in the first half of the century, with even stronger emphasis than before on African self-government on traditional

African foundations. Our policy in a sentence, should be to establish confederations of autonomous tribal communities under British protection, economic support, and (in the ultra-provincial sphere) political suzerainty.

"I pray for this re-appraisal of British policy in Africa all the more fervently because of my conviction that if we destroy Africa's indigenous democracy by driving our European mattocks through its tribal African roots, it will not be the freedom of Western Christendom but the slavery of Communism, which will triumph in Africa."

CHAPTER SIXTEEN

Other writings, eccentricities and cats

Katharine Fannin's true talent for writing did not lie in the field of political journalism, where her emotions tended to get the better of her judgement. From 1952-1959 the Kenyan Press was strictly censored, permitting no criticism of the Government in the interests of national security. This put a strain on journalists, who had to be careful what they wrote and on editors who had to make sure their newspaper copy did not contravene the press laws. Katharine found this increasingly difficult as, although she respected the establishment and the reasons for censorship, she was also forthright in her views and believed in saying things as she saw them. Rather than compromise her integrity, she withdrew from journalism altogether. After 1955 she was often to be found reading *The Times* in the Mombasa Club and she would like to tease Edward Rodwell by asking: "Do you read *The Times*, Mr Rodwell?" *The Times*, printed in London, was not subject to the tiresome restrictions of the locally based newspapers and printed many viewpoints, particularly in the Letters to the Editor. So this was a deliberately pointed remark, not lost on Edward Rodwell, who had by then succeeded Katharine as Coast Correspondent for the *Kenya Weekly News*.[304]

Although deeply interested in politics and holding strong views on most subjects, Katharine was really at her best writing in a more lighthearted vein. As Coast Correspondent, her column had been read chiefly for the lively description and portrayal of contemporary life in Mombasa, amusing and enjoyable material, which the readers liked.

In addition to her column in the *Kenya Weekly News*, between 1949-1951 she also wrote for the *Mombasa Times* Saturday edition under the pseudonym 'Shellback.' [305] To begin with she called this column

'Seascape,' but later changed it to 'Saturday Scrapbook.' In it she wrote about whatever caught her fancy; nursery rhyme characters, childhood games, superstitions, mythical beasts, local history, personal experiences, anecdotes and titbits of miscellanea to amuse and titillate the jaded reader and provide a moment or two of escapism. She drew her inspiration largely from a 'Commonplace Book,' which she had kept before the war. This consisted of a magpie assortment of newspaper articles, extracts from books, poems, unusual items, absurd or curious that appealed to her and she had saved, first of all in a capacious box-file and then later sorted out and put into a scrapbook.[306] The keeping of a Commonplace Book was a Victorian habit, which she must have learnt from her aunts.

Censored news seldom makes inspiring reading, and all good quality newspapers need a journalist or two who just write to entertain. Katharine's great rival and successor in this field was Edward Rodwell, who wrote his weekly column called "Coast Causerie," under the pseudonym 'Watchman,' first for the *Mombasa Times* and then for the *East African Standard* with which the *Mombasa Times* was amalgamated.[307] He had started this column in 1943 and when he stopped in 1949, due to pressures from other work, Katharine took over from him with her Saturday column until 1951, when he once more took over.

Rodwell went further than Katharine's scrapbook device and in one of his articles entitled "Mandarin and a Miniskirt"[308] described how he liked to take a few names and occasions, shake them up and see what came out of the cocktail shaker. This form of journalism, meant to be mildly brain teasing, but not at all serious, is extremely difficult to write successfully over a long period. As it does not rely on reportage, gossip or sensationalism, it needs constant ingenuity, a continuous stream of new ideas and a deft touch to hit just the right note to amuse the reader. Katharine Fannin, if not quite such a master of the form as Edward Rodwell became, had nevertheless considerable talent for this style of creative journalism.

Here, in a typical piece written in 1951 for "Saturday Scrapbook" entitled "Home Sweet Home," she reflected on how living conditions for Government servants had changed since she first came to Mombasa in the 1920s.[309]

> "A little while ago I was shown round some of the new quarters Government has built for its civil servants; in

Kenya an unappreciated tribe. My eyes popped as I beheld the roomy cupboards, electric stoves, aluminium sinks and draining boards, running water, fitted basins, sanitation and indeed other signs of an effete modernity in the works of that Department its victims have long been known to refer rudely as the R.I.P.W.D.[310] As the ageing chattel of an ex-civil servant I contrasted these frivolities with the stark realities we pioneer women had to put up with during our own husband's service and, I reflected, what is Kenya coming too? If young government housewives are pampered like this how will they ever acquire that moral toughness needed, for instance, to face down the meat marketeers when they whack another shilling on the miserable pound of edible offal, now, alas, the mainstay of so many an official meal; joints being beyond the rapidly dwindling purchasing power of fixed salaries. So lets have done with this modern nonsense of government quarters equipped with baths, h & c, cookers that cook, plugs that pull, pleasing furniture, and nice clean colours on the walls and return to the good old days when men were men and we women followed the (early) British way of life. I will describe it as I knew it for nearly twenty five years and in almost as many government bungalows, some modest, others imposing, all without exception minus running water, sanitary sanitation, reasonable stoves or anywhere to store things.

"Our first bijou PWD residence was at the Coast, three hot pokey rooms, alleged modern as they were roofed with tiles not tin. Fortunately we exchanged this with an unwary colleague for an antique semi-ruinous but more spacious double decker; two rooms down, one room and a half up; the roof steep as any in Nuremberg, unventilated and the abiding place of not less than five hundred bats. They swooshed out in three well-drilled flights as dusk fell, startling our less hardy visitors. Up the corkscrew stairs we had a little dogbox; alias the bathroom. In it our own privately purchased tin bath. In an idle moment one day I lent against the wall. There was a protesting creak and the next minute through rusty strands of chicken wire and a large hole in the thin stucco so deceptively and nearly disastrously solid looking, I was watching my boys at their daily task of sweeping healthy piles of bat guano - brushed off our clothes, off our food and from floors and furniture into the growing mould outside the kitchen - we were told it made lovely manure.

"But there, the view from our windows was lovely and we liked that hideously inconvenient little house in spite of the fact that one night a crazy Arab walked up our tottery backstairs and (there being no door to stop him) marched into our bedroom where with eldritch screams of laughter he invited us to sign his Kipande;[311] a large filthy piece of brown packing paper."

In October, 1950,[312] she wrote from Nairobi where she had a brush with the horsey set. (Indeed the idea of the vastly overweight Katharine on or anywhere near a horse is incongruous to say the least.)

"For the past week or so I have been frisking about up-country thoroughly enjoying myself, but at the same time profoundly glad that I don't have to live in Nairobi all the time. That seems ill-mannered and ungrateful, but really is due only to the fact that life for me away from the sight and sound of the sea, and all one can do in, on, or beside it, is no life at all. For what may an obstinate 'Shellback' find to entertain him up-country?

Down to Horses

"Once he has seen the admirable lions and other fauna of the National Park, the view from the new Mannion House Bar, the gay city lights and the melancholy Arch of Triumph (from which one is apt to avert the eye) what remains? The horse, now horsey readers had better stop reading here; for I am about to utter equine heresy so black as to make the stoutest blanch. I do not worship the horse; an incalculable and obstinate animal. I do not enjoy bumping up and down on its concave vertebrae; I do not credit for a moment the nonsensical tales of its sagacity put about by people old enough to know better. In fact I declare roundly that I (as do others, though few are honest enough to admit it) find the horse to be a large unmanageable four-footed creature which bites with one end and kicks with the other; give me a large, powerful, biddable motor-car every time, and as for the horse - well! you can have it."

Katharine may not have been fond of horses, but she certainly liked cats. When she first arrived back in Mombasa she brought with her two elegant Persian cats, called Black Mischief and Gentleman's Relish. However by the early 1950s her cat family had increased to 27 and these multiplied to number over 70 by the early 60s. A keen member of the Kenya Society for the Prevention of Cruelty to Animals (KSPCA), she was always rescuing stray cats from rubbish bins and other unlikely spots and, well known for her weakness for cats, unwanted kittens would often be left on her doorstep. Arthur Ratcliff, Mombasa's Town Clerk for many years, remembered visiting the Fannins in their first big house in Cliffe Avenue, near the old Police Mess. Even then, he said, she was mad about cats and had a large cage where she kept the stray kittens she found and the mother cats would feed them indiscriminately through the mesh. She had such a mania, Ratcliff said, that you had to brush the cats off the chairs in order to sit down and they swarmed about so that it was quite unpleasant. They were all waifs and strays with injuries and diseases, not smart sleek cats, but nevertheless it did not stop them breeding.[313]

In one of her articles for the *Kenya Weekly News*,[314] she described how she rescued two owls, which were being jerked on strings head down along the road by some wretch who had captured them. One died but she managed to nurse the other back to health. The survivor became a pet but had to live in a special box on the top of a mangrove pole so the cats did not disturb him during the day. As she whimsically put it, "I have to report that Owl has now joined the Welfare State." Providing for the Fannin Animal Welfare State was an expensive business and she used to go round the hotels and butcheries looking for handouts of leftovers and offal to feed her ever increasing population. Millicent Reeve, whose husband Eddie sat on the Municipal Board with Charles Fannin, recalled how Katharine always went for lunch on Fridays to the Mombasa Club. The Mombasa Club, founded in 1896, is the oldest club in Kenya and in those days was very exclusive. Originally membership had been restricted to males of Anglo-Saxon origin, but in the 1920s and 1930s the rules were relaxed to admit women and other Europeans, but until 1960 the colour bar was in operation and it was a Whites only club. [315] Despite the heat, strict dress regulations were followed meticulously. Jacket and tie were required to be worn by gentlemen, and ladies had to wear a dress or skirt; if not they were turned away from the dining room. Katharine used to come in for lunch with a big straw basket (kikapu) and persuade her extremely thin husband to have a second helping he didn't want and then scrape the leftovers into her basket for the cats. Mrs Reeve commented, "She was a very peculiar woman."[316]

Arthur Ratcliff once, and only once, gave her a lift. He was not too pleased when she insisted on stopping to pick up a large parcel of oozing meat, which she dumped unceremoniously on the back seat of his new car. She then asked him to stop several times along the route back to her house to feed cats who popped out from nowhere immediately they heard her voice.

By 1953 the Fannins had moved onto the mainland to a spot called Mkomani. Here they rented a bungalow on the waterfront overlooking the island and Mombasa Town,[317] near the pontoon bridge that connected the north mainland to the island.[318] In 1953 the north mainland was just beginning to take the overflow from the town on the island, a far cry from the crowded suburbia, it has since become. Pythons and monitor lizards lived in the coral cliff below the Fannin's bungalow and on one memorable occasion a python entered the house and swallowed several cats, which appeared as bumps along its length. Most upset, Katharine called the Game Department who immediately came and shot the snake and then opened it up to find some of the cats still alive.[319] The monitor lizards were less trouble and she used to feed them at the same time as her cats. Although monitor lizards, which can grow to a length of 6 feet, are not averse to a tasty kitten for breakfast, they also eat snakes, so she must have felt they provided some protection for her cats.

Katharine was always happy to find a good home for her many kittens and when the local shipping company, Southern Line, was started she provided a ship's cat. The captain never forgot visiting her to pick up the kitten and seeing how cats covered every available space and had completely taken over the house.[320] There may well have been a psychological reason behind such excessive cat mania. Perhaps it was thwarted motherhood, or disappointment in love. Katharine liked to play the universal mother figure, dispensing advice and bullying people into action for their own good. She was the kind of older woman who enjoyed the company of young men, who flattered her and listened to her words of wisdom delivered in a fast clear voice, and did not mind her bossiness. Her involvement with cats increased after the death of her husband and in the end became a fatal obsession.

In middle age she became increasingly eccentric and Edward Rodwell described how she wore a monocle and on most days could be seen reading *The Times* on the verandah of the Mombasa Club. Jean Wallwork, who lived in Mombasa between 1950-1953 recalled: "Mrs Fannin used to be seen in the Club Pool, her not inconsiderable bulk clad in a navy blue bathing costume (I think the expression is more appropriate than swim suit), a wide brimmed straw hat on her head, elbows on the edge of the pool, pencil in hand and a crossword, almost certainly *The Times*, spread out in front of her. Those of us who were inconsiderate enough to splash the paper were completely ignored, but I think most people endeavoured to walk around the paper and to avoid splashing."[321] She had become increasingly overweight and her style of clothing by this period was odd. She wore no bra and favoured droopy flowered frocks down to her ankles. Oblivious of her appearance, her clothes were often torn with buttons missing, but, when the occasion demanded it, she could still dress up in grand manner.

As she grew older her interest in the occult and supernatural increased. Flying saucers and strange appearances of stars and heavenly beings fascinated her. On September 5, 1954, in her *Kenya Weekly News* column, she reported a greenish star had been sighted in the heavens, which gave her special cause for concern. She attended spiritualist sessions and believed in telepathy and second sight. Her diaries for 1962-1964, which are the only ones to survive, are filled with messages written in green and red ink with capital letters marking favourable dates for certain types of activities and meetings or warnings of mood swings and hazards ahead. After her husband's death in 1960 she astonished Edward Rodwell by her firm conviction that her husband was still with her, guiding her at every turn, and not buried in a hole in the earth, as everyone thought.[322]

She became interested in African customs and took the Giriama and Swahili belief in witchcraft and magic very seriously. Just before her death she thought a spell or a curse had been laid on her by a servant she had dismissed for stealing, and this caused her great distress. Despite her unorthodox beliefs, she considered herself a devout Christian, attending St Peter's Church, Nyali, regularly on Sunday mornings, though she was sometimes very critical of the content of the sermon. She was still involved in important charity work, belonged to the League of Mercy, the East African Women's League (EAWL), was an active member of the KSPCA and interested herself with municipal affairs and African welfare.

In September 1953, she reported on a meeting in Mombasa where A G S Harrison, the Deputy Officer for African Affairs, gave the Annual Report on the welfare work of his department. This article clearly expressed her views on the subject, as she viewed with disquiet the increasing government tendency towards 'spoon feeding' and felt in the long run this type of assistance would not benefit the African.[323]

> "Perhaps Mr Harrison's most significant and disquieting comment is that 'the African tendency in expecting almost everything to be done for him by the Government is to-day accentuated through his lack of spirit of self-help. Curiously enough this was not the case before the Europeans came.' I have underlined these words because I think that the whole sentence deserves the closest attention of all who have anything to do with the administration and education of Africans. If native people's not very robust self-reliance is sapped by olympian spoon feeding inevitably the day will come when their initiative on their own behalf will be destroyed entirely. Here the unhappy process has already begun and a striking instance of the younger generation's outlook…was a question asked during the lecture in Mombasa. It was: 'As Africans are poor and weak is it not the duty of the Europeans and Asians to help them become their equals?' In giving a report

> of the extraordinarily able address I instanced this question as being most disquieting for it showed only too clearly the view of the younger generation that just because Africans are Africans and backward the good things of life should be handed to them on a plate without commensurate effort on their part. Mr Harrison unwittingly confirms that view because he concluded by saying, 'Unless there is a change of heart, effort and hardwork, co-operation and perseverance exerted, coupled with faith, hope and sincerity I am afraid the lot of the African will remain obscure indefinitely.'"

Katharine's husband, Charles, is described at this period as a silent man, seemingly completely overpowered by his voluble domineering wife. According to Arthur Ratcliff, who knew him well, Fannin, being a South African, had a low opinion of Africans, but despite this he never treated them badly and was much respected for the good work he did. He was an experienced surveyor and after retiring from government service worked freelance on contracts for the government. One of his most interesting projects was the African Housing Development at Kongowea, which he laid out with an assistant, Dixie Dean, in 1954 on a 15-acre plot. The Kongowea experiment, which was based on a traditional African village layout with all the houses built by and for Africans but supervised by Municipal rules, proved very successful and set an example for other developments, which were later built in Majengo and Likoni where cheap housing was desperately needed to accommodate the population explosion in Mombasa.[324] Originally when he surveyed the area, he demarcated it into 184 plots allowing for a main 60 foot road through the estate and secondary lanes of 25 feet. An open space of 25 feet was left around the border of the estate and in the centre another large open area was planned with a well to provide water for the residents. This housing estate was one of the first attempts to provide low cost housing for Africans at the Coast. All the houses had to be constructed to an approved Municipal plan and the prospective residents were given credit facilities to help them purchase the plots and build the houses. In the first year 1954, 87 plots were taken up and by 1958, 123 houses had been built to municipal specifications. As Katharine reports: "The Swahili loves his cool, airy mud and makuti house and Municipal by-laws ensure that the rooms in it are of good size, 13ft x 8ft with a wide centre passage and at the back a kitchen store, proper pit latrine, a concrete washing place for pots, pans etc., and a small open yard."[325]

Charles Fannin sat on the Mombasa Municipal Housing Committee for nearly ten years and was a guiding light behind the Municipal housing and town planning schemes of the 1950s. His dedication was rewarded in 1960, when he was unanimously elected one of four aldermen for the town. Unfortunately the excitement of the election was too much for him and he died a few days later, aged 70. The schemes he initiated are still to be seen in Mombasa and the housing estate at Kongowea, enormously extended from the original intention of 184 houses, has become a teeming populous suburb. After his death, Katharine, was offered his position as alderman, but she refused, preferring instead to contest on her own merits a seat on the newly created Municipal Council.

Katharine must have been thinking of her husband when she wrote her six part broadcast series for the Kenya Broadcasting Service (KBS) entitled 'Memories of the '20s and '30s in Kenya.' These short 15-minute programmes, which were very popular judging by the many letters of appreciation she received, were broadcast from the new regional station that had been opened in Mombasa and came on the air in November and December, 1960.

Cricket had been Charles' favourite pastime and in her second talk she made a special mention of how he used to play in the Officials vs the Unofficials match at the Mombasa Sports Club, which was always held in August when the whole Legislative council and the Governor would move to the Coast for the month.[326] In 1926 Lord Delamare, as leader of the Settlers,[327] captained the Unofficials and Sir Edward Grigg, the Governor, was captain of the Officials. C G Fannin, at that time a junior surveyor attached to the PWD, was eligible to play for the Official side and proved a very useful addition to the team. It must have been a proud moment for him and a battered photograph taken at the occasion of this match had been one of his most treasured possessions. The idea of the Settlers and Government Officials amicably settling their differences and playing cricket together, obviously appealed to Katharine. By including this passage she implicitly suggested that by 1960 Kenyan politics no longer ran on the old principles of fair play and cricket.

The 1920s and 1930s had been a happy time for the Fannins, and her radio series of personal reminiscences and memories of Kenya was Katharine Fannins last attempt at serious journalism, and contains some of her best and most entertaining writing. Many of the quotations found in the earlier chapters have been taken from this source. In her final talk[328] she tried to decide what had been the colonialists' most important contribution to the ordinary Kenyan. It wasn't, she decided, Western education or even modern medicine or the civil service, the railway or electricity. Not communications or air transport, which although in one way had improved life enormously, in another way had made things worse, as busybodies could now descend from all quarters of the globe in a few days to complicate things and, usually, waste the time of people who would be much better employed getting on with their own jobs. No, in her opinion it had to be something more fundamental. She recalled a conversation she had had with a Turkana elder on the occasion of the great firework display given at Government house to celebrate the Prince of Wales' visit to Kenya in 1928. Dressed in his mud and mutton fat hair-do, carrying his spear and small wooden head-rest, he had spoken his mind and had gone straight to the heart of the matter.

> "About the Prince of Wales he said: Was that truly the King's eldest son? If so, why does he dress in khaki shirt and shorts like my young District Commissioner? A great Chief's eldest son wouldn't dress like that; he had his doubts. Next: Fireworks; very pretty, but give him the moon and stars every time. Fireworks fizzled out, he'd heard, you couldn't light them again; what was the use of that? But what he and all the other Turkana and desert tribes considered absolutely miraculous were the magic iron sticks in their camp near the Railway. There they were just sticking up out of the ground and yet you could get a rushing river of clean, fresh water from them, any time of the day and night. His tribe would like to buy a hundred of these iron sticks and they didn't care how many head of cattle they might cost; they'd be worth it. Also they'd like a couple of sacks of seeds, to grow for themselves those strange shiny transparent gourds full of sweet fizzy

> red, green and white juice; they'd nothing like that in Turkana. Well I thought then, who are we to assume unadorned Royalty and a firework display would be more impressive than an unfailing piped water supply and bottled Coca Cola."

She concluded by saying that she did not find Kenya a better or happier place despite all the so-called modern improvements and, blind to the bitterness that Settler-dominated colonial rule had engendered, she maintained that the 1920s and 1930s had been infinitely preferable for their general friendliness and good will among races.

CHAPTER SEVENTEEN

Politics and independence for Kenya

The three years immediately preceding Independence in 1963 was a period of intense activity for Katharine. In an effort to forget her loneliness after the death of her husband and to shut out her forebodings for the future, she drove herself harder than ever. Although during marriage their relationship had not seemed close, with husband and wife taking separate holidays and pursuing independent interests, there is no doubt she missed Charles greatly when he was gone. His quiet good sense had kept her more wayward tendencies in check, but now without his stabilising presence her personal life and monetary affairs began to slide out of control. She was deeply unhappy during the early 1960s. Not only had she lost her husband, but her whole life and all the principles she held dear were being turned topsy-turvy with the political upheavals in the country. By this time she was bitterly disillusioned by the British Government, whom she had seen break promise after promise and betray the trust of its most loyal supporters. Responsibilities were cast aside, duty shelved as the British rushed to rid themselves of the financial burden and political hot potato their once favoured colony, Kenya, had become. Katharine's trusting belief in the wise and benign rule of the British Government was rudely shattered; even her patriotism was shaken to the core.

1955-1959 in Kenya saw the swan song of the Colonial Office, when they once again wielded great power. The Settlers' wings had been clipped; the Colonial Official took control and guided Kenya toward power sharing and self-rule. However, like the Settlers, most of the colonial officials did not want change either. They did not want to lose their jobs. Consequently the training of Kenyan personnel in administration and local government proceeded very slowly. They pushed the timetable for eventual independence well back.[329]

With strict press laws still in operation, press releases from the information officer were the chief source of local news. Any official who spoke out of turn was summarily dismissed.[330] Kenya was ruled by bureaucrats, who kept the lid tightly closed. Sir Evelyn Baring, the aristocratic Governor, himself a former employee of the prestigious Indian civil service, went around reassuring the Settlers and calming their fears.[331] He assured them of British support; Kenya would become a fortress colony, providing a vital link in Britain's global defence network. As late as January 1959, Alan Lennox-Boyd the Secretary of State for the Colonies, on a tour of the White Highlands said: "I am unable to envisage a time when it will be possible for any British Government to surrender their ultimate responsibilities for the destinies and well-being of Kenya". Settler confidence was deliberately encouraged as the Settler population was the economic mainstay of the colony.

The lid came off in 1959 when the policy of slow steady change under the cautious management of the Colonial Office was blown apart by the scandal of the Hola Camp Massacre, which hit the British press in March. The knowledge that thousands of Mau Mau were still being kept in detention camps all over Kenya in conditions of penal servitude and undergoing brutal beatings sometimes resulting in death, shocked the world. Kenya suddenly came into the limelight. There were endless discussions in the British parliament and more pressure was put on for independence. Fearing another rebellion and reprisals by Mau Mau, the timetable was put forward for immediate self-rule. The Governor Sir Evelyn Baring was relieved and first Sir Patrick Renison and then Malcolm Macdonald was appointed to organise a quick and painless handover. However ill-prepared for self government Kenya might be, political considerations had forced the pace. In October 1959 the purchase of land in the White Highlands was opened to all races, then the restrictive press laws were repealed and detainees released. The Emergency was officially declared over by January 1960.

At the Lancaster House Conference held in London in February 1960, it was made clear to all delegates that Kenya was destined to become an African-ruled country and the claims of a handful of Europeans would not be allowed to stand in the way of African rule. (In 1960 it was estimated that there were roughly 60,000 European Settlers and about 6 million Africans.)[332] African delegates were offered 33 out of the 65 seats in the Legislative Assembly. The main Settler party, The United Party, refused to accept this, but eventually Michael Blundell the leader of the Liberal Party, The New Kenya Party,[333] supported the proposals of Iain Mcleod, the Minister of State for the Colonies, and yet another important constitutional change was ratified as Kenya took the final step towards an independent African government.

The Settler community in Kenya was appalled by the outcome of the Lancaster House Conference. Group Captain 'Puck' Briggs, leader of the United Party, went on the record as saying: "I regard the outcome of this conference as a deathblow to the European community in Kenya." The speaker of the Legislative Assembly, Sir Ferdinand Cavendish-Bentinck, resigned accusing the British Government of breaking its many pledges to the Settlers.[334] When Michael Blundell returned to Nairobi he was met by angry demonstrators, one of whom threw a bag of thirty silver pieces at his feet. He explained that he had acted to keep peace in Kenya and in the long term interests of all Kenyans, as no one wanted a resurgence of Mau Mau or a full scale civil war. Nevertheless many of the older Settlers regarded him as a traitor.

Olivia Rodwell, who was raised on a coffee plantation in Kiambu just north of Nairobi and lived through this unsettling period, explained that when the results of the Lancaster House Conference became known, the European community suffered a deep sense of shock. When they asked for guidance and assurance from government officials they received none. When they asked what to do and what provisions had been made for them in a post-independent Kenya, the officials could not reply. The only Government advice given was, wait and see, make sure you behave yourselves and keep out of trouble, then maybe you will be all right. Just as if, as Olivia said, they had been children asking awkward questions.[335]

Many Settlers left for South Africa, Rhodesia, Australia or went back to England, selling their farms at throwaway prices. The British Government bought one million acres in the former White Highlands for re-distribution. Houses and valuables were sold off in panic-selling and unscrupulous speculators made a killing. Those who stayed on felt great uncertainty and depression about their future. Many felt an overwhelming sense of abandonment. The Settlers, who had been the driving force of the colony, who had been encouraged by successive British Governments to come to Kenya and make it their home, to work ever harder and produce ever more, were now cast aside as expendable items, their usefulness forgotten, their efforts unrecognised. Even today many white Kenyans have ambivalent feelings towards Britain and find it hard to forget how they were 'sold out' by the Home Government, given false promises and then dumped.

In a letter dated October, 20, 1960, addressed to the editor of *The Times*, but apparently not published, Mrs Fannin spoke her mind on the subject.

> "Sir,
>
> The Prime Minister's fine phrases about the value of British settlers in Kenya and the Rhodesias, and 'Britain's obligations not merely of interest but of honour to them' are, as far as Kenya is concerned eight months too late. The time for them, backed by decisive action to allay any apprehension about the stability of Kenya's future was last February during the Lancaster House Conference, which instead, witnessed the sell-out of those same Kenya settlers, and other non-Africans, to noisy, importunate African nationalism. That sell-out directly started the economic blizzard which has since swept the Colony - and continues; so that trading conditions in Kenya are as depressed as those of the terrible slump of 1929-31. It also gratuitously embittered race relations to a degree unachieved by local bickerings of the past 30 years.
>
> "If before the Conference, the Prime Minister and his advisers had taken the elementary precaution of consulting agricultural and business interests in Kenya and the big banks they would have learnt that by last Autumn after the disastrous Mau Mau years… the whole colony was beginning to go ahead again.
>
> "In the light of what happened at Lancaster House one can only conclude there was no previous economic consultation; for in the imposed provisions

of the Conference we saw the loyalty and effort of Britons and other non-Africans during the past 60 years apparently judged expendable in as unworthy an example of appeasement and surrender to clamour, as any in the past.

"Thousands of Britons and other non-Africans have made Kenya their permanent home, and intend to stay, valued friends of all races and creeds. For some time we have realised that sooner or later majority rule would become inevitable so, quietly and genuinely, we have done what we could to improve inter-racial understanding to bridge the gaps between black and white. Despite Lancaster House that attitude still obtains, and we can of course be counted upon to help make any reasonable future Constitution work. But Kenya's tragedy is that so far, no African political leader of selfless integrity has arisen to merit unanimous respect and support either of his fellow-Africans or of the numerous long-established resident European, Arab, and Asian population. Until one does Kenya's economic prospects are unlikely to inspire confidence as a reasonable financial risk, or to attract from overseas that substantial investment which is absolutely essential if the Colony and its peoples are to progress.

"Sir Ferdinand Cavendish-Bentinck's selfless stand for the moral obligations of Britain's past pledges, his factual presentation of Kenya's economic plight, the disturbing flight of capital and catastrophic drop in local share values seems at last to have brought HM Government and its advisers partially to their senses. About time too; realistic thought and action in Westminster are eight months overdue! Even so it is discouraging to note how enjoyment of high office appears to blunt statesmen's inner recognition of the paramountcy of moral values. One could wish that in his speech about British settlers in Kenya and the Rhodesias, Mr MacMillan had said 'Britain's obligations

of honour, not merely of interest…' thereby putting the
moral obligation first - where it should be.[336]
Yours faithfully
Katharine Fannin"

A few British politicians of the time, for instance Lord Colyton, were genuinely sympathetic towards the Settlers' plight, but most were not. They were simply seen as a nuisance, an additional complication in the decolonisaton process, which was proving difficult enough.

One of the difficulties lay in the Northern Frontier District (NFD), which was largely populated by ethnic Somalis, who wanted to join an already independent (since 1960) Somalia. There was also a problem at the Coast. The coastal dilemma stemmed from the fact that the Coastal Strip, stretching from Kismayu in the North to Vanga in the South and extending 10 miles inland, still technically belonged to the Sultan of Zanzibar. The Coastal Strip was a British Protectorate rented from the Sultan and administered under the conditions of a treaty, which had been signed in 1895. However, an independent Kenya without an outlet to the sea was clearly not a viable proposition. Jomo Kenyatta, who had been released from prison in 1961 and was clearly the only leader with enough charisma to head the new government, refused to take on the country unless it included the Coastal Strip and the NFD. Nothing less would be acceptable.

However at the coast, the prospect of Kikuyu rule from Nairobi did not appeal to the majority. A group of Europeans headed by Major 'Jacko' Heath, Chairman of the Mombasa and Coast Province European Association (MACPEA), and Dick Cleasby, the European Reserved Member for Mombasa, got together with the leading Arabs and plotted to bring about an autonomous Coastal State known as Mwambao,[337] which would be ruled separately, having its own ministries, but recognise the suzerainty of the Sultan in Zanzibar. They approached the Sultan and sent a secret delegation to various countries in Arabia to seek approval and possible financial assistance. In 1961 a representative of Kenya's Coast Peoples Party (CPP),[338] Said Mohamed, submitted a memorandum to the Colonial Secretary in London formally requesting independence from Kenya for the Coastal Protectorate. As a result, Sir James Robertson was put in charge of a Commission of Enquiry into the Coastal Strip.

Hopes were raised, but when Omar Salim Bassadiq represented the case for Mwambao at the Lancaster House Conference for 1962, he came away bitterly disappointed. As Edward Rodwell reported in his column "Covering the Waterfront" in March 1962:[339]

"The lack of interest at the London Conference on the question of Mwambao must have caused gratification to the leaders of the Nationalist parties. I think it was all summed up in a remark made to me recently by a Nigerian minister: 'Jomo Kenyatta must win. The British Government gives in to the strongest.' We used to have a tradition of gunboats for the underdogs. Now might is always right."

The Sultan of Zanzibar, whose position was weakened with severe problems in Zanzibar, could only bow to superior pressure and issue the statement:

"The sultan has always said that the Coastal Strip people should live in harmony with the rest of the people of Kenya and that any decision reached on Kenya should be agreeable to the Coastal Strip people themselves and should not be detrimental to the political and economic structure of Kenya."[340]

Repeating the words an ancestor of his, Seyyid Hamid Bin Thuwain, had said once before in the face of British Imperial Demands, the Sultan said he was "like a little bird in the claws of a powerful eagle." In 1962, this final demand by the British deprived the sultan of his mainland possession.

Even if the prospect of Mwambao was dead, at the elections for 1963 at Mombasa and the Coast, the Kenya African Democratic Union (KADU), headed by the Giriama politician Ronald Ngala and the Union Leader Tom Mboya, did better than KANU, Jomo Kenyatta's predominantly Kikuyu party. Coastal voters favoured federalism (Majimbo), rather than centralism and although complete autonomy was clearly not possible, most people at the Coast voted for a regional solution. As Hyder Kindy explains, what most of the 'Mwambaoists' had wanted was not really to have their own independent Government, but to use the possibility as a bargaining counter. The Swahili and the other small tribes at the Coast, including the Europeans and Asians, feared that as minorities they would be discriminated against by larger groups, and would not have equal rights in a Kenya run by the Kikuyu, who many coastal people still equated with Mau Mau terrorists.[341] However, Kenyatta and his winning KANU party opposed both the idea of regionalism and separatism. Independent Kenya would have a strongly centralised government based in Nairobi.

Amongst her private papers Katharine Fannin kept a copy of the tenancy agreement between the British and the Sultan of Zanzibar, which had been drawn up in 1895. She felt the British Government's setting aside of the treaty and total disinterest in the Mwambao claim was yet another example of the bad faith shown by 'perfidious Albion.'

Along with Edward Rodwell, who had openly supported the idea of Mwambao and had even been offered a ministry in this proposed Shangri La at the Coast, as it was jokingly called by one up-country journalist of the time,[342] were numerous others who had nursed secret hopes for autonomy at the Coast. One of these was James Kirkman, the erudite and energetic archaeologist, whose excavations at Gedi in the 1950s had first excited international interest in the ancient Islamic settlements along the Kenyan Coast. (In 1960 he was in Mombasa excavating the Portuguese Fort, which was later opened as a museum and is now one of the most important tourist attractions of the Coast). He had many conversations with Katharine Fannin, who sat on the Advisory Committee for the Museum and whom he had first met in Cairo in 1942, when they had both worked for the Ministry of State. He had later worked for British Intelligence in Baghdad and was very pro-Arab. According to his wife, Dorothy Kirkman, Katharine would often come to dinner in Fort Jesus where the Kirkmans lived in a pleasant pink stucco house built into one corner of the Fort.[343] James Kirkman was an intellectual and a great talker and he and Katharine had much in common. Dorothy, who did the cooking, said she generally kept out of the heated academic and political discussions, but remembered on one occasion that Katharine gave her a Wedgewood teapot as a present. This was part of Katharine's original wedding trousseau, which she had brought to Kenya in 1926; Dorothy kept it in her house in Cambridge, England, until her death.

Besides her keen interest in the national political scene, Katharine was also deeply involved in local government. When the elevation of the Mayoress Mrs S H M Simpson to the Aldermanic Bench left a vacancy, Katharine was elected onto the Mombasa Municipal Council on June 21, 1961, as Councillor for European Ward 3 (Nyali, Bamburi, Shanzu, Three Hills and Kisauni) North Mainland. She polled 119 votes, easily beating her opponent Squadron Leader McCormick who polled 47. It was said she gained votes by taking the trouble to translate her election manifesto into Polish and Italian.

Katharine sat on the Municipal Council for two years, 1961-1963, troubled years when the European domination of the Council was constantly called into question. Out of the 40 members of Council, 15 were European, but despite their numerical minority they remained the most influential group and were often accused of 'ganging up' against the others. An Indian, Dr Rana, succeeded Mrs Simpson as mayor and he in turn was succeeded by an African, Mr Kayanda, in 1962. Katharine chaired the Health Committee, which she took on as her chief responsibility. During her tenure, she extended the Municipal Almshouse accommodation and her committee oversaw anti-malarial drainage schemes, collection of rubbish and supply of dustbins to home owners, building of new public toilets and the provision and training of a centralised midwifery service. Despite her efforts and tremendous dedication, the constant sniping and infighting amongst committee members made the meetings increasingly stressful.[344] She had particular trouble with one of the Councillors, Mohammed Jahazi,[345] an outspoken supporter of Africanisation who liked to rant on about Imperialists and their stooges, which annoyed Katharine considerably. The endless meetings of the Finance Committee was another embattled area, with the inevitable insinuations of dishonesty and favouritism in allocation of funds, all of which served to give Katharine an increasing distaste for the whole business. When on July 14, 1963, the Council held a large banquet to celebrate the elections and welcome Jomo Kenyatta as Prime Minister,[346] she wrote on the back of her invitation card:

"Sat at end table as far away from K and the rest of his Mau Mau crew as possible. Had Dick Cleasby on one side of me and Mussa Jetha on the other so enjoyed myself. A good lunch but most indifferent vin ordinaire."

Soon after that she resigned her seat. New elections were held giving the vote to a much wider section of the population as the Municipal Council entered yet another phase in its history and Mombasa became an African-ruled town.[347]

Sadly, the only other memorable occurrence of her time as councillor was her feud with the Bamburi Portland Cement Company. The company had bought a plot of land and had decided to put up cement silos next to her house at Mkomani. She opposed this fiercely on the grounds that the cement dust would pollute the area and disturb the residents, not to mention the cats. However, the industrialists won the day, but not before Katharine on behalf of the Municipal Council had exacted a promise from them that the landing stage would only be used for loading cement and no other commodity as she did not wish to see her back garden turned into an extension of the port. She kept a strict eye out for any infringement of this agreement and nursed a grudge against Dr Mandl, managing director of Bamburi Cement Factory, who had spoiled the pleasant ambience and outlook of her home. Not long after the death of Charles, the Captain of one of the Southern Line ships, which carried the Bamburi cement, offered her a free trip to Dar es Salaam, to cheer her up. This she accepted, but when she discovered the ship was carrying cargo other than cement, she became furiously angry and sent Dr Mandl a cheque for the estimated cost of the trip and a letter accusing him of breaking the agreement. The whole matter was much publicised, causing him great offence, and they exchanged letters of recrimination. The extra cargo turned out to be empty paper bags for putting the cement in and machinery for the new cement factory being built at Dar es Salaam. Eventually, however, the matter was smoothed over and Mandl, a charming Swiss, produced a large chocolate axe to make amends and declare the hatchet well and truly buried.[348]

There is no doubt that Katharine at this period became increasingly difficult to deal with. She was short tempered, impatient, quick to take offence and had no time for fools. She suffered from high blood pressure and seldom felt well. Worry over money was continually at the back of her mind as she struggled to make ends meet. Charles had left her the house in his will but probate took two years and it was not legally in her possession until the end of 1962.[349] By 1963, when she tried to sell, the state of the market was so depressed that the value of her property had dropped by over 60% and even then it took her a year to find a buyer. In the end she sold out for £5,000 to an insurance broker.

Although Charles Fannin had held a good position in the Colonial Office, he had never been a rich man. The modest government pension he received in retirement was eroded by inflation and to supplement this he had worked as a surveyor right up until his death. Katharine Fannin had no idea of money management and without his input her financial situation grew steadily worse. The pre-Independence slump virtually wiped out her locally invested savings and she had to rely on precious reserve capital in order to live. At one stage she took a temporary job at the bank to pay off her overdraft, and later took on the position of chief supervisor and examiner for Pitmans School of shorthand and typing in Mombasa. This brought in some cash, although the payments were irregular. In 1964 she sent antique furniture and house contents for auction. To compound this sorry state of affairs, her health gave out and in 1964 she spent long periods in Mombasa Hospital suffering from dangerously high levels of blood pressure and hernia problems, which further depleted her slender resources. For Katharine Fannin the years leading up to independence in Kenya proved disastrous, bringing both personal heartbreak and financial ruin.

CHAPTER EIGHTEEN
Final decline and death

After leaving her spacious bungalow with the splendid view overlooking Mombasa old town, Katharine moved to a small two-storey house on the mainland north of the bridge in the area known as Kisauni or Freretown. Her house was situated on the creek, well off the beaten track, where few Europeans penetrated. Along with her came her cats, her Giriama servant Hamisi, her faithful ancient typewriter and the treasures and mementos she could not bear to part with. It was a sad state of affairs for a woman who had enjoyed the glitter and pomp of public life and had mixed with the great and mighty.

Occasionally Mombasa residents glimpsed her driving her battered black Rover car, which rattled and choked and was held together with pieces of string. Or she was seen on the roadside bending over to feed and comfort a stray cat. It is extraordinary how many of her former acquaintances cannot remember this last period of her life. It was as if for most people the increasingly portly woman simply vanished from their view.

Kenya's first years of independence proved better than anyone had expected. The Settlers' worst fears were allayed at the famous meeting at Nakuru[350] when Jomo Kenyatta spoke to them and urged them all to stay on and join with other Kenyans to work for the benefit of Kenya and show the other countries of the world that different racial groups can live and work together. "Continue to farm your land well and you will get all the encouragement and protection of the government," he promised. The grateful farmers took him at his word and became among his most faithful supporters. In 1962 it had been calculated that the Settler community produced 80% of all Kenya's exports. Kenyatta understood what a vital component this was for the country's economy and with great shrewdness and humanity he encouraged both Europeans and Asians to become citizens and to continue to manage the big farms and industries which provided the income needed for progress.[351] The Settlers could no longer dictate how the country was run, but they were still needed to supply the wealth. With that not inconsiderable role allotted to them, Kenyans of all races took heart and joined in willingly to help make independent Kenya a stable and successful country. Teachers and trainers were also welcomed as Kenya transformed itself into a modern state with all the necessary infrastructure and attendant parastatal bodies, fully owned and operated by Kenyans.[352]

Katharine, ever eager to do her bit, joined the Economist Intelligence Unit (EIU). This was an international market research company owned by the *Economist* weekly magazine. In the 1960s market research had become big business and the EIU published quarterlies reporting on economic conditions throughout the world and sold commercial information regarding markets, etc. The East African branch was coordinated by June Knowles, the young wife of Oliver Knowles, one of several British colonial officials, who stayed on to provide their expertise in the smooth transition to a wholly Kenyan administration. June operated out of her home in Nairobi and recruited Katharine Fannin in 1965 as the Mombasa stringer. She found Katharine a most valuable assistant as her familiarity with the Coastal area, her fluency in Swahili and her contacts with local businessmen, proved very useful in gathering information. June remembers that questions had to be narrowed down as Katharine tended to go off at a tangent.[353]

Katharine compiled extensive reports between 1965 and 1969 for the EIU. In 1965 and in 1967 she did comprehensive surveys on the production and export of salt at the Coast. In 1966 she compiled import figures and data on the types of woollens and yarns used for men's suitings, which included research into the main merchants and retailers operating in Mombasa and a separate section indicating the potential for growth in the market for men's suits. The last survey she did, for which she was paid £50 in February 1969, looked at the market for clocks and watches and listed in detail the main outlets in Mombasa. This report included a confidential section on smuggling and counterfeit production.[354] Katharine's background as a journalist, her natural curiosity and flair for getting information from people gave her access to detailed material few other people would have managed to find.

This job revealed the clue to her success as a spy. As June Knowles recalled, Katharine was the rare kind of person who could persuade an Asian businessman to open up his safe and show her all his stock and reveal his closely guarded secrets of supply and delivery. She was wonderful at making people talk and from her manner no one would guess her questions had serious import. No one could possibly think she was a tax officer or a customs official, or even a businessperson about to set up a rival firm, so they answered her questions openly. One can picture Katharine at this period as an overweight and rather shabby 'Miss Marple' pottering in and out of the Mombasa shops asking seemingly harmless questions. She enjoyed her work as it got her out and about, meeting and talking to the shopkeepers and businessmen of Mombasa, most of them Asian, whom she had known for many years. June Knowles' contact with Katharine was almost entirely by letter but she does remember meeting her on two occasions for lunch, once at the Nairobi Club and once at the Mombasa Club. Her main impression, recalled after many years, was of a scatterbrained but colourful character who proved an entertaining lunch companion and had a decided ability for market research.

June Knowles left Kenya in 1969 and the EIU was taken under the wing of East African Engineering Consultants. Katharine's new contact was a Mr Symes. One last letter in the Fannin papers, dated June 7, 1969, is addressed to W J Symes Esq. Her trusty old typewriter, now in need of major servicing, no longer obeyed her instructions and leapt madly about as she explained how she loved meeting people and would be glad to be of service and would be more than happy to do something to keep her wits from "rusting solid." This was the letter of a lonely but still entirely sane woman. The rot, it appears, started soon after this, perhaps triggered off by the death of her faithful Giriama 'boy' – Hamisi – who had been with her for almost 40 years. He had become her companion and she depended on him to run the household. After his death she could not find anyone to work for her who suited her, and her house, never very tidy or clean, grew more chaotic and the cats more uncontrolled. She could not manage and after another illness, suffered a complete nervous collapse.

From the end of 1969, Katharine Fannin dropped out of the Mombasa social scene. She became 'a poor white,' whom no one wanted to know. Her eccentricities, which previously had been mildly amusing talking points, now became unacceptable and anti-social. Her shapeless figure in 'reach-me-down' frocks with missing buttons and her swollen feet in cracked shoes were viewed with distaste, while her untidy house swarming with cats was considered a health hazard.

Desmond and Phyllida Forbes-Cockell are two of the few people who remember Katharine from this last phase. Desmond had first met Katharine in 1954, when she came into his office and introduced herself suggesting they were distantly related. It turned out that Katharine's mother's sister, Aunt Lena, who had married Cedric Forbes-Cockell, was indeed Desmond's aunt by marriage. Their paths did not cross again until 1959, when Desmond was working again in Mombasa as the Shipping Director for Smith Mackenzie, the leading shipping agency in town. Phyllida, whom he married in 1965, was the daughter of George Nicol, a previous Chairman of Smith Mackenzie, who had spent much of his working life in the shipping offices of Zanzibar and Mombasa.

Desmond remembers originally visiting Katharine at the house at Mkomani and taking a film of her feeding her cats and monitor lizards, which he took back to England to show his Aunt Lena, who was still alive. Aunt Lena was not at all interested to see the pictures of her niece and simply muttered, "Disgusting," and turned away. Evidently she still had not forgotten or forgiven Katharine for her behaviour in 1926.

Desmond, however, back in Mombasa saw quite a bit of Katharine. He acted as one of her proposers during the Municipal elections of 1961 and in her diaries for 1962-1964 there are frequent mentions of 'dear Desmond,' whom she had quite clearly adopted as nearest kith and kin. Later when the Forbes-Cockells lived in the grand Smith Mackenzie house 'San Jose' on the ridge above the Mombasa Golf course and Katharine was in financial difficulties living at Kisauni, Phyllida invited Katharine together with other elderly Mombasa residents to their regular Christmas Eve dinners. Katharine must have especially appreciated this as the December 24 also happened to be her birthday.[355]

According to Phyllida, after Katharine's mental breakdown, she rather hoped the Forbes-Cockells would invite her to live with them, as they had no children and plenty of space. This was of course impractical as Katharine was not an easy person at the best of times and in her deteriorated mental condition would have been an impossible burden.

Her own house by this time was in a filthy and dilapidated state. The roof leaked and according to eye-witnesses it was an ordeal going to visit her as the place was dirty and stank of cats. She had run out of money, could no longer pay the rent or support herself. The KSPCA, of which she had been a founder member in Kenya, were called in to dispose of her 50 cats and Katharine was taken first to the Mombasa Hospital and then transferred to the Sunset Lodge, an Old Peoples Home run by the Salvation Army.[356] She had written about this home when it was first opened in 1954 in her column for the *Kenya Weekly News*.[357] Little did she realise she herself would one day be a resident.

Unfortunately her condition did not improve and she was returned to the Mombasa Hospital. She had the fixed impression she had been bewitched by one her staff she had sacked for stealing and she was most distressed about her cats, which had all been put down by the KSPCA. After the removal and murder of her cats, she became understandably hostile and negative and her mental condition rapidly deteriorated.[358] It was suggested she be sent to Nairobi for electric shock treatment. Phyllida Forbes-Cockell drove her up to Nairobi with a young doctor and remembered the journey as a nightmare. Katharine was by this time totally unresponsive to her surroundings and could not even be roused from her torpor when a herd of elephants crossed the road right in front of the car.

Phyllida delivered Katharine to the Nairobi Hospital, where members of charitable bodies visited her regularly. She received electric shock treatment, but it was unsuccessful and Katharine remained in Nairobi Hospital until she died on November 27, 1970.[359] The League of Mercy tended to her final days and after her death made all the necessary arrangements and sent her cremated ashes down to Mombasa. Her funeral service was held on December 1, 1970, at the All Saints Cathedral, Nairobi and she was honoured with a long but inaccurate obituary notice in the *Standard* newspaper the following day.[360] The Forbes-Cockells arranged for a small service to be said in Mombasa and her ashes were buried in her husband's grave in the European cemetery in Mnazi Moja Road, near the Mombasa Sports Club and the cricket ground he had enjoyed so much.[361]

After Katharine's death Phyllida had the sad task of disposing of Katharine's house contents at Kisauni. She turned out the rusted tin trunks, which contained bundles of stamps, a collection of fans, quantities of books and an old fur coat, which fell to pieces. Everything was in a terrible condition, badly damaged by humidity and eaten away by insects, rendering the stamps and books, some of which were rare and valuable items, almost worthless. Lofty Davis, the one time engineer of Nyali Estates, and his wife Margaret, who by the time of Katharine's death had retired and moved to South Africa, were the main beneficiaries of her will. They had been neighbours and had looked after her when she first became ill. At their instigation the better pieces of furniture were shared out among those who had known her and the rest were sold at auction and the proceeds donated to charity.

In the Forbes-Cockells' pleasant retirement house in England stands a Lamu glass fronted cabinet, which belonged to Katharine Fannin and came from the house at Kisauni. Elegantly carved and graciously proportioned, it must have once displayed Katharine's most treasured possessions. Now it houses an array of heavy silver anklets and silver ornaments, mementos of the Forbes-Cockells' long connection with Zanzibar and the East African Coast. I was also shown a small tin medicine chest, for taking on safari, complete with original bottles and bandages, and a canteen of bone-handled fruit knives with the original initial 'B' embossed in silver on the lid, carefully picked out – the last remaining treasures of the vast trousseau that had accompanied a naive young girl across the sea to Kenya in 1926.

Endnotes

NOTES TO CHAPTER ONE

1 *Mombasa Times*, December 24, 1949. As it was her birthday, she decided to treat her readers to some autobiographical details and reminiscences of Christmas days in India and England.

2 India Office Records (IOR), Bengal Ecclesiastical Records & Returns N-1-303-62. The baptism entry reads: Dec. 31, 1902, born Dec 24, Katharine Mary, Female, to William & Maude Trood, Dooars, Teaplanter. Church of Scotland.

3 *Mombasa Times*, December 24, 1949.

4 IOR Bengal Ecclesiastical Records & Returns, N-1-463-266. This burial entry reads: Trood William, August 29, 1922, aged 57 Tea planter: cause of death: heart failure. Church of England, buried in the Military Cemetery of Fort William, Bengal in the archdeaconry and diocese of Calcutta.

5 B C Ghose: The Development of Tea Industry in the district of Jalpaiguri 1869-1968, (Calcutta), 1970.

6 *Mombasa Times*, December 24, 1949.

7 IOR Bengal Ecclesiastical Records and Returns N-1-403-261. This burial entry reads: Trood, Maude Elizabeth Jan 11, 1915, aged 39 cause of death: intestinal obstruction. Church of England buried in the Military Cemetery of Fort William Bengal in the archdeaconry and diocese of Calcutta.

8 *Mombasa Times*, October 17, 1950.

9 A dhoolie was a simple litter or palanquin made of cane and filled with cushions, it was apparently not very comfortable.

10 IOR Bengal Ecclesiastical Records and Returns, N-1-334-78. This baptism entry reads: July 27, 1906, born 1904, William Geoffrey, Male, to William and Maude Elizabeth Trood, Dooars, Tea planter. Church of Scotland.

11 Patrick French (1994): Younghusband, the Last Great Imperial Adventurer (London) p.8

12 *Mombasa Times*, October 17, 1950. This article was devoted to the subject of relations and contains some very revealing material.

13 The spacious and solid Victorian house in Exton still stands. It originally had a large garden with tennis court and vegetable patch,

but the land has been subdivided and built over and the house renamed 'Elbowacre.' (Information from Sheila Unwin) Katharine recalled playing in the attics on rainy days with her cousins. See: *Mombasa Times*, July 12, 1951.

14 *Mombasa Times*, August 30, 1951.

15 *Mombasa Times*, October 17, 1950.

16 The life of Sir Francis Younghusband (1863-1942) shows some interesting parallels with that of Katharine Fannin and the families may possibly have been acquainted. Roughly the same age as Katharine's father, Younghusband was educated at Clifton College and was the son of a tea planter who lived at Murree just north of Rawalpindi. As a child he was brought up by aunts in England, who treated him very strictly, and he had an abnormally close relationship with his eldest sister. After school at the age of 19 he went out as a soldier to India where his interest in adventurous travel on the Northern Frontier and his expertise in mapping and surveying led him to become one of the major players of the Great Game. However, coming from a relatively humble background and without personal funds to cushion him, the promise of his early career faltered and he returned to England, where he took up writing. During World War I he set up a patriotic movement called Fight for Right. In later life inspired by his religious experiences in the high mountains of the Himalayas and Tibet he became a mystic and preached a doctrine of free love and life after death. His daughter Eileen was born in the same year as Katharine. She dedicated her life to helping the poor and never married.

17 *Mombasa Times*, November 25, 1950.

18 This was Leonard Atkinson, who rose to became a senior curator in the Public Records Office (PRO), and was later to help Katharine acquire old prints and maps of Ethiopia to take with her on her second Ethiopian journey, see Chapter 9.

19 Article on relations, *Mombasa Times*, October 17, 1950.

20 William Trood left an estate of over 200,000 rupees which was bequeathed entirely to his second wife, with one proviso which read, "subject on provision being made by her for the education of my children Katharine Mary Trood and William Geoffrey Trood until they reach the age of 21 years," IOR Wills & Probates L/AG/34/29/168. Katharine's mother had made a will in 1911 in Exeter but for some reason probate

was delayed until 1925, ten years after her death. She left a small estate valued at just over 1,000 rupees and her jewellery to her daughter, IOR Wills & Probates L/AG/34/29/170.

21 Information from Desmond Forbes-Cockell, son of Cedric's younger brother.

22 This was a standard arrangement in East Africa at the time. See Elspeth Huxley, **Out in the Midday Sun** (London) 1985, p.10.

23 First long letter home, written between September 10-22, 1926.

NOTES TO CHAPTER TWO

24 The following quotation comes from part I of the series which was broadcast by the Kenya Broadcasting Service (KBS) on November 2,1960.

25 British India Steamship Navigation Company, always abbreviated B I, had many passenger ships plying the East Africa run.

26 By 1960 Kilindini had become the busiest and most modern port on the East African Coast, overtaking Zanzibar, Dar es Salaam and Tanga.

27 The Palace Hotel, now three storeyed and renamed the Castle Hotel, is still in existence at the top of Moi Avenue (Kilindini Road), but the Catholic White Father's Mission has been replaced by shops and office blocks.

28 Elspeth Huxley, **Out in the Midday Sun** (London, 1985), 49.

29 First letter home, dated September 10-22, 1926.

30 Told to Phyllida Forbes-Cockell by her mother.

31 Information from Edward Rodwell.

32 Phyllida said Katharine had at one time many letters from George Buchanan, but none of them survive in her papers.

33 Elspeth Huxley, **Out in the Midday Sun** (London, 1985), 77. "Clarence Buxton's own story ended sadly. Despite his attractive wife and their four children his eye roved and he was named co-respondent in a suit for divorce heard in Nairobi. The wronged husband was another official, but very much junior in rank and status - in fact the government analyst. This raised some unkind smiles, since Clarence not only had rather grand connections (son of a baronet) but had been looked upon

as a model of rectitude. Such lapses were severely frowned upon in the Colonial Service. Clarence was not dismissed, but transferred to Palestine, the next worst thing." Clarence left the Colonial Service after two years in Palestine, married the former wife of the government analyst and took up farming. Maeve Buxton in 1995 was still living at Vipingo, on the Coast just north of Mombasa, where she and her husband, Clarence, retired after selling their up-country farm at Limuru shortly before Independence.

34 1960 Broadcast Series, Pt 1, ibid.

35 In 1926 the European population of Mombasa was 869.

36 Information from daughter-in-law, Nicole Benazeth, living in Mombasa.

37 Robert Foran, **A Cuckoo in Kenya** (London, 1962).

38 The original meaning of a Boma, was an enclosure to protect domestic animals from wild predators, or an improvised shelter, usually made of thorn bushes, where hunters sat vigil. The term is used in Kenya to describe the headquarters of the colonial administration in an outlying district.

39 Letter to her uncle, dated September 10-22, 1926.

40 Small settlement at the coast a few miles from Kwale, now a beach resort.

41 Letter to uncle, September 10-22, 1926

42 Ibid

43 Ibid

44 Elspeth Huxley, **Out in the Midday Sun** (London, 1985), 5.

45 C.J. Duder, "Men of the Officer Class - The participants in the 1919 Soldier Settlement Scheme in Kenya," African Affairs (Oxford, 1993), 69-87.

46 In her "Memories of the Twenties and Thirties in Kenya," Part 2, broadcast on KBS November 16, 1960, Katharine recalled that when Charles first came out as a soldier settler, he was befriended by the famous Settler pioneer A.C. Hoey who tried to teach him the rudiments of farming. He then travelled to Londiani on the Uasin Gishu Plateau, where his farm was, by ox-wagon. Here he found the game so thick on the ground that he had to push his way through solid herds of kongoni, eland, zebra and impala, and the local jest was that there was more game than grass. Soon realising that he had absolutely no bent for farming it

was fortunate that in 1920 he met A.G. Baker, the Surveyor General at a cricket match, who offered to employ him as part of his surveying team.

NOTES TO CHAPTER THREE

47 "Memories of the Twenties and Thirties in Kenya," Pt 3, KBS, November 30, 1960.

48 That raised part of Nairobi, above Nairobi River, where George Whitehouse, the railway administrator built his house overlooking the railway sidings. In the 1920s it was the fashionable part of Nairobi, where all the senior government officials and the Governor lived. Now called Museum Hill.

49 **Out in the Midday Sun**, 49.

50 "Memories of the Twenties and Thirties in Kenya," Pt 3, KBS, November 30, 1960.

51 Letter to her Uncle dated February 8 -13, 1927.

52 "After the wagon came the motor car, at first the 'box body' loaded up with spades, axes and chains, with spare springs and gaskets, with cans of petrol and water, with iron rations, first aid kits, dogs and guns and other equipment needed to cope with anything from a flooded river to a charging rhino." Elspeth Huxley, **Nine Faces of Kenya** (London,1990), 60.

53 Letter to Uncle dated January 12, 1928.

54 Ibid

55 Ibid

56 Letter to her Uncle dated March 11, 1928.

57 This formal invitation headed with a crest and the words "To meet the Commission," reads: "The Governor and The Honorable Lady Grigg request the pleasure of Miss Trood's company at a Garden party on Wednesday 15th February, 4.30 o'clock, Government House, an answer is requested addressed to the Aide-de-Camp in waiting."

58 Letter to her Uncle dated March 11, 1928.

59 Letter to her Uncle dated May 14, 1928.

60 Ibid

61 Ibid

62 Letter to her uncle dated May 22, 1928.

63 Letter to her Uncle dated March 11, 1928.

64 Letter to her Uncle dated October 7, 1928. "I've been in such a rush of interesting things recently.... what with State Balls with the Princes and Government House and assemblies of 2000 native chiefs....I seem to be having all the luck in this colony don't I?"

65 Letters dated February 6, 1929 and April 29, 1929.

66 Letter to Uncle dated April 29, 1929.

67 Uncle John had a habit of putting a pencil line through the parts of Katharine's letters he disagreed with, or annoyed him. Significantly there is a pencil line scoring out the section where Katharine warns her uncle of Charles' impending visit. Letter dated March 11, 1928.

68 According to Desmond Forbes-Cockell, who also remembers seeing a wedding photograph showing Katharine looking unusually slim and elegant. The Church of Scotland is less strict than the Church of England on marriage of divorcés.

69 I was unable to track down a record of their marriage either in Somerset House or the Public Record Office, as the section for Kenya 1924 -30 is unaccountably missing. Though one of my informants speculated the Fannins may not have been formally married, this seems unlikely as any irregular liaison among the European community was an immediate source of gossip and it would have been almost impossible to keep such a matter secret. It is more likely that by now Katharine had realised she had made a mistake in promising to marry Charles, as there were many far more eligible men to be had in Nairobi, but although she regretted it she had determined to make the best of things as there was no other way, if she wanted to remain in Kenya. Her hopes for financial independence had received a severe setback with her failure to overturn her father's will.

NOTES TO CHAPTER FOUR

70 Shimo La Tewa in literal translation means the Rock Cod's Hole.

71 Takaungu is a corruption of the Swahili nataka ungu, meaning I want to go back, dating from its days as a trading port.

72 Even 30 years later, in 1995, The Boma, or the 'Old DO's Building' as it is more usually called these days, remains the same despite increasing dilapidation. There is a move afoot to gazette it and restore it

as a museum for Malindi, but at present, although the DO no longer lives there, it still contains government offices.

73 "Memories of the Twenties and Thirties in Kenya" Pt 4, KBS, December 14, 1960.

74 Letter to Uncle dated February 1, 1931.

75 Ibid

76 Ibid

77 Information taken from letter to Uncle dated March 10, 1930. Sefu came from Mwanza and had been with the German army and then the British Carrier Corps in World War I, but even these experiences had not prepared him for an English Memsahib.

78 "Nowadays people can have little idea of the tremendous authority and personal standing (heshima is the Swahili term) of those old Mnyaparas. You worked through them and their word was law. No porter thought of questioning it. Such a headman could make or break any safari. In his youth Jascho had himself twice walked from Mombasa to Uganda and back carrying his 60 pound loads as a member of those huge foot caravans of the 1890s. He'd helped to fight off Maasai attacks in the Kedong, and seen Europeans and fellow-Africans fall out and die by the way of illness and exposure. He'd become an incomparable headman, who served the Government faithfully for over forty years. He's dead now; of all things, knocked down and killed by a lorry in Mombasa." "Memories of the Twenties and Thirties in Kenya," Pt 4, KBS, December 14, 1960.

79 "Memories of the Twenties and Thirties in Kenya," Pt 2, KBS, November 16, 1960.

80 See Charles Chevenix Trench: **Men who Ruled Kenya**; The Kenya Administration 1892 - 1963 (1993, London). Only one chapter in the entire book mentions the Coast and that concentrates on Lamu, which was renowned for its eccentrics. The chapter is entitled 'Sloth Belt.'

81 This still stands and is now the headquarters of the Kenyan Navy.

82 Letter to uncle dated November 21, 1930.

83 "Memories of the Twenties and Thirties in Kenya," Pt 2, KBS, November 16, 1960.

84 Letter to Uncle dated August 4, 1930.

85 Ibid

86 Ibid

87 It is perhaps significant that this act of German provocation should have taken place in Tanga, which was where one of the most embarrassing and complete British defeats in World War I took place. Tanga in present day Tanzania is situated close to the Kenya border and in 1930 was a much busier port than it is today.

88 Letter to Uncle dated August 4, 1930.

89 IOR Wills & Probates. Ethel M. Trood left an estate in excess of 225,000 rupees mostly invested in shares.

90 Letter to Uncle dated February 1, 1931.

NOTES TO CHAPTER FIVE

91 Charles was promoted from an Assistant District Surveyor to a District Surveyor in 1932.

92 Karen Blixen, **Out of Africa** (1937).

93 According to the government census of 1932, the population of Mombasa consisted of 930 Europeans, 10,860 Indians, 1,077 Goans, 6,699 Arabs, 458 others, and 20,670 Africans.

94 Once situated on Mbarak Hinaway Road, Old Town Mombasa, this clinic no longer exists. The recently modernised building, now rented to the National Museum, once housed the office of Old Town Conservation Project and has residential flats above. The full-length portrait of Sir Ali bin Salim, which once hung on the wall in the entrance, has been transferred to Fort Jesus Museum.

95 Freretown, founded in 1874 and named after Sir Bartle Frere, closed down in 1934.

96 From a letter written to J.D. Mckean, District Commissioner, Mombasa, September 16, 1937.

97 Letter to Uncle dated September 8, 1933.

98 Ibid

99 The Wakf Commissioners who administered many of the mosques and religious properties in Mombasa and held the purse strings of the charitable donations given in the name of Sunni Islam, were an influential body in the town. As a religious organisation, which was not tied to the Colonial administration, they obviously disliked being told what to do and how to spend their money by the wife of a minor colonial official.

100 Two handwritten letters dated February 13 and 14, 1933.

101 Letter to Uncle dated September 8, 1933.

102 Handwritten note of interview with Mr. Foster at 4.15 p.m, on May 6 at his house. She considered the trouble was caused by Pedraza and Bahamadi, who she called mischief makers. R. Pedraza worked in the District Commissioner's office in Mombasa and Bahamadi was an Arab who looked after the temporary almshouse scheme on behalf of Sir Ali bin Salim. Both men obviously disliked Katharine Fannin and found her overbearing and refused to work with her.

103 Letter to Uncle.

104 Full page article on the opening of the Almshouse in *The Coast Guardian*, September 11, 1937. See also the *Mombasa Times*, September 11, 1937, article entitled "Ceremonies in Mombasa. H.E. Opens New Almshouse."

105 The Governor unveiled a bust erected in memory of Allidina Visram on the same day.

106 1937 articles ibid. *The Coast Guardian* article came in for particularly bitter attack.

107 "Caring for the Aged and Infirm in Mombasa," *Mombasa Times*, November 26, 1962, report on the history of the Mombasa Almshouse.

108 Information from Edward Rodwell who as a young and unmarried man in Mombasa remembers seeing Mrs Fannin in action, chaperoning the girls - too well.

109 This article and photograph, found in the Fannin papers, unfortunately is undated, but the interview probably took place after September 1936, by which time she was living in Nairobi.

NOTES TO CHAPTER SIX

110 No letters from Katharine survive from this period, but there are one or two photographs taken of this safari amongst the Fannin papers, which show that Charles Fannin must have been employed in the Rift Valley where considerable road building was taking place. There is also a letter from Charles to Uncle John dated November 23, 1936, where he describes surveying an area of 500 square miles of arid and mountainous terrain and complains about the difficulties he had in setting up triangulation points. Unfortunately he does not mention the exact

location of his survey or why it was carried out, though his report no doubt is available somewhere in the archives of the Kenyan mapping department.

111 See Fannin papers for records of committee meetings, etc.

112 The *East African Standard*, weekend edition October 1936: Article on "Value of the Guide Movement" and "Girl Guide Ball."

113 Dated May 3-5, 1938.

114 Letter to Uncle dated May 3-5, 1938.

115 Anecdote told to author by Edward Rodwell.

116 Letter from Charles Fannin to Uncle John, dated July 24, 1938.

117 Ibid

118 Letter to Uncle dated May 3-5, 1938.

119 December 6, 1934, fighting broke out at Wal Wal.

120 Eritrea had been an Italian colony since 1885 and Somalia since 1889.

121 This body was the fore-runner of the United Nations.

122 Laval's dream was to give the Germans a free hand to crush the Soviet Union while keeping Hitler and Mussolini apart to preserve the French balance of power. The British Government at this stage also were more interested in preventing the spread of Bolshevism and had not fully recognised the dangers inherent in the Fascist and Nazi political systems. In 1934 Russia rather than Germany or Italy was viewed as the more serious enemy

123 At one stage the British suggested offering British Somaliland to Selassie if he would agree ceding territory to Italy, while the French proposed ceding Djibouti to the Italians if they would give up their designs in Abyssinia. Both suggestions were unacceptable. Robert Rhodes James: Anthony Eden, (London 1986) p 142,149.

124 This was the first time that the method of sanctions, so popular nowadays, was used in an international dispute to try and prevent conflict.

125 Letter from M D Kampf Ltd, dated September 10, 1938: "In this connection we would like to mention that we do not advise Mrs Fannin to make the journey to Addis Abeba from Mogadiscio as this is to be undertaken either by motor car or lorry, there being no railway between these two places. Also the distance from Mogadiscio to Addis Abeba is considerable and the journey rather hazardous. Besides, your client will

be required to procure permission from the Governor of Addis Abeba before she can enter Addis Abeba. From the above difficulties, you will please realise that such a journey will not be advisable."

126 This was indeed to happen in 1941.

127 Dated October 18, 1938, the letter is marked secret in red.

128 Letter dated November 4, 1938.

NOTES TO CHAPTER SEVEN

129 Foreign Office Correspondence File PRO F.O. 371/22030.

130 PRO FO 371/23382.

131 The letter addressed to Sir Bernard Reilly, dated October 29, 1938, survives in its original envelope amongst her papers.

132 Italo Zappoli, Royal Italian Consul General, Nairobi, to the Governor of Somaliland, dated November 1, 1938.

133 This elderly lady was much respected by the Somalis for her kind and charitable acts and she was popularly known as the 'Mother of Somaliland.'

134 First letter posted from Belet Uen November 10, 1938.

135 Dated April 30, 1939.

136 *Sunday Post*, April 30, 1939.

137 Letter dated November 13, 1938.

138 First Report, p. 2/3 & 30/31.

139 First Report p. 29. Francesco Savio Caroselli was Governor of Somalia 1937-1940.

140 Italian East Africa was divided into 5 provinces (Governatorate), which were subdivided into numerous areas large and small under the administration of commissioners, residents and vice-residents. Separate from these was the Independent province of Addis Ababa, where the Governor General resided.

141 A guidebook for Ethiopia was brought out in end 1938 and there is a letter in the Foreign Office Correspondence files (ref: F.O. 371/23377) reporting that Count Ciano wished to present one to Mrs Fannin. However, as this is not mentioned in the Fannin papers, she presumably never received her copy.

142 Information from Dictionary of National Biography (D.N.B.) Also see section on Henry Salt, R. Pankhurst: **Travellers in Ethiopia**

(London, 1965). Pankhurst says Salt was the first traveller to describe the country since the time of James Bruce, but his travels were limited to the Northern province of Tigre and his interests confined to the promotion of trade. See also: Deborah Manley and Peta Ree: **Henry Salt, Artist, Traveller, Diplomat, Egyptologist** (London, 2001).

143 First Report, p. 33. In the Abyssinian Campaign of 1941 he defended Gondar and held out against the Allies longest of all.

144 FO 371/23382 contains telegrams sent from the consul in Harar in cypher to FO in London about build up of military, March, 1939. Robert Eldon Ellison was a career diplomat, who came originally from Ireland, near Dublin. He had a great interest in butterflies and worked closely with his boyhood friend and fellow butterfly enthusiast, Philip Graves, the writer, journalist and later editor of *The Times*. After the war he was posted to Panama.

145 First Report, p. 36 "I saw a great deal of him and judged him to be an engaging, but entirely unreliable Neapolitan. Perhaps one could call him an Italian 'Vicar of Bray,'"

146 The *Sunday Post*, June 11, 1939.

147 Letter dated November 24-26 written aboard *SS Sandro* off Massawa.

148 Ibid

149 Ibid

NOTES TO CHAPTER EIGHT

150 Information from letter dated November 24-26, on board *SS Sandro* off Massawa.

151 *Corriera della Sera*, December 3, 1938.

152 Saturday/Sunday edition of *Il Piccolo*, December 3/4, 1938.

153 Letter to Charles Fannin dated December 13-16, 1938.

154 Ibid

155 Ref: FO 371/22030.

156 Letter dated December 13-16, 1938.

157 This mistaken version of the facts had appeared first in the Italian newspapers - "Salt became my grandfather in some papers and my uncle (1810!) in others." Letter to Charles ibid.

158 Letter to Charles Fannin dated December 29, 1938.

159 Information from letter to Charles Fannin dated January 10, 1939.

160 Ibid

161 She was often described by the Italians in their press as "Buona amica d'Italia e intrepida viaggiatrice." Katharine particularly liked the intrepid voyager bit!

NOTES TO CHAPTER NINE

162 See front page article *The Daily Telegraph* and *Morning Post*, January 12, 1939, where Mussolini is quoted as saying: "The Italo-British accord which has recently entered into force has put the relationship between Britain and Italy on a solid basis and not only has it reconstituted a new phase of friendship and understanding of new Mediterranean and African realities, but has opened a road for the collaboration which, as the necessary element to the peace of Europe, we hope will be a lasting one and a fruitful one."

163 FO 371/23382.

164 Seven articles which appeared weekly between April 30 - June 11, 1939.

165 According to the FO reports from Ethiopia, Teruzzi made himself extremely unpopular during his visit January 4 - February 6.

166 See Fannin Second Report p. 11,12, Section 3, (political). Ruth Ricci Eltse (1894-1977) returned to the US after the war. Her papers are in the Hoover Institution Archives, Stanford University, California. Collection No 77068.

167 Dates of this trip February 8-17, according to 1939 diary.

168 *Sunday Post*, April 30, 1939. Henry Salt had been one of the first Europeans to see the huge stelae at Axum standing high in a field in the middle of the village. He measured them and drew them and Katharine was fascinated to see nearly the same scene, but with one stela missing. This had been taken by the Italians, cut into three pieces and reassembled for a Piazza in Rome.

169 The Abuna, head of the Ethiopian Church, was traditionally a Coptic Prelate, although the beliefs and practises of the Ethiopian Church differed from the Coptic or Egyptian Church.

170 These treasures obviously impressed her greatly and she took a

film of the occasion with her ciné camera. The film still survives.

171 "A grave and polite gentleman in a hat like the funnel of a French liner. I mention him as he is the spiritual father of the majority of Eritrean native troops who are devout Copts. The Italians are building him a beautiful new cathedral in Asmara, which seems tactful." Fannin Second Report, p. 5, Section 4 (people).

172 Fannin Second Report, p. 5,6, Section 1.

173 According to Richard Pankhurst in his article "A page of Ethiopian History: Italian Settlement Plans during the Fascist Occupation of 1936-41," *Ethiopia Observer* (1970), XIII, No 2, pp.145-56, all these settlement schemes were a failure.

174 See *Sunday Post*, May 7, 1939, where she discusses these Italian settlement schemes at length.

175 La Colonizzazione Demografica dell Impero, 1939.

176 Dated May 14, 1939.

177 Source of the Blue Nile. Footage of Katharine's visit to Lake Tana can be seen in her film that survives. It shows Katharine and Ruth sailing on the lake with some Italian officials.

178 Felix von Luckner was famous in World War I as 'The Sea Devil,' who as a lone yachtsman caused considerable damage to British shipping in the Pacific before he was finally caught and interned in New Zealand. He was the subject of a popular biography and was a well-known figure, especially in Germany.

179 Note in 1939 Diary for February 18-19.

180 Enrico Cerulli later became famous as a historian and ethnologist. He wrote many books on Somalia and Ethiopia.

181 Katharine Fannin was told this was because Italian Colonial Officials were very poorly paid and no other section of the community would have accepted such hardship and such responsibilities for so little remuneration. Others would have disagreed. "Millions have been spent to build luxurious villas with modern style furniture, Persian carpets, silver cutlery and so forth for the Heads of Government Departments and Vice-Governors" (Bonacorsi Report) see note 184 below.

182 Fannin Second Report, p. 2, Section 3 (political).

183 Fannin Second Report, p. 10, Section 3 (political).

184 Bonacorsi Report, Rodwell archives. 'Being an appreciation written in April, 1940, by General Arconovaldo Bonacorsi, Inspector

General of the Blackshirts, Italian East Africa, of the situation in Italian East Africa, translated from the original Italian Document which was captured at Addis Ababa,' Nairobi November 7, 1941. It has been suggested that this document was not quite what it claimed to be. It paints a very black and completely hopeless picture and was possibly a piece of deliberate misinformation put about by the Allies to cause maximum despondency amongst the Italians or it was deliberately leaked to the British in Kenya by the Italians before the start of the Abyssinian Campaign. Conversation with Edward Rodwell, who was the press officer in Mombasa during the period.

185 *Sunday Post*, April 30, 1939

186 Fannin Second Report, p.10, Section 3 (political). She was so horrified by this she remonstrated personally with the Duke of Aosta. He said he had abolished public flogging, which was a traditional form of Abyssinian punishment, in 1937 but had had to re-institute it in order to check the rise in violent crime.

187 Ras Hailu, one of the most powerful chieftains in Ethiopia, supported the Italians. He was one of several Rases, who did not want to see Haile Selassie reinstated. His peaceful submission was bought by the British on payment of 300,000 Maria Theresa Dollars, in 1941.

188 *Sunday Post*, May 14, 1939.

189 Ibid

190 He signed his name in Henry Salt's book on that date and there is a terse entry in her diary for that day, "Lunched Mandera wired Tizz."

191 Fannin Second Report, p.15, Section 4 (people).

NOTES TO CHAPTER TEN

192 This article entitled "Kenya Lady's Abyssinian Journey - 7,000 Miles on New Roads Across Italy's Colony," appeared on March 26, 1939.

193 FO 371/23382

194 In the Emperor's triumphal address in Addis Ababa in May 1941, the number of Italian troops was put at 150,000 - but G.L. Steer in his book **Sealed and Delivered** (London, 1942) gives the number as 300,000.

195 This of course was wishful thinking, as the visit never took place and by March 1941 the British invasion of Abyssinia was well underway.

196 Fannin Second Report, p. 2, Section 2 (Military).

197 Her last article May 28, 1939, described "What I didn't like in Abyssinia."

198 Dated May 26, 1939.

199 Dated June 27, 1939, Colonial Office, Downing Street.

200 FO 371/23382, dated June 19, 1939.

201 Ibid, scribbled comment dated April 28.

202 The Honorable Mrs Evelyn Emmet was the daughter of Lord Rennell of Rodd and Lady William Percy was the daughter of Lord Perth, the British ambassador in Rome. Both ladies were pro-Italian. Katharine Fannin had quarrelled with Lady Percy on March 7 (See 1939 Diary). It seems the two aristocratic ladies were somewhat put out to find plain Mrs F staying as a favoured guest of the Viceroy, while they had to stay at the British Consulate. Mrs Emmet also wrote a brief report of her visit, which can be seen in the same Foreign Office File as the Fannin report, but unlike the Fannin report it excited little comment.

203 FO 371/23377, letter from Bird to Bentinck dated March 8, 1939.

204 There is no date for these newspaper clippings stuffed in amongst the Fannin papers on Ethiopia.

205 Correspondence File FO 371/23377 contains two articles written by G.L. Steer for *The Spectator* entitled "Ethiopia in 1939" and "Italy and the Sudan." According to the FO comment : "Mr Steer as we know is violently anti-Italian. He has not been in Italian East Africa since he was expelled after the fall of Addis Ababa and he gets a great deal of his information from Ethiopian émigrés in Jibuti. Mr Steer's description of armed opposition to Italians in Abyssinia is exaggerated."

206 For further reading see Patricia W. Romero: E. Sylvia Pankhurst, **Portrait of a Radical** (Yale University Press, 1987).

207 This appeared in the July 17 edition.

208 *Manchester Guardian*, July 20, 1939.

209 *Manchester Guardian*, August 18, 1939.

210 Information about this comes from a letter to her bank manager, Mr Alcock, of which she retained a copy, written February 16, 1940.

Apparently she informed him about this matter "in case my ship is sunk."

211 It is not known whether this transaction with the Italians came off or not. Two films survive amongst her papers. Unfortunately they are duplicates and both show scenes from her second journey. The film of her 1938 journey is unfortunately missing. Nevertheless, the film that remains provides incontrovertible proof of her journey and is a valuable pictorial record.

NOTES TO CHAPTER ELEVEN

212 Fannin Third Report dated May 24, 1940.

213 She notes that the regiment took with them 95 copies of a map her husband made showing the complete road system in Italian East Africa, based on a map she had been given by the Duke of Aosta in 1939.

214 Fannin Second Report, section 2 (Military).

215 Moyale was captured by the Italians.

216 Information given to the Author by Edward Rodwell.

217 See Richard Frost: **Enigmatic Proconsul: Sir Philip Mitchell and the Twilight of Empire** (London, 1992) pp. 117-118. Frost claims the Emperor was only with much difficulty dissuaded from invading Ethiopia immediately at the head of a small army, and that Anthony Eden, at that time Secretary of State for war, initially supported Emperor Haile Selassie's proposal. It was General Platt who argued forcibly against the idea, pointing out the many potentials for disaster and after considerable discussion the compromise of an organised rebellion to occupy the Emperor and soften the Italians up before the start of a properly co-ordinated campaign, was agreed upon.

218 Fannin papers.

219 Ref: J497/15/16 in lists of Foreign Office Correspondence for 1941.

220 Lord Rennell of Rodd: British Military Administration of Occupied Territories in Africa During the Years 1941-1943, (London,1948) p. 33.

221 Born in India in 1903, and a converted Zionist, he was an unconventional officer who believed it was his destiny to lead some wronged and beleaguered people to victory. He specialised in raising insurrections, and fostering resistance movements within enemy countries.

However, he received little thanks for his handling of the Gideon Force and was recalled to Cairo, where he was reduced in rank and accused of insubordination. In despair he tried to commit suicide but, fortunately for the success of the Allied Cause, he lived to go on to yet greater exploits in Burma. He was killed in an aircrash behind Japanese lines in 1944. He was considered by many a dangerous maverick.

222 For an account of Thesiger's part in the Abyssinian Campaign see: Michael Asher: **Thesiger** (London, 1993), chapter entitled "The one Great Emotional Cause of My Life, "pp.177-205.

223 British Government pamphlet printed by HMSO (His Majesty's Stationery Office), (London, 1941).

224 Ibid

225 On March 20, 1941 she authorised Cattermoul to hand over her films to His Majesty's Armed Services, but in fact her instructions were lost in the general wartime confusion and the films were never sent.

226 Official Account of Ethiopian Campaign, (1941), HMSO.

227 1,370 miles in 50 days.

228 Official Account of Ethiopian Campaign, (1941), HMSO.

229 Letter dated June 4, 1941.

230 Ewart Grogan employed 900 Italian prisoners of war on his estate at Taveta, where they worked on his schemes for irrigation. An Italian engineer also designed and built his extraordinary house at Girigan Hill, called Grogan's Castle. Leda Farrant: **The Legendary Grogan** (London, 1981) pp. 199-200.

231 Major the Hon Peter Rodd, Evacuation Officer Asmara: 'Report on the Evacuation of Italian Civilians from Italian East Africa 1941-1942,' (Rhodes House, Oxford, Mss British Empire 5360) According to his report there were in addition 55,000 in and around Asmara, 12,000 in Mogadishu and 12,400 elsewhere.

232 Orde Wingate had disobeyed orders in bringing Haile Selassie and his army into the capital so soon, which may account for the degree of panic. The agreed plan had been that the Emperor would not occupy the capital until after the surrender of the main Italian army at Amba Alagi.

NOTES TO CHAPTER TWELVE

233 Letter dated November 3, 1940. His reply in the negative dated November 18, 1940.

234 During the war Lord Francis Scott held the position of Assistant Military Secretary in Command Headquarters, Nairobi, and was responsible for posting officers to the different units and for all military appointments. Ever hopeful, Katharine no doubt thought he might pull strings for her return to Kenya, but her appeal to him met with no success. Lord Francis Scott was European Elected Member of the Legislative Council for the Rift Valley, represented the so-called Arab interests in the Legislative Council, and after Lord Delamere's death in 1931 had been the leader of the Settlers in Kenya. He was therefore one of the most influential men in the Colony.

235 Copy of letter no date, but sent after June 6, 1941, in reply to his thanking her for her assistance in the Abyssinian Campaign.

236 Letters in Fannin papers. Katharine worked for the Government censor the whole time she was in Accra.

237 Copy of letter to Mr Edmet, undated.

238 Dated June 20, 1940, broadcast on Accra local news.

239 As per various letters from the Commissioner, Gold Coast Police, Accra, whose signature is unreadable, and handwritten memorandums from a Mr L. Chapman, C.I.D. who seems to have been her main contact.

240 This was the pseudonym for William Joyce, a supporter of the British Fascist Party, led by Oswald Mosley, who transmitted his broadcasts on behalf of the German war effort from Jersey, in the Channel Islands.

241 Dated November 4, 1941:

Inspired! To save Verdun the Humble came
And flung the invader back on either hand
Rallied by Pétain's brotherhood and name
A flame to keep white honour in your land

Rank upon rank in thousands where they fell
Heaping the graves our common foes defile.

Forever sons of France they served so well
The Brave lay silent, watchful for a while.

But now They rise again, who never die!
Great souls who guard in death their country's fame
And call to each where'er his path may lie -
"True Frenchmen Rally to this other Name!"

242 Letter to Mrs Fannin dated May 13, 1944, from Martinique, where he had been appointed Governor. Cantonments or Cantoonments literally means quarters for troops. Although the Fannins were not military personnel, the housing provided in Accra for Colonial Office employees followed the same principle as that of military quartering, usually in a separate compound with houses graded according to rank and precedence.

NOTES TO CHAPTER THIRTEEN

243 General Sir Alan Cunningham (1887 -1983) did not, however, end his career here. He was eventually appointed High Commissioner and Commander-in-Chief Palestine from 1945-1948.

244 See Michael Carver: **Dilemmas of the Desert War, A New Look at the Libyan Campaign 1940-1942** (London, 1986) pp. 27-53. The subject has been extensively discussed by most historians of World War II. This is one of the more recent analyses.

245 Entry in 1942 pocket diary for Monday, January 19.

246 Ibid

247 Ref PRO FO 921 2 1942 1 (18).

248 Formerly Australian Minister to the U.S. 1940-1942.

249 Transferred from the Colonial Office.

250 Conversation with Dorothy Kirkman.

251 FO Correspondence lists for 1942/43: R 2639/403/44 also K 5102/60/289, K2370/60/289, K 6673/59/216 etc., but virtually none of this is available in the PRO.

252 PRO FO 921 89(45) 13, FO 921 90 (45)15.

253 Long letter to Charles written over Christmas 1942, finally finished

January 6, 1943. It is headed: Flat 23, 215 Sharia Khalif el Masry, Midan Saida Zeinab, Cairo. Her other letters are all on headed office paper.

254 Letter to Charles dated May 30 - June 3, 1942.

255 1942 Diary entries April 17-21.

256 Letter to Charles dated February 6, 1943.

257 "It may interest you to hear that my husband as part of his job had to dish out over £5,000,000 sterling in compensation for land compulsorily acquired in 1941 under the wartime Lease Lend Agreements when America got Chaguaramas and other naval and air bases in Trinidad in exchange for the fifty destroyers Britain needed so badly then." Katharine Fannin: 'Memories of the Twenties and Thirties in Kenya,' Pt 2, KBS, November 16, 1960.

258 There are five letters from Charles written during this period, which survive in the Fannin papers. The post was severely disrupted during the war and we know that their correspondence between Trinidad and Cairo was often delayed and sometimes lost altogether.

259 *Mombasa Times*, November 1, 1950.

260 By summer 1942, the British Secret Service had a last succeeded in breaking the German Enigma code and were intercepting many of Rommel's radio communications with his high command. This gave the Allies an important advantage as they had forewarning of German movements and battle plans. It is possible that Katharine in her position knew of Britain's most secret weapon, code-named Ultra, and it may have been this type of knowledge that caused her so much anxiety "not to unwittingly give a line on something."

NOTES TO CHAPTER FOURTEEN

261 See Colonial Lists.

262 Their house was next to the present police headquarters in Kaunda Avenue.

263 Ethiopia, a landlocked country, has always been concerned to secure itself an outlet to the sea.

264 *The Times*, April 21, 1949.

265 *The Times*, October 21, 1949, published in the Correspondence Column under title 'The Future of Eritrea.'

266 Letter dated September 16, 1949. He had seen her letters

translated into Italian, which appeared in *Il Tempo*, Rome, August 28, and in the Eritrean news on August 19, 1949. Katharine sent him a letter and a Christmas food parcel to cheer him containing butter, coffee, golden syrup and lard.

267 Letter from the sculptor, Prof Romano Romanelli, dated April 29, 1949, from Piazza Bellosguardo, Firenze.

268 *Eritrea Nuova*, August 19, 1949.

269 Letter dated September 1, 1949, signed by E Guidotti.

270 Paresce had written to her in 1939, offering to purchase her films of Italian East Africa on behalf of the Italian Government.

271 Letter dated October 5, 1949.

272 See letter from *New York Times* editor, L P Huger, dated November 7, 1949.

273 Katharine had met Brigadier Longrigg in Cairo in 1942-1943. She had this to say of him: "He himself is a pleasant man, an Arabic scholar, very pro-Ethiopian and anti-Italian, and not particularly receptive of ideas that run counter to his own: I fear I remain profoundly unimpressed by his advocacy of Ethiopia and deplore his anti-Italian bias that blinds him to all save their shortcomings."

274 Letter dated November 25, 1949. R G Woolbert was a professor of History in Denver University, whose Harvard dissertation had been on the subject of the origin of Italian territorial expansion in Africa. He was an advisor to the State Department on East African affairs.

275 Letter to Woolbert dated December 6, 1949.

276 Ibid

277 Woolbert by his own admission had never been nearer to Ethiopia than Cairo, but had joined with the Pankhurst lobby in denouncing the Italian rule and specialised in writing strongly anti-Italian articles.

NOTES TO CHAPTER FIFTEEN

278 Martin Meredith, **The First Dance of Freedom: Black Africa in the Postwar Era** (London, 1984).

279 The Legislative Council, usually abbreviated to LegCo, was set up in 1907, largely as a result of early settlers, such as Lord Delamere, lobbying for some say in how the colony was run. To begin with the Settlers had only two representatives, but in 1917 this was increased to

ten and in 1922 the Asians were also given minimal representation. Arab and African interests continued to be represented by Europeans until the 1940s. It was a very small and select body, that sat with the government officials to debate the laws and internal policies of the colony.

280 For information on Jomo Kenyatta see Guy Arnold, **Kenyatta and the Politics of Kenya** (London 1974).

281 Many Kenyan African soldiers fought in the Burma campaigns under extremely unpleasant and harsh conditions. Treated as equals in the army, they found it difficult on their return to accept the strict colour bar and differentiation between the treatment of races that existed in colonial Kenya.

282 For a balanced account of the events that lead up to Mau Mau see: Frank Furedi, **The Mau Mau War in Perspective** (London, 1989).

283 Sir Philip Mitchell, the Governor, was in part to blame for ignoring the evidence of growing unrest and for not taking action of any kind. When his successor, Sir Evelyn Baring, arrived in the Autumn, 1952, he found he had been left with an explosive situation. It has been suggested that by 1952, Sir Philip was a seriously sick man, and for a recent and favourable account of his governorship see: Richard Frost, **Enigmatic Proconsul: Sir Philip Mitchell and the Twilight of Empire** (London, 1992).

284 Frank Furedi, ibid, pp.119-122.

285 He was kept in prison at Lokitaung in northwest Kenya until 1961.

286 Figures taken from: Denis Holman, **Bwana Drum: The Unknown Story of the Secret War against the Mau Mau** (London, 1964) pp. 186-187.

287 James Griffiths replaced Arthur Creech Jones as secretary of State for the Colonies in 1950 and visited Kenya in May 1951 to discuss the problem of African representation on LegCo. Griffiths wanted more Africans to be nominated to LegCo without any increase in Settler membership, but the Settler members refused and for the time being the principle of 'parity' in LegCo, maintaining a Settler majority over all other races, was guaranteed.

288 The Haj or pilgrimage to Mecca, is one of the pillars of Islam and the festival of the Haj, which ends the official period of pilgrimage, is the second most important feast day of the Muslim calendar. Idd ul

Fitr marking the end of Ramadhan, the month of fasting, is the most important one. On these occasions it was traditional that the Sultan or his representative would hold a baraza, a gathering of the important inhabitants of the town, to exchange congratulatory speeches before the main festivities started.

289 *Kenya Weekly News*, September 12, 1952.

290 Mombasa's famous Portuguese fort, Fort Jesus, at this point in history was being used as the Government Prison.

291 Information from "Mombasa Social Survey," unpublished typescript, n.d., Chapter on 'Demographic Factors and Population' by G M Wilson pp. 149-173 and 'The Development of Municipal Government in Mombasa' by P Burke pp. 173-230.

292 On March 6, 1951, a bill was passed through LegCo, which required that everyone should carry a national registration card, which would include their fingerprints. Previously only Africans had been required to carry a Kipande, but this was now extended to all races. However, many Settlers felt that having to give their fingerprints, as if they were criminals, was degrading and there was considerable opposition to the bill.

293 In the end the proposals for the Federation were shelved, as no agreement could be reached and Mau Mau overshadowed all other considerations.

294 Shirley Victor Cooke was an Irishman with decided opinions. His career as an administrative officer had ended in 1930 when as DC Lamu he had clashed with his superior officer H. R. Montgomery, then the PC for the Coast. After leaving the administration he went into politics and, despite his reputation as being unduly pro-African, he was elected to LegCo time and again by the European voters at the Coast. "As a parliamentarian he was often inspired, but rarely predictable, except in siding always with the underdog." Charles Chevenix Trench, **Men who Ruled Kenya: The Kenya Administration 1892-1963** (1993, London).

295 Settler power was further eroded in 1957 with the Lennox Boyd constitution, which provided 15 new seats for Africans in LegCo, which meant that the Settlers no longer had the dominant voice on council.

296 This party later changed its name to The New Kenya Party to differentiate it from the main Settler political party, The United Party. For an account of the politics in Kenya in the 1950s see Michael Blundell's

autobiography **A Love Affair with the Sun: A Memoir of Seventy Years in Kenya** (1994, Nairobi), which clearly states his political thinking at the time.

297 *Kenya Weekly News*, August 15, 1954.

298 "Mombasa Social Survey," unpublished typescript, n.d., ibid p. 162, which gives the final figures for the 1958 census carried out in Mombasa Municipality. Thirty-five years later the population of Mombasa had quadrupled and stood at over 500,000. The largest increase in the population has been in the African sector, while the other three main ethnic communities have either declined or shown only marginal increase. The figures for the 1989 census list 24,619 Asians, 7,000 European and 22,000 Arabs living in Mombasa.

299 Tom Mboya was a young Luo leader of considerable popularity and ability, who was later to be appointed a minister in Kenyatta's cabinet. However, his radical ideas and outspoken views caused him to fall out with Kenyatta and he was assassinated in Nairobi in 1969 by a Kikuyu. The Luo tribe, who come from the banks of Lake Victoria, were strong and reliable workers, who made up the majority of the workforce in the port and Kenya Railways.

300 *Kenya Weekly News*, March 11, 1955.

301 The *Mombasa Times* ceased publication in 1954, when it was amalgamated with the *East African Standard*.

302 Information from Edward Rodwell. There is nothing in the Fannin papers about why she suddenly stopped writing for the *Kenya Weekly News*. Although she never said anything, it is clear that she was bitterly disappointed and jealous of Edward Rodwell, who had taken her job.

303 (Lord) Altrincham, **Kenya's Opportunity** (London, 1955).

NOTES TO CHAPTER SIXTEEN

304 Information from Edward Rodwell.

305 Apparently she chose this 'nom de plume' because an up-country reporter once referred to people from the Coast as 'Shellbacks.' She thought it most appropriate because, as she explained, "The name has a salty tang, it connotes a crusty exterior concealing a kind heart, suggests sturdy independence - not to say obstinacy, a weather eye, kept lifting,

and a philosophic attitude towards life. So with due acknowledgement...I subscribe, myself, nobody's obedient servant; Shellback."

306 Although her scrapbook has not been preserved in the Fannin papers, she describes this in her column for *Mombasa Times*, December 17, 1949.

307 Edward Rodwell's Coast Causerie column, one of the longest running columns in the world, ran for 57 years. See: Aldrick, J, *Kenya Past and Present*, Issue 33 "Edward Rodwell 1907-2002, A Profile," pp. 31-36.

308 Edward Rodwell, **Coast Causerie I: Experiences from 48 years of Rodwell's Column** (Kenya, 1972, reprint 1992), p. 41.

309 This article, which appears in draft form amongst her papers, was never published.

310 These initials R.I.P.W.D. must stand for Rest in Peace, (the standard phrase placed on a tombstone) Public Works Department.

311 A Kipande was an official certificate of employment; see note 292 for further information.

312 *Mombasa Times*, October 28, 1950.

313 Information from Arthur Ratcliff, who as Town Clerk for Mombasa from 1952 - 1965, knew the Fannins well. He stayed on in Mombasa after independence and was first bursar of Shanzu Teachers Training College and later office manager for the legal firm, Bryson, Inamdar and Bowyer. After retirement in 1977 he lived on his boat Little Gypsy at the Mombasa Yacht Club where, sadly, he was murdered in 1993.

314 *Kenya Weekly News*, July 1954.

315 See Edward Rodwell, **The Mombasa Club** (Mombasa, 1988).

316 Information received from Millicent Reeve.

317 Commanding spectacular views, this site is now occupied by the famous Tamarind Restaurant and Tamarind Village.

318 This first pontoon bridge was built in 1931. It was 1,300 feet long and one of the longest pontoon bridges in the world, however it was single lane and by the 1970s could no longer take the increased traffic. The present dual highway Nyali Bridge, which links the island at Buxton to the north mainland at Ras Kisauni, was opened in 1981 and the old bridge was demolished in 1982.

319 Story told to the author by Millicent Reeve.

320 Information from Tom Miller and Eddie Gregory.

321 Information in a letter sent to the author by Jean Wallwork.

322 Told to the author by Edward Rodwell.

323 *Kenya Weekly News*, September 18, 1953.

324 "Mombasa Social Survey," typescript n.d., Chapter entitled 'Kongowea,1956-8, A case study of African built housing on a temporary village layout, supervised by Municipal Rules' by G M Wilson, pp. 461-491.

325 Kenya Weekly News, August 13, 1954.

326 During the 1920s and 1930s LegCo was made up of Government Officials, 11 elected European Settlers and two Asians, who sat together as an embryonic parliament for the colony. The 11 Settlers conveniently made up the side for a cricket team and cricket matches Unofficials versus Officials were played up and down the country.

327 Lord Delamere, who came to Kenya in 1897 and died in 1931, was the great champion of the Settlers. He almost single-handedly organised and focussed the Settlers into a powerful group who challenged the Colonial Government and demanded a leading voice in the running of the Colony. Ultimately the Settlers' aim was self-government by whites.

328 "Memories of the Twenties and Thirties in Kenya," Pt 6, KBS, December 28, 1960.

NOTES TO CHAPTER SEVENTEEN

329 Martin Meredith, **The First Dance of Freedom: Black Africa in the Postwar Era** (London, 1984).

330 Information from Edward Rodwell.

331 Evelyn Baring was Governor of Kenya from 1952-1959. See: Charles Douglas-Home, **Evelyn Baring, The Last Proconsul** (London, 1978).

332 In the last 30 years the population has grown explosively to well over 30 million in 2010. The Asian population in contrast has declined by 50% since 1960 and the European population has dwindled even more.

333 Michael Blundell, who arrived in Kenya in 1925, was elected after the war to LegCo as member for the Rift Valley and subsequently to the leadership of the European Elected Members. He formed the New Kenya Party in 1959. It was open to all races and campaigned for co-

operation with the British Government to ensure a peaceful transition from colony to independent nation.

334 One of these pledges was the Closer settlement scheme which started in 1948, whereby the British Government offered tenancies to Settlers wishing to farm on a 44-year lease, after which period they were to be given the title deed for the land. Settlers were encouraged to come to Kenya on this scheme up until 1960. No provision had been made for what would happen under independence, when the title deeds promised by the British Government would no longer come under British jurisdiction. After the Lancaster House conference, the scheme was wound up and the tenancies lapsed.

335 Information from Olivia Rodwell. Her father Monthermer Stanley Hume Montagu was one of the early Settlers, who started farming coffee successfully at Kiambu. He came to Kenya in 1910 and was a great friend of Denys Finch Hatton, whom he introduced to Kenya, inviting him for a safari in 1911. Denys was so taken with the country that he decided to settle. During the 1920s Montagu (always known as Monty) sat on LegCo and the family was always deeply involved in Settler politics.

336 Harold MacMillan was Prime Minister of Britain during Independence in Kenya. He had little interest in or sympathy for the Colonies and thought Britain's future lay in closer union with Europe.

337 Mwambao means coastline in Kiswahili. See chapter on "The Mwambao episode," Hyder Kindy, **Life and Politics in Mombasa** (Nairobi, 1972) pp. 184-191.

338 There were two parties at the Coast that supported Mwambao; the Coast Peoples Party (CPP) who wanted complete autonomy and the more moderate Coastal League, to which Europeans and Asians and Arabs tended to belong, who wanted to retain ties with Zanzibar.

339 *Kenya Weekly News*, March 16, 1962.

340 Sheikh Ali Muhsin's statement on behalf of the Sultan of Zanzibar, March 1962, quoted from Rodwell article ibid.

341 Hyder Kindy, ibid, p. 190.

342 This was Paul Pry, who wrote an article in the *Sunday Nation*, January 22, 1961, entitled "A Tale of Two Independents" where he angrily denounced the idea of autonomy for the Coast as "dangerous balderdash." This article was probably written by a colonial official as the name Paul Pry is certainly a pseudonym and employees of the colonial service were

not allowed to write in the newspapers under their own names as they were meant to be apolitical and impartial.

343 Information from Dorothy Kirkman, who lived to be over 90.

344 Fannin Papers, diary for 1962, makes almost daily mention of her troubles on these committees. She often attended two or three in one day.

345 Later a Kanu MP for Mombasa and vice Chairman of the Mombasa Kanu Party.

346 Kenyatta and his KANU party won the general elections in May 1963 and Madaraka, internal self-government, was attained on June 1, 1963. Uhuru was proclaimed on December 12, 1963, when the Union Jack was hauled down in Nairobi and Kenya officially became independent. The following year December 12, 1964, Jamhuri was proclaimed when Kenya became a republic with Jomo Kenyatta as its first president.

347 August 10, 1963, the Mombasa Municipal Council was reconstituted and new elections were called.

348 Information about this incident is taken from letters in the Fannin Papers and Edward Rodwell.

349 Although no evidence for this surfaces in the Fannin Papers, it is probable there were complications in the will, as Katharine was Charles's second wife and he still had family from his first marriage living in England.

NOTES TO CHAPTER EIGHTEEN

350 August 12, 1963.

351 Guy Arnold, **Kenyatta and the Politics of Kenya** (London, 1974).

352 1968 Africanisation policy was introduced. Many Asians left the country as their shops and businesses were taken over by Africans and white farmers were forced out of their farms by compulsory purchases.

353 Information from June Knowles.

354 All these reports can be seen in the Fannin Papers.

355 Information from Desmond and Phyllida Forbes-Cockell.

356 Information from Desmond and Phyllida Forbes-Cockell.

357 *Kenya Weekly News*, 1954. Mombasa Salvation Army Eventide

Home was opened, a “hostel for ageing European men and women who would otherwise be destitute.”

358 Information from Lorna Hayes.

359 It was rumoured that Katharine Fannin ended her days in Mathare Mental Hospital, in those days a place only for Africans and the absolutely destitute. However, Phyllida Forbes-Cockell categorically denies this story.

360 The *Standard*, December 2, 1970.

MRS KATHARINE FANNIN DIES IN NAIROBI

Standard Staff Reporter

“The funeral service of Mrs. Katharine Fannin, aged 68, widow of the late Alderman Charles Fannin, formerly Kenya Director of Surveys, took place at All Saints Cathedral, Nairobi yesterday.

“Mrs. Fannin, who was born in Bhutan of an Indian civil service family arrived in Kenya in 1927. She took an interest in social work for which she was awarded the Jubilee medal in 1936 and also served on the Mombasa Municipal Council. Later she wrote of coast life for the *Kenya Weekly News*.

“In the late 1930s Mrs Fannin travelled extensively by road on her own in Ethiopia and Somalia and became the first Englishwoman to cross the Danakil Desert. She wrote of her experiences for the then *Manchester Guardian* and the articles provoked a lively correspondence with Miss Sylvia Pankhurst, then an Ethiopian resident who disagreed with her views on that country.

“Mrs. Fannin’s solitary travels - although in some areas she was provided with an Italian military escort,- were inspired by a rare first edition in her family’s possession, which had been written by a relative.

“She gave the volume **A Voyage to Abyssinia and Travels 1809-1810**, to the Duke of Aosta in appreciation of the help she had received during her travels. The Duke was then viceroy in Ethiopia.

“Mrs. Fannin was widely read and took a close interest in world affairs. Her lively conversation and sense of humour attracted a wide circle of friends from all walks of life to her home at Kisauni, where she lived after the death of her husband.

"She continued her work for the KSPCA as well as the League of Mercy until shortly before her last illness which resulted in her death at Nairobi Hospital on Friday."

361 I searched for Charles's grave in the Anglican section of the European cemetery but could not find it as it was not marked by a headstone. I like to think it was the grave with a simple metal cross and the initials R.I.P.

Index